# Creative Planning Resource
# for Interconnected Teaching
# and Learning

# Studies in the
# Postmodern Theory of Education

Joe L. Kincheloe and Shirley R. Steinberg
*General Editors*

Vol. 174

PETER LANG
New York • Washington, D.C./Baltimore • Bern
Frankfurt am Main • Berlin • Brussels • Vienna • Oxford

Lyn Ellen Lacy

# Creative Planning Resource for Interconnected Teaching and Learning

CONSULTING EDITOR
Ann Watts Pailliotet

PETER LANG
New York • Washington, D.C./Baltimore • Bern
Frankfurt am Main • Berlin • Brussels • Vienna • Oxford

**Library of Congress Cataloging-in-Publication Data**

Lacy, Lyn Ellen.
Creative planning resource for interconnected teaching and learning /
Lyn Ellen Lacy; Ann Watts Pailliotet, consulting editor.
p. cm. (Counterpoints; vol. 174)
Includes bibliographical references and index.
1. Curriculum planning. 2. Interdisciplinary approach in education.
3. Education, Humanistic. 4. Learning, Psychology of.
I. Title. II. Counterpoints (New York, N.Y.); vol. 174.
LB2806.15 .L33    375'.001—dc21    2001034682
ISBN 0-8204-5185-1
ISSN 1058-1634


**Die Deutsche Bibliothek-CIP-Einheitsaufnahme**

Lacy, Lyn Ellen.
Creative planning resource for interconnected teaching and learning /
Lyn Ellen Lacy.
Consulting ed.: Ann Watts Pailliotet.
—New York; Washington, D.C./Baltimore; Bern;
Frankfurt am Main; Berlin; Brussels; Vienna; Oxford: Lang.
(Counterpoints; Vol. 174)
ISBN 0-8204-5185-1

Composition by Deirdre Smith
Figures by Brian Plantenberg
Cover art by William Capel Slack
Cover design by Dutton & Sherman Design

The paper in this book meets the guidelines for permanence and durability
of the Committee on Production Guidelines for Book Longevity
of the Council of Library Resources.

Printed in the United States of America

For my children
Ruth, Peter and John

and in loving memory of
Ann Watts Pailliotet
1955–2002

"All things are connected, like blood which connects one family. Whatever befalls the earth befalls the children of the earth. Man did not weave the web of life—he is merely a strand in it. Whatever he does to the web, he does to himself."

—Chief Seattle

# Table of Contents

# Figures

# Acknowledgments

Finishing *CPR* would not have been possible without the support, help and loving patience of my family—my mother and best proofreader Virginia Hammack; my daughter Ruth Grim, her husband Bob and their baby Allison; my son Peter Lacy; my son John Lacy, his wife Karin and their sons Nick, Luke and Marcus; my companion and problem solver Dave Gatewood; his daughter Deirdre Smith, her husband Mark and their daughter Jasmine.

I am enormously in debt to the writers, teachers and educational researchers whose exemplary ideas and insights I have tried to synthesize creatively in *CPR*, especially Philip Chinn, David Considine, Carlos Cortes, Arthur Costa, Howard Gardner, Donna Gollnick, Gail E. Haley, Bernice McCarthy, Robert Marzano, Vito Perrone, Cornel Pewewardy and Theodore Sizer. Ideas from many, many others are cited here, and I thank them all for sharing their expertise in print, at workshops and in conversations.

I appreciate contributions and encouragement of staff members at Cooper and Keewaydin Community Schools and colleagues in the Information Media and Technology Department of Minneapolis Public Schools.

I am indebted to the 1992 Board of Directors of the American Council of Learned Societies (ACLS), former president Stanley N. Katz and Michael Holzman of the ACLS Staff for offering me the opportunity to study for a year with my ACLS team of teacher fellows.

I have been inspired on my journey by the ancient Peruvian culture that outlined elegant creatures in rocks on the Nazca plain. By the words of Chief Seattle. By the Native American Educational Philosophy of Cornel Pewewardy. By fiction writers Frank Herbert and Tony Hillerman. By the art of Bill Slack. By my friend Bob Muffoletto who asked, "Why not?"

Cornel Pewewardy's "Holistic Circle of Learning" is reprinted by permission of the author. All rights reserved. William Capel Slack's "The Wind Beneath Our Wings" is reprinted by permission of the artist. All rights reserved.

I acknowledge individuals who have been particularly generous with their time and talents—Brian Plantenberg for doing computer graphics, Dave James for turning *CPR* into a computer program and Deirdre Smith for doing prepress formatting.

I am especially grateful to series editors Joe Kincheloe and Shirley Steinberg for their willingness as always to listen to a school teacher's voice. And to Ann Watts Pailliotet for her friendship and guidance as contributor and consulting editor. As this book went to press, we received word of Ann's death. She loved teaching and researching, teachers and researchers, and all who knew and loved her will miss her vibrancy, humor and brilliance. She was a shooting star, brightest in the firmament.

# Introduction:

## A *Sunwise* Journey

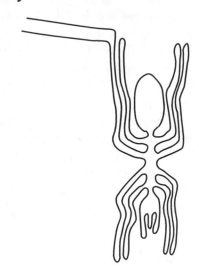

Figure 1: Nazca Spider

Faced with writing an introduction, what author can resist quoting the first line from Frank Herbert's classic, *Dune* (1965): "A beginning is the time for taking the most delicate care that the balances are correct." After quoting such eloquence, however, comes all the hard work of trying to live up to it.

Interestingly enough, help comes for me in the decidedly *unbalanced* form of Spider, a 150-feet-long beauty outlined by rocks over 2000 years ago by a pre-Incan culture in Peru. One of Spider's legs inexplicably goes off at an awkward angle into the Nazca plain, which seems an intriguing thing for such an elegant creature to do. She is one in a zoo of giant creatures—including a monkey, a hummingbird, a whale—some of which are as large as football fields and are seen in their entirety only from the air. The tantalizing mystery of why they were created remains unsolved.

Ruminating about balance and mysteries and such, I dug out my treasured old *National Geographic* (1975, p. 728) with photos of

Nazca and asked artist Brian Plantenberg to create the computer graphic above, as he has for other illustrations in this book. Spider's legs remind me to search for balance—for instance, ideas in this book are organized in multiples of two, especially in fours and eights. That wandering leg, however, reminds me to reach out and not be timid in the face of the unbalanced, the awkward, the unexplored.

More help is offered to me in another novel, *The Dark Wind* (1982) by Tony Hillerman, in which Navajo Tribal Police sergeant Jim Chee wrestles with problems and is advised by an uncle to think *sunwise*. Chee is told to start at the east, then to turn his thoughts south, west and north to gather unique energies offered by the four directions. In the Diné (Navajo) way of thinking, he will achieve wisdom or the balance of mind and heart.

I have a strong belief in insights to be found in diverse ways of knowing and in their applicability for my students in Minneapolis Public Schools (MPS)—African Americans and recent immigrants from Somalia, Asian Americans (primarily Hmong), European Americans, First Nations People (Ojibway and Dakota) and Hispanic Americans recently from Mexico. I decided to try thinking *sunwise* in my search for balance and, if I were successful, perhaps introducing *Creative Planning Resource (CPR)* would be easy. After all, I know a lot about the chapters that follow, having lived with them and field-tested their ideas for a very long time.

Herbert reminds us, however, that care must be taken to achieve *correct* balance, and I admit I have not learned all I should know, want to know or need to know in my journey. The delicate balance of mind and heart—wisdom—I know little about, and I ask those who find flaws in my efforts to realize that the hard work is simply not over yet.

My favorite quotes about wisdom are by young people, like seventeen-year-old Andy Pfeiffer (1997) who says, "Knowledge is power. The more information a person acquires, the more of an individual he becomes. Every time I learn something new I feel a little more *alive*" (p. E12). Then, third-grader Sonya Garelick (1997) describes a world without wisdom: "If we all do not listen and learn, then in the future everybody would be dumb and boring" (p. E5).

Improving interactions with children is the primary goal for my *sunwise* journey, and what follows is a description of my travels so far (including what happened to Spider). My introduction is intentionally long and serves as an eighth chapter—not only does this help me achieve balance but also process is as interesting for many readers as product. "Why" and "how" are often valued as much as "what." As First Nations People believe, all things are interconnected and a journey is more important than the destination. I hope that Sonya might agree I have been a good listener and learner in my travels.

### East

The Diné way of *sunwise* thinking says that turning first to the east gathers energy for such things as clarifying values and setting standards for oneself. My attitude when I began my journey was anything but this reflective. I had become crabby and resentful over a multitude of increasingly prescriptive demands on me as a teacher.

I was experiencing overload. Many educators are experiencing this tension today. We sense that if we do not feel inadequate, we are probably not doing our job. We work hard to plan the teaching and learning in our classrooms and become frustrated by mountains of material representing other people's ideas about how we should do that job.

At inservices and workshops, we gather handouts, black-line masters, notes, statistics, articles, bibliographies and essays about standards-based reform, learning styles, thinking skills, classroom management, gifted and talented education, interdisciplinary instruction, whole language, cooperative learning, gender-fair disability-aware education, children at risk, diversity, site-based management and educational leadership.

Usually the intentions of the presenters, materials and our own participation are the best, but unless we use the ideas very soon, unless we internalize them to make them a part of what we routinely do, we file them where we hope to find them later when we need them, and then we lose them. Many we forget we even had.

In electrical overload, a need for electricity is more than electricity stored; one too many appliances is plugged in; a fuse blows; the lights go out. Information overload is the same. We have all these ideas that we need to plug in to our teaching jobs, but one-shot, drive-by inservicing and our own retrieval system often provide inadequate wiring. When the fuse blows, teachers simply turn off a few ideas and make do in the classrooms with less information.

However, during today's nationwide effort of educational reform, teachers are well aware of their need for new information because it has been said that public education does not, can not and must not exist solely as we have experienced it. We are being asked to teach in distinctly different ways from how we ourselves were taught and how we have been teaching. School is no longer viewed as a shopping mall of knowledge, with teachers as salespeople and students as customers, but as a center for collaborative exploration requiring diverse strategies.

Teachers are also aware of a common feeling by the public that educational practices inside the buildings too often fail to keep up with societal changes outside them. Government, business and the community all call for their own kinds of changes—with every person an expert about school because every person went to one—and as the saying goes, if you try to rescue everybody, you can get lost.

Keeping up with changes in the classroom is difficult, because it takes courage for teachers—just like anyone else—to let go of old practices in favor of new. Dramatic changes, for example, in digital and electronic ways for teachers and students to gather and use information now play a central role in the learning process but take time for teachers to internalize and make significant impact system-wide.

Obstacles to reform also lie in teachers' paths—large class sizes, heavy schedules with a variety of classes to prepare for, obsolete buildings, unavailability of resources or nonsupportive community or school climates. Institutions of higher education are not being required to reform in the same ways, which results not only in a lack of continuity for students but also a lack of modeling by many professors in new methods for beginning teachers.

Research (Wang, Haertel and Walberg, 1994) additionally points out that many of the most powerful factors affecting learning come from outside the school itself—poverty; housing problems; lack of English language skills; unstable home lives; high mobility; abuse of all kinds; health, crime and safety issues; dysfunctional peer group influence; and a lack of clear and enforced behavioral standards at home and in the community (p. 74–79). Some psychologists have posited that today's children come to school with different brains that have been physically altered not only by these changes in our society but also by television, environmental hazards and the technology-driven phenomenon of multitasking.

As one reporter points out, "Much of the burden of solving society's problems is on schools even as they try to teach math and spelling, reading and science. This increased pressure to address social as well as educational needs raises the question of how much one institution can be expected to do" (Smetanka, 1992, p. A8). Susan Fuhrman (1993) adds, "There's no easy answer except to say that social reform has to accompany school reform...[and] while some analysts say the entire school system should be junked and designed anew, there's no reason to think that better learning can't occur under the current structure...like reconstructing the house while you live in it" (p. A8).

What is easily forgotten in reform rhetoric is that in the United States today, a larger number of children representing a wider diversity of intellectual, physical and cultural identities go to public schools for a longer period of time than ever before in the history of any country. Equally as important, I see the quality of what children learn and how they learn it improving daily, as creative people in the public system not only participate but also play leading roles in the reform movement.

The public school practitioners I know are enthusiastically involved in a search for the best changes to make in education, and together we can help identify the roles that schools perform well. Teachers are said to understand better than anyone the many problems encountered by students as they balance their lives inside and outside school, and they search for the best practices to incorporate our learners' diverse cultures, experiences and expectations. Those among us who know what works in the classroom can lead the way for shaping standards for which our students and we ourselves are to be measured.

As a high school social studies teacher (Levitsky, 1990) has said, "Teachers are among the handful of adults who deal with the essence of civilization—Shakespeare, the diversity of other cultures, the latest scientific discovery—on a daily basis" (p. 73). Another fellow teacher (Shulman, 1986) adds, "We reject Mr. Shaw and calumny—`He who can, does. He who cannot, teaches'—and with Aristotle we declare that the ultimate test of understanding rests on the ability to transform one's knowledge into teaching. Those who can, do. Those who understand, teach. Those who teach, do better" (p. 44).

My advocacy reflects the view of columnist Molly Ivins (1996) who remarks, "One of the odd problems about every problem associated with public education is that someone somewhere has already solved it. Around this shining land, teachers are managing to interest inner city kids in physics, getting bored little snots in the 'burbs excited about trigonometry and taking tough young punks and turning them into a literate basketball team" (p. A17).

My stance also mirrors the opinion of a majority of voters in the fall of 2000, who resoundingly defeated private school tuition vouchers. This nonpublic initiative exasperates researcher and reformer Howard Gardner, who called it a "commodification of education [that] will destroy public education in the process. You can't have a country with 100,000 schools where no one knows what is going on; it's just madness" (Smetanka, 2001b, p. E2).

I set out in the east to identify exactly what I needed from my mountain of materials to avoid blowing a fuse. I committed myself to the effort and patience it would take to rewire, reflect and rejuvenate. I backed up to begin at the beginning and clarify what I value about teaching.

High on my list is the kind of creative teaching that results in meaningful learning, which may be a simple way to put it but is by no means as easy as it sounds. To know how to engage children in challenging opportunities for learning and to authentically assess their understanding of important concepts and skills is no stroll through the park.

Teachers' own creative improvement in how to teach is the single most important action to be taken in educational reform. In the teaching profession, creativity most often means finding new ways to look at old ideas or perhaps using old ways to explore new ideas. Creative teaching is putting pieces together with students to make a new whole, a time when teachers demonstrate that they too are lifelong learners.

The creative process is well known to teachers, because a part of their job is to teach it to students. Many educators believe creativity in adults is encouraged by working alongside the children, thinking like they do, seeing what they see and becoming kids again themselves. This appears to be the case with Max Sawochka's (1998) fourth-grade teacher: "I have no idea how she can stand all of us kids. She blows in a conch shell to quiet us down sometimes. She often sings, 'Don't cry for me, Argentina'" (p. E10). Sonya, that other student I mentioned, would never find *this* teacher boring.

My favorite adult quote about the creative process is by David Perkins (1986b), who said that "the romantic image of creativity is it bubbles up or blossoms out spontaneously. But biological data suggest that a lot of creativity comes about because that's what the person is trying to do...(like) scientists who've proven themselves creative by quite deliberately seeking out a problem that is a little off to the side" (p. 14).

Fourteen-year-old Matt Reichert (1997) painted a similar picture: "If you are creative, you will do well at almost anything you do in life. If you are taking a walk, put a little bounce in your step, get a rhythm going, and you'll find that this makes the walking process more fun and you want to keep walking. I learned creativity from my teachers and mentors who have never ceased to let their creativity shine" (p. E12).

Creative thinkers in education welcome such whimsical, rhythmical, off-to-the-side suggestions (and kind words from students) about improving children's learning. Creative teachers take sensible risks, question assumptions, stir things up, face obstacles head-on and rarely take no for an answer when it comes to effecting change.

There are many ways, times, places and situations in which teachers are willing to grow creatively, but there are also many administrative, parental and public demands to be satisfied, and teachers have to fulfill the unique requirements of their own environments. They must evaluate whether a creative plan is appropriate by candidly asking themselves, "Is this going to be acceptable (does it fit my professional environment)? Is it going to be workable (does it fit what my students need to do and can learn to do)? Is it going to be doable (are my students and I personally cut out to try this particular approach)?"

In addition to valuing teacher creativity in public education, I value the changing perception about teaching and learning that says our job must be to plan for the latter rather than the former. A focus on *what the student will do* is a constructivist attitude, described by Jerome Bruner (1960, 1986) as an emphasis on students actively discovering principles themselves and *going beyond the information given* to make their own meaning, rather than stopping at spoon-fed facts or figures.

I value teachers who play the role of mediator in order to guide, model, support and coach students in constructing meaning. These teachers not only connect subjects but also emphasize concepts and help students understand the big picture.

I value creative teachers who focus on the development of the whole child as unique individual while also developing that child's interconnectedness with others. If Abraham Lincoln had been a teacher, he might have said that some content, methods and tools are effective for some of the students all of the time and for all of the students some of the time and for some of the students some of the time but not for all of the students all of the time. Plus, he would have done something about it, just as creative teachers do.

As I clarified what I value about creative teachers in public education, I began to envision a long-term plan for strengthening my chances to become one. I would need my creative colleagues in MPS, because given time, resources and supportive school climate, they are some of the most creative people I know.

We know there is no cheap, quick, easy, sound bite that describes what is needed in educational reform. There is no one answer since there is no one single problem, and even if there were only one problem, there would be more than one solution. Much must be done, and there is a long way to go, and people who work in public education know how hard it is to make effective schools that are student-centered, empowering and valuing of all who teach, learn and work in the building.

For over a quarter of a century, I have taught in public schools and join my colleagues in applauding common-sense ideas about reconstructing the house while we live in it. We value quality public education as an institution that must remain vital in a democracy, and reform means working alongside the landlords, relatives and neighbors who have come in to help. It requires the support of government and policy makers; business partnerships with fewer strings attached; funders that adequately finance salaries, building improvements and learning materials; and communicative, supportive and involved parents who send their children to school ready and willing to learn.

In the east, as I defined what I value about public education, I struggled with planning exactly how to raise my teacher's voice. I realized I needed to climb my mountain of material about how to teach and bring back what is creatively acceptable, workable and doable in my classroom today and what might be possible in the future. I needed to study current educational theories and listen to the ideas driving today's reform movement.

I struggled through the mess-finding part of the creative process and emerged with a tentative goal of creating a resource tool that organized the most useful ideas I could find into a new coherent whole. Its purpose would be to help me make more creative choices in my classroom and thus contribute myself to reform.

That was the beginning of *CPR*. Eager to the point of exhilaration and more than a little naive, I did not realize I had started on what would be a most formidable journey.

### South

In the Diné *sunwise* journey, turning south offers energy for such things as practical, day-by-day living. I began by looking at important issues in my own backyard before I discussed with colleagues what would be the most helpful kinds of information to include in a creative planning tool for addressing those issues.

Minnesota holds a position as a national model for public education (Shaubach, 2001, p. 1). Since 1997, our state's Graduation Rule is divided into two parts: Basic Skills standards in reading, math and written composition and challenging, rigorous High Standards called the Profile of Learning, which has been called "a major retooling of education of exactly the sort we need as a state and nation" (Partridge, 1998, p. A19). The purpose of the Profile is for students to demonstrate in a variety of ways what they know, understand and are able to do with what they have learned.

Also noted is that Minnesota student scores on ACT exams remain among the highest in the nation, a full point above the national average (*Minnesota Educator*, 2000, p. 1). Minnesotans have concerns, however, about basing promotion and graduation on the results of single tests, and their objections rose to an uproar in 2000 when 8,000 students were told they failed the Basic Skills math test when they actually passed. This included 336 seniors, 54 of whom were kept from graduating because of a scoring error made by the state's contractor, National Computer Systems (*Minnesota Educator*, 2000, p. 3). Within the year, Minnesota Sen. Paul Wellstone worked to amend the U. S. Senate education bill to require all states to use "multiple measures for assessment" (Gordon, 2001, p. A1).

Even though our state's Profile was intended to provide for that, it has been declared seriously flawed by some teachers, parents and state legislators. Repairs are needed regarding the lack of practical ways to address standards for special-needs students, a preponderance of standards to be met at certain grade levels and the scarcity of tools and training that teachers have had for implementation.

Too many secondary school students who were not the beneficiaries of earlier Preparatory Standards have little or no chance of meeting the new, tougher high school graduation requirements, an opinion fueled by the alarming fact that less than half of MPS students who entered ninth grade in 1996 went on to graduate (Shah, 2001, p. B1). National criticism of Minnesota's Profile was also evident when the state was among six that failed *Education Week*'s report card for standards and accountability because of a lack of clear and specific performance requirements in English and social studies (*Education Minnesota*, 2001, online).

Full implementation of the Profile is now voluntary statewide, even though weakening Preparatory Standards can cost elementary schools their federal Title I funding (Lonetree, 2001, p. B1). However the Profile may be altered, MPS remains committed to a standards-based, performance-based approach to teaching and learning rather than an input-based system and continues to move forward with implementation (Vana, 2001, p. 1).

When it comes to urban education, educators and observers say that MPS is one of the best systems in the nation (Shah and Drew, 2001, p. B1). It is featured in a report by the American Federation of Teachers (2000) that highlights districts making substantial progress in raising student achievement because a comprehensive set of reforms has been put in place (p. 3). While state test scores for our students are below where we would like them to be, they are steadily on the rise, and students' improvement on the Northwest Achievement Level Tests exceeds the national average.

Three-fourths of Minneapolis voters expressed appreciation of public school efforts by supporting passage of a $42 million excess-levy in 2000 (Shah and Drew, 2001, p. B5). Even so, they mirror the nation-wide sense of dissatisfaction with the enormous problems shared by urban school systems, as demonstrated by a *Star Tribune* poll in 2001 showing that a majority think public schools do only "a fair to poor job of preparing students for the future, which is little change from polls taken in 1995 and 1997, despite major improvement efforts underway" (Smetanka, 2001a, p. A1).

Eighty different languages are spoken in our district, and one in five of our students is learning English. Minnesota emerged from the 2000 census (Peterson, 2001) with 142,000 Asian/Pacific Islanders, the greatest number of any state in the interior of the United States, with the Hmong community the largest group (p. B1). The population of Minneapolis (382,618) is almost eight percent Hispanic/Latino, and the African American population is over twice that amount. It is also the seventh largest urban concentration of American Indians (8, 378) in the country.

The president of the Minneapolis Urban League (Suddeth, 2001) explained the impact that racial diversity has on our schools by saying that an educational model adopted in the 1920s for the education of white children of northern European heritage does not accommodate nonwhite children of today. "Most students come from homes that are different from their teacher's home. Not better, not worse—different. Homes where people look at the world through different lenses. It seems logical that these students might also have a different way of learning" (p. A14).

Student diversity and controversy over assessment are two of the primary issues in my own Minnesota backyard, much like ones in every other state. State and district educators recognize that all of our schools for all of our children are not yet good enough, and because of our problems and solutions, I spent a long time gathering facts in the south on my Diné journey. Now it was time to approach my colleagues with the idea of a creative planning resource that might address those issues.

An important aspect of embedding professional development into our everyday practice in MPS is collegial dialogue, which is where I began. I wanted planning for my resource tool to be an exercise in creative problem-solving itself. I wanted to participate with my colleagues in types of behaviors below that Robert Sternberg

(1995) identifies as those which teachers use to foster creativity in students:

**Creative Teacher Behaviors** (Sternberg, 1995)

- Encouraging questioning of assumptions
- Allowing mistakes
- Encouraging sensible risk-taking
- Designing creative assignments and assessments
- Letting students define problems themselves
- Rewarding creative ideas and products
- Allowing time to think creatively
- Encouraging tolerance of ambiguity
- Pointing out that creative thinkers face obstacles
- Being willing to grow

I began my dialogue with two colleagues in the staff lounge on a cold winter morning. I don't recall how many inches of new snow we had outside, but count on the fact that there were lots. Humorist Garrison Keillor calls Minnesotans "God's frozen people" and during the winter in question, we were not just frozen but "colder than the vast majority of the world's population will ever experience" (Pratt, 1996, p. B10).

I was rattled after driving to school in the bad weather, and I complained to my friends that our turn at lounge duty—making coffee, cleaning up and setting out treats—was an extra hassle I did not need. We spoke of last-minute things we each had to do to get ready to teach before buses arrived.

"Is it me," I asked, "or is there just an infinite number of things we do? I'm so frazzled all the time—couldn't we organize better? What if we turned things around about what we need to do to teach? Instead of an infinite number of stuff we think about, can't it be organized into a finite number of categories?" I admitted it was a simple idea but one with merit, one that we had probably heard before in staff development.

"Categories *we* feel are important?" asked Eleanor. "That could help us every day?"

"At our school? In our rooms?" asked Kathi.

"Across the curriculum. For all our kids," I insisted.

"I would like one place to go for information about kinds of materials," Eleanor said, "descriptions about technology and other resources I could choose from for teaching to standards."

"I'd want one place for an overview of strategies," Kathi added, "so I could compare and decide which ones to use with different kids."

I told them my idea to create a tool for alleviating our stress—not about lounge duty or even winter snowstorms—but about information overload, especially about student diversity and assessment. Their suggestions defined a place to start and, after school a few days later, we gathered again in the lounge. Other teachers wandered in, so I explained a second time that I wanted to create a planning resource for "pedagogy—how teachers teach and how students learn—[which] is at the heart of school change" (Tyner, 1998, p. 198).

I showed them what I had been reading by Lee Shulman (1986, p. 13–15), who elaborates on the following two kinds of knowledge that teachers juggle simultaneously:

**Content Knowledge** (Shulman, 1986)

- Subject matter content knowledge: understanding the organization of basic concepts and principles of a discipline
- Subject matter pedagogical knowledge: understanding the most useful strategies for representing ideas in a discipline
- Curricular knowledge: understanding the materials available

**Teacher Knowledge** (Shulman, 1986)

- Propositional knowledge: understanding theoretical teaching principles (i.e., checking for understanding, never smiling until Christmas)
- Case knowledge: understanding specific instructional events (i.e., instances of practice for a disciplinary concept or principle)
- Strategic knowledge: understanding situations in which principles contradict one another (i.e., a longer wait time is supposed to produce higher levels of cognitive processing but discipline problems may increase if the pace of the classroom is slowed too severely)

I asked my colleagues for their direction and input to create one tool to turn to for a variety of approaches to both content and teacher knowledge. On that day and on many others during the school year, interested teachers and I periodically discussed what types of information we felt were most important. Starting with the two categories from Eleanor and Kathi—resources and strategies for teaching to diversity and assessments—all of us plugged in as many ideas as we could find from our mountains of materials (my colleagues had them too) and generally exercised our creative muscles to dig deeper and wider.

I brought in Roger von Oech's "Creative Whack Pack" (1992), a set of 64 cards that "whack you out of habitual thought patterns and allow you to find information, generate new ideas, make decisions and get your ideas into action." Throughout our work together, we were encouraged by the "Whack Pack" to question assumptions about our categories, let go of previously cherished ideas, eliminate something if it didn't feel right, tolerate ambiguity and sometimes see what was right in front of us.

We looked for ideas off the beaten path, in contexts outside teaching and from totally different viewpoints. We looked below the surface and made random associations in order to play with different ways of looking at what we were designing. We began to devise new categories for what we do as teachers and were often frivolous with analogies, like comparing our categories of teaching decisions to types of decisions diners make from menu boards on the walls of fast food restaurants.

We were reminded of novelty "flip books," in which combinations of head, torso and legs are changed to make 1,001 funny monsters. We made one that some of us still find not only fun but intuitively useful for flipping among ways to teach. We also made a simplified one for students to use in planning how they could study—what resources and strategies they might use.

We used index cards to make our own version of a "Whack Pack"; we arranged color-coded post-it notes on large poster displays of our categories; we made all kinds of graphic organizers like webs and charts. One teacher's husband used software to program our categories, giving us the ability to select from categories on the computer, key in notes and print out our plans.

Inevitably, the process of working on the project began to influence what we were doing in the classroom. I remember a colleague exclaiming one morning before she hurried away, "This just reminded me of a box of stuff I have in the storeroom. You just made my lesson plan for today."

By the end of the school year, my colleagues trusted in me, the writer in the bunch, to make something happen as a result of all our efforts. One thing we agreed on was that we wanted lists of ideas to choose from—alphabetically when reasonable, not chronologically or hierarchically prescriptive—in categories that could prompt us to think in new, more creative ways to teach.

Over the summer, I distilled most of our work into the following four categories of basic decisions that teachers make several times every day:

## CPR Categories of Practical Decisions

- How many students and teachers are involved in a lesson, unit or course of study (see grouping arrangements in Chapter 4)
- What resources we need (see forms of media in Chapter 5)
- How we find information with students (see strategies for accessing and processing in Chapter 6)
- How we communicate understandings with students (see strategies for reporting and evaluating in Chapter 7)

These categories are nothing new to teachers, administrators, theorists or instructional designers. However, I feel that a key element—creativity—is missing in what most other writers present. I sense that, once categories and subcategories are listed, teachers can put together ideas in their own ways to improve learning by their own students. The idea offers infinite potential for combinations, a lot like creating 1,001 monsters, but more importantly, the plan reflects the fact that no single model of teaching is sufficient to achieve all the aims of schooling because each teacher has his or her own unique situation to satisfy.

Over the next several years, I showed my colleagues what I was working on as I continued to expand *CPR*, and they recognized themselves and their ideas as it developed. This nurturing group environment is behind the efforts I present in this book, and only with help and enthusiasm of my colleagues was I able to build the fledgling idea I envisioned in the east into a plan of action in the south. I salute every one of my friends and hope they find here at least one more "Aha!"

## West

To the west in a Diné *sunwise* journey is found, among other things, energy for thinking and learning. In the south, I had tackled practical aspects of craft knowledge that Shulman described—the "how" and "what" of teaching. For a creative planning resource, my colleagues and I also wanted academic knowledge about the "who" and "why" of our profession.

In the west were the times I examined current research about child-centered, holistic education; curriculum that is balanced and comprehensive; and nonprescriptive instructional design that supports constructivist teaching and learning. Presented in Chapters 1, 2 and 3 are ideas by persuasive and creative researchers who are experienced teachers themselves, describing what they see the best of our colleagues already doing in the schools and suggesting what could and perhaps should happen next. I encourage the reader to study their books cited in my bibliography and look for their articles in such periodicals as *Educational Leadership, Learning, Education Week, Teaching Tolerance, The Council Chronicle, American Educator* and *NEA Today*.

I attended workshops and conferences that influenced *CPR*, each in its own way. Instead of gathering a new mountain of material that might get lost or forgotten when I returned to school, I was now searching for kinds of information that would add to the creative planning tool I had begun with my colleagues. I sought out ideas that were acceptable, workable and doable in my classroom and found writers who are committed to bridging from theory to practice. The fact that my own efforts are derivative of their exemplary efforts lends credence to their usefulness.

My first area of study—holistic and child-centered education— began with a workshop entitled "Multiple Intelligences and the Medicine Wheel" by Cornel Pewewardy (see Chapter 1), award winning Comanche-Kiowa educator and one of twenty founders of the National Association for Multicultural Education. The theory of seven multiple intelligences in *Frames of Mind* (1993), first published in 1983 by Howard Gardner (see Chapter 1), had already made its impact on the classroom, and thousands of teachers like me were refining our methods so that students demonstrated in more than one way that they could apply ideas appropriately in new situations.

In Pewewardy's workshop, he modeled for me that educators also can and should apply ideas to new situations (as I was later to do in *CPR*). He helped me to understand that our American educational system develops three components of human existence as seen on the Medicine Wheel—mental, emotional and physical well-being, represented by Gardner's seven intelligences. However, when we do not develop an awareness of the fourth component— represented by Pewewardy's own contribution of an eighth intelligence, the spirituality of "seeing the big picture"—we deny an intelligence possessed by many of the very students we serve. Many of our children today come from cultures around the world that have world views related to the "big picture" of interconnectedness, and the concept need not conflict with individual beliefs, cause offense to faith communities or trespass across the boundary between church and state.

In my career, I have intuitively sought connections and bridges to be found among curriculum areas, lesson planning and my day-by-day interactions with children. I realized that my plans for *CPR* could benefit from further research about interconnectedness and reflect a better path I believe we could all travel in education for the new century.

Gardner himself later made public not only his own eighth "naturalist" intelligence but also discussed the possibility of an additional "existential intelligence that refers to the human inclination to ask very basic questions about existence. Who are we? Where do we come from? What's it all about?" (Gardner, 1997, p. 9). Among many books about the nature of intelligence are those cited in my bibliography by Gardner, Campbell, Silver, Wahl, Kincheloe and Steinberg, Sternberg, Perkins, Nelson and Clark. Gardner's work with Harvard's Project Zero is found at www.pzweb.harvard.edu; Pewewardy's "Holistic Circle of Learning" is also available online at busboy. sped.ukans.edu/~rreed/NAedPhilosophy.html.

I found more information about interconnectedness in a workshop on cognitive coaching (1993) by Arthur L. Costa and Robert Garmston (see Chapter 1), which introduced the concept of *holonomy*, or the ability of people to grow as individuals while playing part in a larger group. Robert Marzano and Debra Pickering (1997) allude to this ability when they say that results of individual scholarship have usefulness for the group and knowledge is used for the benefit of all. Carlos Cortes (1999) describes the same when he says, "People can come together to create a larger sense of community without having to surrender their smaller sense of affinity communities...One of our challenges is to forge an inclusive, horizontally multicultural *Unum* that can coexist with a healthy, constructive *Pluribus*" (p. 15).

My research about interconnectedness revealed not only that aspects of a child's education do not exist independently but also that disconnected, fragmented and passive learning, without meaningful connections, is thought today to be wasted and harmful. Analysis in Chapter 1 of holonomy and interconnectedness indicate how holism —an integration of world views and multiple intelligences with micro-cultural identities and learning styles—impacts the classroom.

A second search was for information about a balanced and comprehensive curriculum. During the early days of educational reform, my fellow teachers and I were dismayed over the fact that standards were intended to be written only for core disciplines. One teacher (Howe, 1995) wrote that this was the "wrong problem, wrong solution" since surely much more than English, math, science and social studies were essential to prepare students for the 21st century (p. 22). Today, most practitioners and researchers alike agree on the need for a deeper and wider variety of understandings and skills.

To help in my search, I was granted a teacher fellowship in 1992 to participate in a Humanities Curriculum Development program of the American Council of Learned Societies (ACLS), a private non-profit confederation of sixty national scholarly organizations that advance studies in the humanities and related social sciences. The program involved teaming in a seminar setting with fellow MPS teachers and faculty members from the University of Minnesota and Carleton College to discover the very real benefits of preK-16 collaboration and scholarship. I was challenged by the program to reach beyond the practical needs of my day-to-day classroom situation to consider the changing perceptions of teaching and learning—what students and I should be doing together and why we should do it.

One result of my year with ACLS is a balanced curriculum proposed in Chapter 2 that provides only the broadest of academic fields—the humanities, mathematics and the sciences. Although the term *humanities* is not often used in the preK-12 setting, it is defined by Stanley N. Katz (1998b) to incorporate familiar areas that we simply organize differently in the schools—dance, drama, history, language, literature, music, philosophy, the visual arts and humanistic aspects of the social sciences (p. 40).

A majority of these areas were not included in early reform efforts, but today an increasing number of educators express the belief that the humanities are "best suited to drive school renewal in a way that will result in educational, not structural reform" (Purrington, 1994, p. 17). As Richard Ohmann (1994) says, "Our society has never needed more than it does now the kind of vision and critical thinking offered, at their best, by the humanities and by public education…What better place might lead toward friendly cohabitation of the world's peoples on this beleaguered planet?" (p. 6).

I was also encouraged by my studies to recommend in Chapter 2 a combination of single-discipline and interdisciplinary approaches among all areas of the curriculum as the best way to capitalize on strengths of both approaches and to examine diverse ways of teaching and learning. Books that discuss integrating the curriculum are cited by Costa, Fogarty, Jacobs and Gardner in my bibliography.

Chapter 2 additionally recommends infusing other areas of study—personal development, multiculturalism and media/technology literacy—to address the reality of students' diversity of backgrounds and experiences. All three of these areas seem to benefit from interdisciplinary approaches because they imply wholeness and unity, confront personally meaningful questions and experiences students can integrate into their own systems of meaning, proceed from a constructivist view and present an authentic integration of affect and cognition (Beane, 1991, p. 9).

Personal development or affective education involves emotional, social and practical intelligence as well as student empowerment. Among books I found helpful are those cited in the bibliography by Goleman, McCown and Williams.

Infusing multiculturalism across the curriculum is best described by Carlos Cortes, James A. Banks, Donna M. Gollnick and Philip C. Chinn, whose works are cited in my bibliography. One of my favorite quotes about cultural awareness is by Walter Parker (1997): "School is not a private place, like our homes, but the first sustained, daily experience of public life where diverse children are gathered together…For this reason, schools are ideal places to nurture the public habits and values that are crucial for democratic living" (p. 18).

Media/technology literacy across the curriculum involves learners not only in educational uses for computers and television but also in the lifelong skills of analysis and production of information from electronic or digital sources. The most unique features of image-based technologies remain their interactivity and ability for precise communication in ways that we have never had before in the classroom. David M. Considine's overview of media literacy is at www.ci.appstate.edu/programs/edmedia/medialit/article.html. Recommended readings in the bibliography are by Considine and Haley, Tyner, Bianculli, Silverblatt, Lockwood Summers and Watts Pailliotet.

A third search was for information about instructional design that supports constructivist education. Several catalysts for the restructuring of today's classroom have influenced the cyclical process in my own Interconnected Design (see Chapter 3). One is *4MAT System* (1987) by Bernice McCarthy (see Chapter 3), who introduced me to a meaningful instructional sequence based on learning-style research. Another is *Dimensions of Learning* (1992) by Robert Marzano (see Chapter 3), who introduced me to the interdependence of climate-setting, learning-centered instruction and students' use of productive habits of mind. Books by McCarthy and Marzano are cited in the bibliography; other resources about *4MAT* are available at www.aboutlearning.com; other materials about *Dimensions of Learning* are available from ASCD and are listed at www.mcrel.org.

Next is Harvard's Teaching for Understanding project, a highly successful nationwide program built on understanding goals for generative topics at the core of any curriculum. I was introduced to the program by Vito Perrone (see Chapter 2), Harvard professor on an ACLS collaborative team from Massachusetts. Last is the Coalition of Essential Schools, founded by Theodore Sizer (see Chapter 2), headquartered at Brown University and one of the most prominent education-reform initiatives with more than 1,000 member schools.

Crucial in both programs from Harvard and Brown Universities are planning backward from big ideas; a focus on concepts (rather than facts and figures) and understanding (rather than simple recall); covering fewer topics but in more detail; concentrating less on texts and more on hands-on activities; stressing problem-solving and creative as well as critical thinking; making learning practical and meaningful by providing connections to the real world; and viewing assessment as an integral, ongoing part of teaching and learning (*Learning90*, 1990, p. 29). Citations are found in the bibliography by Blythe, Wiske, Perkins, Perrone and Sizer. Information is available at www.essentialschools.org; learnweb.harvard.edu/alps/tfu; www.newhorizons.org and www.brown/edu.

After my studies in the west, I added four theoretical components to my previous list of four practical categories from colleagues in the south, and the following revised overview of *CPR* is the result:

## Creative Planning for Interconnected Teaching and Learning

- Who we are: holistic profiles of teachers as well as learners in Chapter 1
- What we learn: balanced and comprehensive curriculum in Chapter 2
- Why we learn: concepts, big ideas and authentic assessments in Chapter 2
- How we learn: Interconnected design for teaching and learning in Chapter 3
- How many are involved: types of grouping arrangements in Chapter 4
- What we need: types of resources in Chapter 5
- How we find out: types of strategies for accessing and processing information and skills in Chapter 6
- How we communicate: types of strategies for reporting and evaluating understandings in Chapter 7

My task in the west had been value-laden, because I entered territory in which I studied the very meaning of school itself, with more and more questions to explore for which the real possibility existed that I might not find answers. I continue to study today, as the reform movement presents an explosion of new and potentially valuable answers in professional literature and online.

For education to keep up with our culturally complex and information-rich world, both recognizing connections and forming our own are crucial for reform of curriculum as well as imperative for our interactions with students. I came away from this part of my journey believing that creative planning for interconnected teaching and learning has a role to play in restructuring, for it is a time when research as well as practical experience shows that schooling is becoming more connected to the whole of students' lives.

## North

North is the direction in the Diné *sunwise* journey where energy is gathered for such things as reflection, wonder and joy about the unifying nature of all things. I am respectful of the spiritual nature of this time for many First Nations People. For my own personal and professional search to be a more creative teacher, I reflected how all I had learned might come together harmoniously.

I had defined what I value about the role of creativity in our schools. I had listened to fellow teachers' suggestions about day-to-day practical improvements. I had delved into theories about teaching to the whole child using an interconnected design for learning across a balanced curriculum. I had compiled a rather overwhelming twenty-page bibliography, in which were cited origins for the ideas found in my mountain of materials. Now I sought a plan of action for teaching and learning that might unify the nature of my studies.

Most public school teachers are unable to find time and energy to study at length as I had done. As a result, researchers and practitioners are sometimes said to ignore each other, and too often disharmony has been described between them. To borrow a favorite line from a Ngaio Marsh novel (1941), I "pronounce the noise usually associated with the word 'Pshaw'" (p. 88). The creative teachers I know have listened to researchers, or they could not speak the language of research as well as they do. The creative researchers I admire have listened to teachers, or they could not analyze what goes on in the classroom as well as they do. We teach and research alongside each other, through each other and for each other; our work is integrated; we ourselves are interconnected.

I had experienced the benefits of collaboration with post-secondary educators during my studies. At the culminating conference for the ACLS program, Katz (1993, p. 2–4) described it best:

> "There is an unnecessary and counter productive fracture within the teaching profession, between those who teach youngsters in the K through 12

years and those who teach grades 13 to 16...What happens educationally in the schools is important to post-secondary educators not only because pre-collegiate teachers prepare some of their students for us, but also because they have both experiential and theoretical knowledge about pedagogy (both teaching and learning) to impart to us, though we have seldom taken their expertise with sufficient seriousness. Conversely, the disciplinary professionals of the colleges and universities have subject matter expertise that is essential to school teachers. Both need to learn from each other...College humanities teachers cannot tell school teachers how to enhance the humanistic content of their curricula, but they can work with them to make it happen."

As a result of my experiences, I continued working with colleagues such as Ann Watts Pailliotet, professor at Whitman College, consulting editor and contributor to *CPR*; David Considine, professor at Appalachian State University, and Gail Haley, award-winning author/illustrator, with whom I coauthored *Imagine That* (1994); and Cornel Pewewardy, assistant professor at the University of Kansas and contributor to this book.

In the north on my *sunwise* journey, I needed to take care that the balance between research and practice would be correct. However, Herbert in *Dune* should have warned that delicate care could be sticky. Predictably, I got stuck. I was stuck for a very long time, going nowhere, writing too much or too little or nothing at all, and there was no wonder or joy to be found in the north. Significantly, it was another bitter winter in Minnesota and on evenings and weekends, I burned up the woodpile and all the scrap lumber in the garage as I sat at my desk, got up to stoke the fireplace and stomped back to my chair.

I reflected on my vision for *CPR* through a variety of filters and settled on one that, however awkward and imperfect, was still the most acceptable, workable and doable. As my colleagues had requested in the south, *CPR* would present short and sound descriptions for a spectrum of ideas from the reform movement that, when put together creatively, have potential for making learning meaningful for students and for coping with changes in our schools.

However, I was stuck in my thinking about all the aspects of creative planning—holism, balanced curriculum, constructivist planning, grouping arrangements, types of resources and strategies. To be stuck in this theoretical web was not moving me forward in the practical world where I lived and worked with my colleagues.

Artist and fellow teacher Bill Slack suggested I take a break from words and draw my ideas. Clever man. He knew that my colleagues and I had devised visual aids such as a flip book, pack of cards, computer program and graphic organizers. Only the last type of tool—a graphic—was possible in a book, so he encouraged me, a nonartist, to give it a try. I needed to know and show what *CPR* looked like as well as what *CPR* said.

Bill gave me a drawing of one of his ideas and then, when I drew my own, writer's block was released. My Interconnected Design clarified how all I had gathered might be arranged for creative teaching and learning. No little doodle, this:

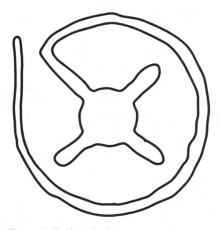

Figure 2: Outline for Interconnected Design

Components that fit into the Design are analyzed fully at the end of Chapter 3, along with the necessary labels that show relationships among concepts. Here, however, in the spirit of planning backward from a big idea, I present only the outline of my organizer as a conceptual base with meaning unto itself that deserves attention before reading Chapter 3.

Even though the drawing was a mere swirl with pen across paper when I did it, it was intuitively correct, and I could see where all the parts of my journey fit in. To me, at first, it resembled the cross section of a seashell. A colleague said it looked like a propeller or maybe a hubcap; another said it was like a section of the double helix, that spiraling staircase of DNA; a third said it was like some

Thing under a microscope from *X-Files*. Certainly not elegant, it was still for me the right graphic for several reasons.

Classically circular, it symbolizes holism. It is not a Medicine Wheel but a spiral, representing a wheel in time, with a gap at the top that is open to past and future. This suits a way of thinking about time for many indigenous people that says we are all moving events within a moving universe, shaped by and shaping our environment, with no starting or ending points.

This same idea was applied to American education by John Dewey as cyclic, recursive or dialectic learning, in which meeting an objective and assessing success are not ends in themselves but remain open-ended. Each educational experience is generated from what went before and generates new experiences, with meaningful ideas growing from and leading to related ideas, questions and problems. Thus was born our time-honored, familiar notion of spiraling curriculum and its companion, spiraling planning, or one coil unwinding into another as we develop a theme.

It did not take long to realize that the left side of my drawing also resembled something which had long fascinated me—the wandering leg of the Nazca Spider, discussed at the beginning of this introduction. In addition, another faintly remembered aspect of the figures in Peru sent me back to my *National Geographic*, in which an art historian said that most of the animals were composed of a single line that never crosses itself. He suggested that if the Nazcas walked on this line, as on a path in a maze, they might have felt "they were absorbing the essence of whatever the drawing symbolized" (Sawyer, 1975, p. 725).

Labyrinths as ancient tools for reflection happen to be well suited to the structural purpose of my Design, as can be seen by some of the following common guidelines for them:

## Guidelines for Walking a Maze

- Bring in a question or intention with you.
- Be a receptive observer of yourself during the process.
- There are no dead ends or prescribed answers.
- Go at your own pace and pause when you need to.
- The path that takes you in is the path that takes you out.

- As you leave, reflect and plan the next walk.
- Each walk is a different experience.

My image, which Brian Plantenberg re-created above using Adobe Illustrator 8.0, is also composed of a single line. If the essence of creative planning for teaching and learning has a chance of becoming absorbed by figuratively walking such a line, I want to be there.

A third influence on my Design is the theory that the number four contributes to harmony and balance, especially when applied to information on wheel analogies. This idea is reflected in my spiral, which is divided into four pie-shaped chambers of time for creatively planning events with and for students.

Drawing with a single line benefited my thinking by opening up the events to those on either side. The Design is thus interconnected, with influences in each event to be understood as flowing back and forth, as do dynamic and evolving aspects of creative planning in real life.

In each event, described in Chapter 3, *CPR* leaves decisions up to individual teachers about when and how fast to move along. The events are driven by the "propeller," if you will, in the center. The four "blades" represent choices to be made among grouping arrangements, resources and two categories of strategies, all of which are described in Chapters 4–7.

At the core of the Design is the whole child, described in Chapter 1, who is surrounded by a balanced curriculum, described in Chapter 2, around both of which all plans for teaching and learning revolve. Looking up through the gap, teachers and learners consider what has gone before and what should come next. The outside rim represents the continuing goal for creative planning: the development of interconnected student behaviors.

Now that I was almost to the end of my *sunwise* journey, I was as close as I could get to a definition of creative planning that might make me a better teacher.

Creative planning for interconnected teaching and learning is based on development of the whole child across a balanced, comprehensive curriculum focused on big ideas. It relies on ongoing meaningful assessments of the child's own construction of understandings. Creative teaching involves planning both backward and forward in a spiraling design with students to meet their needs, through use of interactive grouping arrangements, resources and strategies.

In an interconnected classroom, the move is toward emphasis on personal developmental as well as academic objectives, toward transformed rather than token multiculturalism and toward an expanded definition of literacy that includes the presence of technology in our lives. Less emphasis is placed on teacher control and facts or figures and more emphasis is found on student empowerment and conceptual learning. The move is from didactic teaching toward student exploration, from individual work toward collaborative work, from teacher as knowledge dispenser toward teacher as learning facilitator and from testing of facts and discrete skills toward performance-based assessment.

Constructing knowledge and understanding of interconnectedness itself is the primary focus for America's creative teachers and learners at the start of the 21st century. To do this, we have to understand that a constructivist approach to education serves as the very foundation of interconnectedness. Constructivism blooms from the work of cognitive psychologists who built on Jean Piaget's assertion that real learning involves people reaching their own understandings based on interactions with other people, places, things and ideas.

Global interconnectedness of our very existence reflects much of the educational research of the past, when cultural psychologists not only alerted us to the role of context and community in shaping individual learning but educational anthropologists also illustrated how differences in micro-cultures are assets rather than liabilities.

In the Diné way of knowing, the result of a *sunwise* journey is wisdom or a gathering of unique energies from the four directions that offers access to the union of the intellect and affect, a balance of head and heart (Nelson, 1994, p. 14). For the living of these days, the nation's educational reformers would do well to take such a journey in order to search for wisdom as well as courage to design a concrete, detailed vision of what interconnected teaching and learning looks like when operating at its ideal best.

In the restructuring of our schools, the most important factor remains how creative teachers are allowed to be in designing education that is constructivist, holistic, conceptual and interconnected. We need the freedom to make our vision a reality, to help students understand relationships among all things, all places, all ideas and all peoples. As Patrick Shannon (1991) has said elsewhere in this book, teaching is a continuous discussion of the question, "How do we wish to live together?" (p. 32).

When I finally went through my mountain of papers to throw stuff away, I ended up instead with two stacks to keep. One had classroom ideas that I needed to take back to school. The other had ideas for a new book, and on top was my old *National Geographic*. I had so much fun with Nazca's Spider that I like to imagine what might be done with Hummingbird...

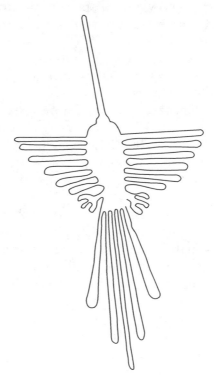

Figure 3: Nazca Hummingbird

# Chapter 1

## Creative Planning for Holonomy and Interconnectedness

"From birth we must struggle…to find some love, some power, some fun, and some freedom. To the extent that we can satisfy these needs on a regular basis, we gain effective control of our lives…All that we get from the outside world is information. We then choose to act on that information in the way we believe is best for us."

—William Glasser,
"The Key to Improving Schools"

When a Minnesota Citizens' Forum was convened in 1997 to address issues of accountability in preK-12 education in the state, participants agreed on an opening statement which reads, "Educate the individual student, using resources of family, school and community—holding each entity accountable for its contributions *to the whole child*" (Hotakainen, 1997, p. B1).

Interconnected teaching and learning is for the student as whole child. A goal of creative teachers is to influence the ways learners act, think and feel, to empower them to have a healthy sense of self— self-confidence, self-assurance, self-restraint, self-reliance and self-worth. Interconnected education maintains that learning for one's entire self is richer than learning for only one's brain, voice, hands or feet.

Interconnected education also empowers learners to respect and value others, to work, learn, play, communicate and solve problems as members of a group. Interconnected educators maintain that building on the ways others are alike and different from ourselves is vital in today's world, when the sense of our common humanity has been threatened by terrorism.

Maintaining a basic integrity of self while simultaneously integrating with others is understood as a universal characteristic of life. Arthur Koestler in *The Roots of Coincidence* (1972) coined the term "holonomy" to describe "the dual tendency of every individual to preserve and assert its individuality as a proud and quasi-autonomous whole, while functioning as an interdependent part of a larger system" (Costa and Garmston, 1993, p. 93).

The authors conclude that holonomy is a natural tendency which creates dichotomies of independence versus integration, competition versus cooperation and individuation versus unity. Creative teachers and learners actively construct not only their own views of themselves but also their places in the world. This inner, constructivist search for meaning is at the heart of interconnected education in which individuality is understood in the context of groupness and the whole is recognized as well as its parts.

Creative planning for the development of holonomy requires an understanding of such aspects of human existence as micro-cultural identities, learning styles, integrated brain processing, multiple intelligences and the world view of interconnectedness. What follows are brief descriptions of these important aspects, and the reader is encouraged to research the work of exemplary educators, theorists and scholars mentioned here.

All aspects will come together in a "Holistic Circle of Learning" symbolizing the Native American educational philosophy of research practitioner and University of Kansas educator Cornel Pewewardy (1999), who calls for "a new recognition of the organic, subconscious, subjective, intuitive, artistic, mythological and spiritual dimensions of our lives" (p. 28). The chapter concludes with a reflective analysis of how holonomy impacts the interconnected educator's classroom.

## Micro-Cultural Identities

Interconnected education places great emphasis on creative planning that takes into account the degrees to which teachers and learners identify with their micro-cultures or the subsocieties to which every individual belongs. Ideas about the cultural identity of an American have been adapted below from *Multicultural Education in a Pluralistic Society* (1998) by Donna M. Gollnick and Philip C. Chinn:

**Types of Micro-cultures** (adapted from Gollnick and Chinn, 1998)
- Age
- Geographical region a person lives in or came from
- Mental or physical exceptionality
- National, racial or ethnic origin

- Place of residence as urban, suburban or rural
- Primary language
- Religion or spiritual philosophy
- Sex or sexual orientation
- Socioeconomic level

Membership in this mosaic of micro-cultures results in traits at a point in time that not only determine what someone looks like but also influence lifestyles, behaviors, attitudes, values and the ways a person thinks, feels and communicates. Carlos Cortes (1999) calls this unique multicultural perspective the *"intersection* of issues that operate within each individual [and] cross-cut to come out differently in every person" (p. 14).

Gollnick and Chinn further explain that each of the subsocieties has distinct cultural patterns shared by those who identify themselves as members of that particular group. Membership in one micro-cultural group can also have an impact on membership in another, and micro-cultures themselves may adapt and change over time or for various reasons. As Joe Kincheloe (1999) observed, "Cultural boundaries are constantly negotiated and transgressed as individuals engage the forces and discourses that shape them" (p. 57).

Members who form a micro-cultural group can not all be stereotyped as being alike in every respect. Subtleties within and among micro-cultures exist in part because identities are really shaped by *how much* someone ascribes to patterns of any particular group (i.e., adolescents who identify with a current fad a lot, some or not at all).

Neither can members be expected to be experts or spokespersons for the group. This has meaning for today's learners who may be struggling to maintain group identities valued by their families while at the same time acquiring and refining skills to participate in the larger society or macro-culture that has different values.

The theory of social development by Lev Vygotsky also centers around identity in which culture and social interaction are prime determinants in cognitive development. "Interaction with others teaches children both what to think and how to think...Every function in the child's cultural development appears twice: first, on the social level, and later, on the individual level; first, between people and then inside the child" (1978, p. 57).

Interconnected teaching and learning draws upon the various ways diverse micro-cultures may access, process, report and evaluate information. Micro-cultures often define intelligence differently than the macro-culture in which they exist, and education for the whole child requires that these differences are taken into account.

Although development of the cognitive function of the brain has been the primary goal of American education, creative planners of today recognize that many of their students, such as those from non-Western European cultures, often think best by integrating cognition with other brain functions. Barbara Clark, author of *Growing Up Gifted: Developing the Potential of Children at Home and at School* (1997) and *Optimizing Learning: The Integrative Education Model in the Classroom* (1986), describes functions of the brain based on Carl Jung's (1964) four types of human behavior or functions of consciousness as follows:

**Functions of the Brain** (Clark, 1997)
- The thinking function (cognitive)
- The feeling or emotional function (affective)
- The physical function (sensing)
- The intuitive function (insightful, creative)

Clark describes integrated brain processing as more than the sum of all functions and different from a single function; the integration creates something new. She explains that when only one of four brain functions—cognition—is developed, the supporting functions of the brain stem (physical sensing, feelings and intuition) are completely left out of the learning process. "While these functions cannot be spoken of or experienced separately, integration of these functions creates high levels of intelligence and the optimal development of human potential" (1997, p. 14).

In light of new information offered by brain research and cognitive psychology in the 1990s, Clark (1996) explains teaching for an integration of the brain functions: "Neuroscientists show integration and association as the overriding functions of the brain…[and] have brought forth a wide base of support to validate the need for teaching to the whole child…Current data show that the integration of all brain functions can better support learning and ensure success to every learner" (p. 2). The author points to the use of such methods as visualization and imagery to enhance higher thought processes, synthesis, creativity and physical well-being.

## World Views

One way that micro-cultural identity may shape our definition of self is by a world view (literally translated from the German "*Weltanschauung*" as "view-of-the-universe") or the understanding of life and society as seen by a person or a group from a particular value system. A world view results in behaviors or attitudes that reflect the value system.

An example of a world view is found in the mystery novel *A Taste for Death* (1986), in which P. D. James describes the viewpoint of a character: "Miss Wharton had been taught to fear in her childhood by her father, and it isn't a lesson children can ever unlearn...And yet, she never blamed her father for past or present unhappiness. She had learned her lesson well. She blamed herself...People, like countries, needed someone weaker and more vulnerable than themselves to bully and despise. This was what the world was like" (p. 162).

Groups from the same country or geographical region also may look at the world in similar ways when they have had common experiences or structural conditions. An example of a national or societal world view is found in a *National Geographic* article in which Alain Mairson (1995) writes the following about his tour of well-kept gardens along the British coast: "It is part of the character and culture of the British people to try to organize and manage land and the things in it to conform to a particular pattern or idea. On the whole we're uncomfortable with allowing free rein to nature and what nature might produce. We're uncomfortable with the possibility that it would make a mess" (p. 56).

Another micro-culture with its own outlook might be called a political or historical group that has lived through the same time period with exposure to the same experiences or events (i.e., the London blitz, the assassination of President Kennedy, the Challenger explosion). Although members of different ages, languages, etc., within the group may differ in their degree of response, they may share a world view because of the common experiences.

An example is given by economists Jeremy Rifkin and Ted Howard, who describe the mechanical world view of Bacon,

Descartes and Newton that science and technology bring order to the world and advance the material self-interests of human beings. As the earth's resources become increasingly limited, the authors call instead for the world view of many non-Western societies—interconnectedness. "Because every event that ever was or will be is interconnected, we share an ultimate responsibility for the infinite past and future...How we choose to live our lives is not only our own individual concern. It is of concern to everything" (1989, p. 252).

The importance of world views in creative planning for teaching and learning is that they broaden the base for a curriculum which stresses interconnectedness. Learners' points of view have limitations because they are often based on incomplete evidence or on the students' own time and place, personal background, direct experience, attitude, interest, need, capabilities or imagination. As Annabelle Nelson in *The Learning Wheel: Ideas and Activities for Multicultural and Holistic Lesson Planning* (1994) elaborates, "People may be very intelligent in their own world views but may not appear to be intelligent in another world view...By incorporating a variety of world views into the learning process, education can be made more whole" (p. 42).

Nelson integrates world views of a variety of ethnic microcultures to define her "Wheel Intelligence Model," in which she lists the following five intelligences (p. 41):

**Types of Intelligences** (Nelson, 1994)
- Practical: learning skills and facts and working with the hands
- Technical: using guidelines and strategies to solve problems
- Conceptual: comparing abstract ideas to discover underlying principles
- Creative: recombining information in novel ways to produce innovation
- Expanded: opening to the intuitive process of the unconscious mind for insight

Nelson suggests including each of her five intelligences in instructional models. She further suggests a shift to teaching strategies that encourage the nurturing of creative and expanded intelligence to foster insights, with conceptual, technical and practical intelligences used to support the insights. "Teachers could reach more students, accommodate individual differences and accelerate learning" (p. 44).

## Learning Styles

Interconnected education also requires an understanding of both teachers' and students' learning styles or the ways people typically tend to think, remember or problem-solve. Robert Sternberg (1994) explains, "A style is a preferred way of using one's abilities. It is not in itself an ability but rather a preference. Hence, various styles are not good or bad, only diverse. We all have a style profile, meaning we show varying amounts of diverse styles, but we are not locked into any one profile. We can vary our styles to suit diverse tasks and situations" (p. 36). Heredity, age, maturation and culture contribute to development of strengths in learning styles, and styles may change over time.

Learning style or cognitive style systems are attempts to explain students' attitudes toward learning, and the systems can have implications for teaching. Creative teachers do not necessarily need to know the specific style of each student for each different learning experience, but they should understand the variety of styles and be able to recognize when students are exhibiting attitudes that are typical of a style.

Vicki Hancock, Brian Moore and Bernard Schwartz (1993) point out that "many students can not learn effectively by just hearing or reading information. For many students accustomed to the visual stimulation of television, learning can be facilitated with charts, diagrams, mind maps, computers, video or other kinds of visual aids. Other students must literally hold ideas in their hands" (p. 8).

A host of theorists apply a variety of terms from neuroscience and developmental psychology to describe style systems, which often are related to integrated brain processing in their social, emotional, physical and intuitive as well as cognitive dimensions. Each system, explains Pat Burke Guild (1997), contends that "the learner is the most important focus...The whole person is educated...The curriculum has substance, depth and quality...and diversity is celebrated...We would be wise to keep the common principles of the theories in mind" (p. 30). Aspects of well-known learning style systems are highlighted below:

## Types of Learning Style Systems

*Conceptual systems theory* (Hunt, 1977): learning by amount of flexibility, tolerance and independence that one brings to authority, conflict and relationship to self, others and the environment (Reiff, 1992)

- Stage 1: rejects information that is not in own belief system; is dependent and needs structure
- Stage 2: has difficulty with seeing viewpoints of others; is breaking away from rigid rules and beliefs
- Stage 3: begins to understand viewpoints of others
- Stage 4: has balanced perspective; can build new belief; is independent

*Conceptual tempo* (Kagan, 1965): learning by acting and reacting to problem situations rapidly or cautiously, accurately or inaccurately

- Impulsive: works fast, is easily bored, is a global thinker
- Reflective: works thoughtfully, concentrates, is a problem solver

*Experiential* (Kolb, 1971, 1985): learning by ways information is perceived and processed depending on positions along the two dimensions of concrete experience as the polar opposite of abstract conceptualization and active experimentation as the polar opposite of reflective observation

- Accommodator: prefers concrete experience and active experimentation
- Assimilator: prefers abstract conceptualization and reflective observation
- Converger: prefers abstract conceptualization and active experimentation
- Diverger: prefers concrete experience and reflective observation

*Field dependence/field independence* (Witkin and Goodenough, 1981): learning by processing information globally (taking in the overall scheme) or analytically (distinguishing parts of the whole)

- Field dependent: enjoys working collaboratively with others; works from intuition; likes and needs concrete experiences; is good at metaphor, analogy and relationships
- Field independent: likes to work alone and is internally-motivated; has a logical, rational, impersonal orientation: likes theoretical and abstract ideas; is good at sequencing and details

*Hemispheric orientation* (Guilford, 1967; Meeker, 1969): learning by dominant use of the left side of the brain (verbally, analytically, sequentially) or right side of the brain (visually, globally, holistically) for processing information. During the 1990s, several educational theorists (Sylwester, 1995; Caine, 1990, 1994a, 1994b; Crowell, 1994; Jensen, 1998; Sousa, 1995; Lowery, 1998) responded to dramatic scientific discoveries about neurons and synapses with their theories of *brain-based education*, a whole-brain approach for dynamic, real-world interactions, as opposed to the hemispheric theory.

*Mental self-government* (Sternberg, 1994): learning by an organization for oneself that corresponds to categories of government

- Functions: legislative (likes to create), executive (likes to follow directions) or judicial (likes to evaluate)
- Forms: monarchic (likes one thing at a time), hierarchic (likes to prioritize) or anarchic (likes no priorities)
- Levels: global (likes the big picture and generalities) or local (likes details and concrete examples)
- Scope: internal (likes to work alone) or external (likes to work with others)
- Leaning: liberal (likes new ways of doing things) or conservative (likes tried and true ways of doing things)

*Modalities* (Barbe and Swassing, 1979): learning by use of sensory channels through which information is processed most efficiently. Most people are multisensory or integrated learners, but some learners have unusual strengths and weaknesses in only one modality

- Visual: prefers pictures and opportunities for mental imaging
- Auditory: prefers talking and opportunities for verbalizing and writing
- Tactual/kinesthetic: prefers touching and opportunities for doing things
- Multisensory: preference may change with task or situation; integrated

*Moral perspectives* (Gilligan, 1989): solving problems in ways that are grounded in different sets of rules for thinking and knowing which influence how a learner looks at self, others and the environment

- Rights perspective: is objective, autonomous, concerned with equality, cares about justice, generalizer

- Response perspective: is subjective, interdependent, concerned with connecting, cares about others, contextualizer

*Perceiving and processing* (Gregorc, 1982a,1982b ): learning by ways information is perceived and processed depending on positions along the two continuums of concrete experience as the polar opposite of abstract conceptualization and processing sequentially as the polar opposite of processing randomly

- Concrete sequential: prefers hands-on experiences, concrete materials and step-by-step details
- Abstract random: is emotional, imaginative, holistic, subjective, reflective and empathetic
- Abstract sequential: is logical, organized and excellent decoder of verbal and visual information
- Concrete random: likes games, experiments, risk-taking, problem-solving and brainstorming

*Personality types* (Myers and Briggs, 1977, 1980; Lawrence, 1982, 1997; Keirsey and Bates, 1984): learning that is influenced by characteristic personal traits (rather than intelligence) depending on positions along four continuums

- Extravert (prefers stimulation) to Introvert (prefers solitude and quiet)
- Sensor (prefers applied knowledge) to Intuitive (prefers abstract knowledge)
- Thinker (prefers logic) to Feeler (prefers sensitivity)
- Judge (prefers making decisions) to Perceptive (prefers open-endedness)

*Physiological styles* (Carbo, Dunn and Dunn, 1986a, 1986b; Dunn, Dunn and Price, 1989): learning that is influenced by preferences in areas of external and internal stimuli

- Emotional preferences for work habits (is motivated by adults, by peers or is self-motivated; has a lot, little or no persistence and responsibility for tasks)
- Environmental preferences for comfort (likes bright lighting or dim lighting; likes warm or cool temperature; likes silence or noise)
- Physical preferences for comfort (moves around or sits still; prefers morning, early afternoon, late afternoon or evening)

• Sociological preferences for teaching methods (works alone, works with one student or works with a group; a lot, little or no adult direction and feedback needed)

## Multiple Intelligences

Interconnected education relies on an understanding of the ways teachers and students exhibit multiple intelligences. Unlike micro-cultural attitudes and values, world views, integration of brain processes and learning styles, multiple intelligences are individual differences in abilities regarding specific subject areas or products.

Similar to Nelson, Robert Sternberg suggests that there are a variety of intelligences, only one of which can be measured by most traditional assessment devices. "Componential intelligence, composed mainly of verbal and logical mathematical abilities, can be assessed by I.Q. and standardized tests. In contrast, creative intelligence and practical intelligence can not be measured with standardized tests even though we know they are of great value" (1997, p. 35).

Howard Gardner (1993) in *Frames of Mind: The Theory of Multiple Intelligences*, advances a theory that shares common ideas with Sternberg (although Gardner does not identify a creative intelligence, indicating instead that strengths or weaknesses in his identified intelligences have an impact on the ability to create in those intelligences). Sternberg and Gardner also worked with others on *Practical Intelligence for School* (Williams et al., 1997), which analyzes "a person's ability to understand herself and her environment, and to use this knowledge to figure out how best to achieve her goals" (p. 1).

Gardner presents evidence for his theory from psychology, biology, anthropology and the arts and describes in familiar language what preK-12 teachers recognize as generally true about how differently children are smart. Gardner continually refines and improves his theory (such as adding an eighth intelligence in 1996 and a new book, *Intelligence Reframed: Multiple Intelligences for the 21st Century*, in 1999), and his work has validated educators' efforts around the country to change traditional assessment patterns from paper-and-pencil tests to authentic alternatives. Much of what teachers understand about multiple intelligences is also due to the work of David Perkins, formerly codirector with Gardner of Project Zero at Harvard and author of *Outsmarting IQ: The Emerging Science of Learnable Intelligence* (1995).

Gardner defines intelligence as the ability to solve problems or make something that is valued or favored within one or more micro-cultural contexts. He urges educators to pay attention not only to learners' biological and psychological inclinations but also to the particular historical and cultural locales where they live and learn. He suggests that we each possess at least eight forms of intelligence to varying degrees, with no two people having exactly the same combination, and they can change over time as children grow, mature and learn new skills.

All intelligences are equally valued, and learners must not only be encouraged to learn in their preferred form but also to transfer strengths to another form, so as to learn in all ways and select goals to achieve in each. Every intelligence can be molded and improved by practice, instruction should appeal to different forms and assessment should be varied to measure multiple forms. Gardner warns educators against trying to teach everything eight ways, creating eight distinct tests and viewing his theory as the only panacea for educational problems.

Gardner's eight multiple intelligences are briefly outlined here:

## Multiple Intelligences (Gardner, 1993, 1999b)

- Bodily/kinesthetic: prefers dance, crafts or athletics and learns best through physical activities, moving and making things; Gardner's outstanding example: Martha Graham
- Interpersonal: is a leader among peers, empathetic and learns best when sharing and cooperating with others; Gardner's outstanding example: Mahatma Gandhi
- Intrapersonal: is self-motivated and learns best by working alone on individualized projects; Gardner's outstanding example: Sigmund Freud
- Logical/mathematical: is interested in arithmetic, strategy games or experiments and learns best by categorizing, classifying and working with abstract patterns and relationships; Gardner's outstanding example: Albert Einstein
- Musical/rhythmic: is aware of sounds and is discriminating listener, always singing or drumming, and learns best using

rhythm and melody; Gardner's outstanding example: Igor Stravinsky
- Naturalist: is good at recognizing objects as members of a class and learns best when exploring the outdoors or from materials related to the immediate environment (i.e., cars, sneakers); Gardner's outstanding example: Charles Darwin
- Verbal/linguistic: is a reader, writer, speaker and/or story-teller and learns best by hearing and seeing words; Gardner's outstanding example: T. S. Eliot
- Visual/spatial: draws, builds and/or daydreams and learns best by visualizing or working with pictures, colors and puzzles; Gardner's outstanding example: Pablo Picasso

### Holistic Circle of Learning by Cornel Pewewardy

Figure 4: Multiple Intelligences and the Medicine Wheel

No one has more completely visualized holonomy and inter-connected teaching and learning than has Cornel Pewewardy in his "Holistic Circle of Learning" (Figure 4). Pewewardy is the author of "Native American Educational Philosophy" (2000b) and has designed the accompanying "Holistic Circle" with the cardinal directions of the Medicine Wheel as passed down from his Comanche and Kiowa traditions.

In the introduction to his online document, Pewewardy (2000a) explains that his philosophical view "encompasses the education of the whole child with many types of learning styles and teaching styles. A child does not live in multiple worlds but lives in one surrounded by sensations, events and feelings impacting him or her from all sides. A holistic educational philosophy is geared toward teaching the whole child and not just separate pieces of the child" (p. 1).

In his article "The Holistic Medicine Wheel: An Indigenous Model of Teaching and Learning," Pewewardy (1999) calls for "educational systems that reflect reality...holistic models of teaching and learning...where cultural understanding is not transmitted accidentally but by design" (p. 31).

The Medicine Wheel or "Circle of Life" is a symbol of wholeness and balance for the self that permeates the philosophy and thought of many indigenous peoples in North and South America. It is a most appropriate icon for holonomy and interconnectedness in education today. Medicine Wheels are carefully and respectfully drawn in several ways, fashioned on the ground as a circle of stones or visualized in a person's mind as he or she stands in what is understood to be the center.

Hyemeyohsts Storm in *Seven Arrows* (1972) explains, "In many ways this Circle, the Medicine Wheel, can best be understood if you think of it as a mirror in which everything is reflected. 'The Universe is the Mirror of the People,' the old Teachers tell us, 'and each person is a Mirror to every other person'. Any idea, person or object can be a Medicine Wheel, a Mirror" (p. 5).

No two people see exactly the same thing when studying a Medicine Wheel and as a reflection of one's personal way of living, it is seen as a life journey in which all things and ideas are connected, related and welcomed as lessons. Found in all parts of the world, circles usually share the same intent: to spatially represent holistic harmony and nonhierarchical, noncompetitive integration of equal elements. They may also represent cyclical thinking and are found as a symbolic motif in art, architecture, science and psychology.

The circle provides a metaphor here for our discussion of micro-cultural diversity, the integrated brain and variety of learning styles and multiple intelligences. Holonomy or the duality of existence is also best represented by this shape as a metaphor for the independent self surrounded by a larger system, various aspects of which may be represented at directional points around the perimeter.

The meaning behind the circle as penultimate metaphor for wholeness of self was described by Carl Jung (1964) in *Man and His Symbols*. Jung remarked that in order to achieve wholeness, one needed to complete individuation, which can be done by recognizing brain functions and the balance between the conscious and the unconscious. Original teaching of the Dakota/Lakota is that balance on the Medicine Wheel is achieved by "traveling the Red Road, when you are in the center. The Red Road is a holistic concept, thus the Red Road for educational synergy would be interpreted as integrated brain processing" (Ross, 1989, p. 30).

David Lazear in *Seven Ways of Knowing: Teaching for Multiple Intelligences* (1991) incorporates imagery of the four directions and four basic elements from the Medicine Wheel for physical exercises that demonstrate how breathing and walking may "intentionally put yourself into more optimal states to face different situations in your daily life" (p. 93). Lazear's four exercises in the use of Gardner's Bodily/kinesthetic intelligence are intended to amplify and deepen one's understanding of the body as a "vehicle for journeying into greater understanding, wisdom and knowledge" (p. 94).

The following examination of Pewewardy's "Holistic Circle" summarizes the discussion in this chapter about creative planning for holonomy and interconnectedness:

**Holistic Circle** (Pewewardy, 2000a)

*Self:* at the center of the circle is the Self or as Pewewardy explains, the individual as he or she learns and grows. The Self is seen as the focus of his Educational Philosophy as it is the focus for interconnected teaching and learning. Placing Self at the core of his Circle, in a position of strength with pathways open to the cardinal directions, he grounds and empowers the individual child in the learning environment. The child not only reflects his/her own micro-cultural identities and learning styles, as has been discussed in this chapter, but the child also changes and adapts those identities and styles as he/she continues learning and growing. Pewewardy (1999) explains, "The inside-out approach means to start first with self—to start with the most inside part of self—with your paradigms, your character and your motives. Look at your own life first, rather than looking at other people's lives, when examining the whole picture" (p. 31).

*Spokes:* emanating from the Self are Gardner's original seven multiple intelligences, with Pewewardy's own idea for an eighth, "Native American World View," which balances the wheel and completes the circle. Pewewardy explains that his addition in 1993 of "Native American World View" is like Gardner's own addition in 1996 of Naturalist, but his World View does not apply solely to nature. Pewewardy defines it as a person's ability to recognize larger contexts about all things or to "see the big picture."

Learners with this intelligence consider the larger spectrum in which any task is embedded, connect one idea to another, like to know backgrounds and reasons for doing things, encourage harmony among their peers and make connections between work and play at school and the outside world. They are interested in large concepts, patterns, biographies, making things work, drawing, stories or mythology and learn best in informal, social situations; by example and modeling; by sharing and helping each other, through peer tutoring and group problem-solving; and in noncompetitive efforts that foster pride in the group.

This world view is part of the spirituality of interconnectedness found in many non-Western cultures, and seeing the big picture can be brought into public schools without infringing on any student's belief system. Donald Oliver (1990) describes it in terms he calls "grounded knowing" compared with "technical knowing": "Technical knowing begins with language describing sharply delineated qualities of events, with a defined object or set of events that can be precisely stated…grounded knowing allows us to feel a connectedness and continuity with the complex natural and cultural relationships in which we are always enmeshed" (p. 65).

Interconnectedness is the second goal of holonomy that Koestler described, at the beginning of this chapter as the self's interdependent functioning within a larger system. As a way of knowing, this concept was also mentioned several times during  discussions of the integrated brain process, learning styles and multiple intelligences. For instance, Vygotsky's social development theory describes the importance of children's interactions with others; Clark and Nelson describe the intuitive function of the brain as holistic learning; several learning style systems speak of holism and connectedness; Gardner's interpersonal and naturalist intelligences are defined in large part by their awareness of connections.

*First ring:* encircling the intelligences are locators for Mental (at the north, representing winter, fire), Spiritual (at the east, representing spring, earth), Emotional (at the south, representing summer, air) and Physical (at the west, representing autumn, water). Pewewardy explains that all of these aspects of human nature are "influenced by the knowledge coming from the Self through the various spokes" and are equally important to develop, balance and integrate for one's lifestyle to be healthy.

Pewewardy has placed "Native American World View" in the Spiritual quadrant along with Gardner's Musical/rhythmic intelligence, because music is of a spiritual nature to First Nations People. In the Emotional quadrant reside the Interpersonal and Intrapersonal intelligences; in the Physical quadrant reside the Visual/spatial and Bodily/kinesthetic intelligences; in the Mental quadrant reside the Logical/mathematical and Verbal/linguistic intelligences.

Some of the cognitive, social, emotional, physical and intuitive dimensions of learning style systems are also echoed in the four quadrants of the Circle, as well as three of the functions of the brain—Mental, Emotional and Physical. Only the brain's intuitive function described by Clark is missing in Pewewardy's work and is replaced in his Circle by the Spiritual aspect of human existence.

Worth repeating is that spirituality is understood here as an awareness of the interconnectedness of all life and does not take the shape of formal religion. A definition of spirituality as the connection between the earth and all living things is shared by many peoples around the world—like the African Gaian and the Australian aborigine—and as such it globalizes education for all children, not just for those from whose culture it may derive.

The Hmong of southeast Asia, for example, believe that "the goal or purpose of life is to maintain balance…balance with oneself; with family and friends; with one's ancestors; with the creatures of earth, sea and air; with forces and manifestations of nature; and with spirits of the unseen world (Willcox, 1986, p. 33).

Pewewardy points out that attention to this fourth aspect of human existence is noticeably lacking in American public education, but for First Nations People it can not be separated out, just as it can not be for other peoples who share this belief. Pewewardy (1999) states that fostering a sense of interconnectedness "enables educators to address the most destructive issues impacting education today: gangs, violence, substance abuse, poverty, homelessness, illiteracy" (p. 31).

He quotes Alex Gerber (1991): "Mainstream educators are focused primarily on objectively-derived solutions...But in today's media-saturated society, and given our eclectic styles of family and religious life, it is not always easy for children to learn that the 'whole' exists. The unity of life on earth may not be self-evident but it can be learned" (n.p.).

Also important to note is that interconnectedness closely resembles Clark's earlier definition of the intuitive brain process as an insightful sense of total understanding for a whole concept, representing the highest-level function of the brain—a synthesis of all functions, providing optimal development of human potential. When Clark (1997) calls for more attention to be paid in public schools to this intuitive function, her words might equally apply to the world view of interconnectedness: "People often repress and devaluate the function because it does not operate in the rational manner western minds have been taught to expect. Activating [it] gives a person a sense of completeness, of true integration, leading to an understanding of concepts and people and to an expansion of the human reach" (p. 14).

In research about common beliefs of indigenous peoples, four aspects for an ideal human existence can be seen to appear again and again—a recognition of universality, harmony with the environment, a sense of group belonging and reflective thinking before taking action. After studying Pewewardy's "Holistic Circle," a philosophical application can be seen for his placement of the eight intelligences by examining intelligences which are opposite each other.

For instance, when someone with the Native American World View strengthens his/her opposite Visual/spatial intelligence, the result might be recognition of connectedness (universality) through visualization or mental imagery. When someone with Musical/rhythmic intelligence strengthens his/her opposite Bodily/kinesthetic intelligence, the result might be an increased sensitivity for and expression of the rhythms and patterns in the environment (harmony). When someone with Interpersonal intelligence strengthens his/her opposite Verbal/linguistic intelligence, the result might be improved communication to pass down traditions, history, stories and wisdom for the benefit of all (group belonging). When someone with Intrapersonal intelligence strengthens his/her opposite Logical/ mathematical intelligence, the result might be a deeper integration of reasoning skills with self-reflection before acting on beliefs, values, needs or feelings (thoughtful action).

*Middle ring:* "Virtue," "Significance," "Competence" and "Power" spaced around the middle ring of the Circle are "societal values influenced by and influencing the child," Pewewardy explains. These values are examined in *Reclaiming Youth at Risk: Our Hope for the Future* (Brendtro, Brokenleg and Van Bockern, 1990), in which the authors believe that a student must possess the following four aspects of self-concept to be healthy:

- Generosity (which reflects Virtue): gained by expression of worthiness and usefulness
- Belonging (which nurtures Significance): found in acceptance, attention and affection from others
- Mastery (which ensures Competence): gained through managing the environment and experiencing success
- Independence (which fosters Power): learned through controlling one's behavior and gaining respect (Farner, 1996, p. 27)

*Outermost ring:* "The global, universal view of the world shows that we are all related and all things are connected, influencing the world and being influenced by the world," explains Pewewardy. This last ring is a reaffirmation of the world view of interconnectedness—seeing the big picture, holism, grounded knowing, intuition—all of which are part of holonomy or the dual existence of individuals functioning interdependently.

In her work about integrative education, Clark (1997) also identifies implications for school reform in the common themes of connectedness, interrelatedness, environmental concern and global awareness that are found today in the research of other fields such as neuroscience, physics, linguistics and systems theory.

By adding his Native American World View to western-European theories of intelligence and by encircling the learner as self within universal interrelationships, Pewewardy solidly places the awarenesses of indigenous peoples into a transformational and workable paradigm for the restructuring of American education. This way of knowing is increasingly important as creative teachers plan for our culturally diverse population in the 21st century.

## Impact on Creative Planning

Creative planners are aware of subtleties of their own as well as their students' micro-cultural identities and use positive behaviors and strategies which respond to the impact that multiculturalism has on learning. Cortes (1999) cautions teachers that "The important questions are 'Are there *patterns* of difference on which I can draw? Are there certain effective ways of dealing with different kinds of students? Can I develop a repertoire of five or six approaches that help me reach more kids?'...The challenge is to use that group knowledge constructively, not destructively; subtly, not stereo-typically" (p. 14).

A goal of interconnected education then is to infuse day-to-day curriculum and assessment with action plans that reflect diversity but that also *cross* micro-cultures so as not to stereotype any one micro-culture. Diversity among all micro-cultures is valued and equality is promoted for all groups not only by including multiple perspectives in curriculum materials but also by incorporating relevant teacher behaviors and instructional strategies that respect the backgrounds of all group members.

Creative planners engage students more than ever before in the informal curriculum of their upbringing, family expectations and community life. All students are afforded the skills for participation in the dominant society while maintaining their micro-cultural group identities to the degree that they and/or their families choose.

More types of learning groups are used from Chapter 4, such as self-managed small groups, individualized learning centers and partnerships with members of the community. Creative uses of learning resources are also the result from Chapter 5, such as "talk radio" sessions for learners to express opinions about current events or documentary videotaping of objects valued by different micro-cultures of age, gender or ethnic origin. Students' lives outside school are seen as a vital resource, and the mass media is scrutinized for its persuasive power to direct young people's lives in negative and positive ways.

The informal curriculum of home or neighborhood is understood to result in varied approaches to social interactions and academic tasks at school. Some national and ethnic micro-cultures strongly identify with the values inherent in rights of a group rather than rights of an individual, in cooperation rather than competition, in measuring success by giving rather than by acquiring, in responsibility for and reliance on a group rather than for and on oneself, in strong kinship ties rather than associations based on common interests and in adhering to a small group's identity rather than assimilating into a larger one.

Other micro-cultures vary in the degree of positive experiences they have had in the past with peer relationships, authority figures and uses of personal time and space. They may or may not relate to the school culture, may consider formal learning as an important part of their lives or may view time at school as unconnected to life outside.

In the interconnected classroom, "the best procedure for inducing an individual to progress toward complexity and flexibility is to match that person's present stage of personality development to an environment tailored to the characteristics of that stage, but in such a way as to pull the individual toward the next stage of development" (Joyce and Weil, 1996, p. 96).

When students exhibit a variety of attitudes toward the learning experience, teachers also creatively plan mutually-agreed upon expectations for working together in the classroom. These expectations may imitate or replicate those that students are familiar with in other settings (i.e., one creative teacher uses numbered cards on a spindle for learners to request help during lessons by silently "taking a number" as they might at a store counter).

Whereas differences in learning styles and micro-cultural identities are respected, only personal behaviors are encouraged which positively promote learning and do not infringe on the dignity and rights of others. Real-world discussions offer students opportunities to relate positive behaviors to lifelong learning in the outside world.

Creative interconnective strategies are used from Chapter 6, such as bridging not only from micro-cultures but also from the past or from the outside world. From strategies in Chapter 7, information is organized about topics in reflective discussions using perspectives chosen by students themselves, and a variety of strategies for research and communication include collaborating, journaling, debating and storytelling. Gollnick and Chinn also suggest strategies in their book that are multicultural and character-building, along with exercises in problem-solving for real-life situations that involve diverse experiences of students.

In support of integrated brain processing, A. C. Ross (1989), a member of the Mdewakantonwan tribe of the Dakota nation, gives examples from his experience of traditional tribal modes of education: learning by discovery; by example; by use of visual aids, diagrams, charts, key words and phrases; by individualized and small-group instruction; by testing that is not in written form; by storytelling with good moral values of generosity, courage and fortitude; by riddles and meditation; and by being given the very best materials to practice on (p. 47–50, 190).

Theorists continue to develop learning style systems to examine different ways learners have for accommodating new or difficult information and skills. Creative teachers are receptive to this research and, as learners themselves, most of them concentrate (in their own stylistic ways) on each theory as it is presented, absorb what is revealed about teaching and learning, retain the insights that ring true in their experiences with students and accommodate what makes sense to them for improvement of the everyday world in their classrooms.

They are keenly aware that an understanding of learning style diversity leads to better interactions and communication among all concerned in the school, family and community, and they achieve, maintain and document a versatile approach to the needs of learners when administrative support of time and resources is present at the school, district and state levels.

What Rita and Kenneth Dunn (1989) have said in their workshops for over thirty years perhaps best reflects the intuitive understanding that creative and reflective teachers have about learning styles: "If children do not learn the way we teach them, we must teach them the way they learn" (p. 4).

Pewewardy (1994) calls for a "culturally responsive pedagogy as an important aspect of the educational reform presently taking place in the nation's schools. Essentially, it is at the heart of all 'good' teaching. It helps teachers meet the needs of each individual in the classroom by addressing cultural and experiential backgrounds and special expertise each student has developed" (p. 30). He offers the following "Principles for Culturally Responsive Teaching" that add to a description of interconnected teaching and learning:

- Teachers use students' prior cultural knowledge as a foundation in the teaching and learning process.
- Classroom practices are compatible with students' language patterns, cognitive functioning, motivation, and the social norms and structures to which they are accustomed.
- Assessment practices and procedures reflect the diversity of student strengths and an appreciation for learning styles and intelligences.
- The attitudes, beliefs, and actions of the school model respect for cultural diversity, celebrate the contributions for diverse groups, and foster understanding and acceptance of racial and ethnic plurality.
- Teachers value cultural knowledge, view students as assets, and integrate these assets into classroom instruction.
- Teachers act as cultural mediators, and provide assistance through the use of questions, feedback, and scaffolding.
- Schooling provides children with the knowledge, language, and skills to function in the mainstream culture but not at the expense of losing their native language and original cultural orientation.
- Schooling helps children participate in multiple cultural or language domains (arenas) for diverse purposes without undermining their connection to their original culture.
- The community and the home validate and support the academic success of its children.

Reading about types of intelligences enables creative teachers to better appreciate the popular culture of students, such as the kinesthetic intelligence of skateboarders and the visual discrimination skills of avid trading card collectors. Instructive in the social studies curriculum is to discuss possible rationales behind the valuing of intelligences by different geographical regions of the country, by rural versus urban or suburban lifestyles and by diverse age groups.

The biggest change in interactions with students of multiple intelligences is that teaching is conducted in different ways and offers them more opportunities to make choices in grouping arrangements, use of resources and strategies for learning. Students are grouped in various arrangements to learn in their preferred intelligence or to strengthen their uses of other intelligences.

Cooperative groups may be organized with members who demonstrate different abilities but with an assessment tool that is a rubric for which members are held responsible as a group. Assessments never measure strengths in intelligences but offer opportunities for learners to demonstrate understanding in different ways. Assessment strategies are more learner-generated and reflective, and self-assessment is crucial to help learners understand their intelligences.

Even with larger group arrangements in which all the students are expected to learn the same material, teaching and assessing the material is conducted in many ways to strengthen intelligences by using resources and strategies creatively. In Chapter 5 are categories of resources that appeal to every intelligence according to how they are used.

Examples of successful learning strategies from Chapter 6 are bridging from one intelligence to another; focusing with multisensory strategies; organizing in a visual, kinesthetic, verbal or linear manner; and questioning using Robert Marzano's framework. Remembering and language-learning strategies can be tailored to different intelligences on an individual basis —such as visualization or storytelling—and all learners need basic skills in sequencing and categorizing.

Successful learning strategies from Chapter 7 are discussing using Socratic dialogue questions with specific roles for teacher and learners; researching; reading and literature responses as well as writing strategies that offer students choices among different study techniques and resources. Also offering learners choices among types of human-based and media-based reporting is basic to an instructional design with goals for strengthening multiple intelligences. These types of endeavors are accompanied by group or peer assessments, self-assessments, portfolios and/or exhibitions, sometimes with rubrics designed by the very learners themselves who demonstrate strength and creativity in the intelligences involved.

After studying Pewewardy's "Holistic Circle," I saw a practical application for his placement of the eight intelligences within the four quadrants. Grouping students who demonstrate strengths in intelligences that are opposite on the circle engages the learners in a complementary manner that results in very productive cooperative work, much like pairing complementary or opposite hues on a color wheel.

For instance, learners who see the big picture are grouped with those with visual/spatial aptitudes to work on art projects; learners who are intelligent in music are paired with those who are intelligent in movement to plan dance performances; those who work best in interpersonal relationships are grouped with those who have strong linguistic abilities to do plays or storytelling; and reflective, intrapersonally intelligent children are paired with logical, analytical peers to engage in thoughtful problem-solving.

Learning resources from Chapter 5 are most appropriate for fostering holonomy when they are human-, object- or environment-based because learners are actively constructing meaning in ways that are hands-on and personal. Learning strategies from Chapter 5 include bridging from the contextual "big picture," the outside world, the natural world, an abstract concept or the four aspects of human nature on the Medicine Wheel. The best focusing strategies are asking the over-riding question "Why are we doing this?", telling a fable or parable, using a visual or playing music and using intrinsic rewards as reinforcements for focused behaviors.

Using advance organizers, closing organizers, big concepts or spatial descriptions offers learners organizing scaffolds on which to connect information. Remembering strategies are those using sensory associations, and use of a whole word approach is best for language and literacy learning in which students learn by making connections. Questioning and discussing that encourage interconnected thinking can be found in "Reflective Questions That Span the Inquiry Process" in Chapter 7.

Human-based communicating and two- or three-dimensional assembling are part of the personalized approach for holonomy. Research tasks that examine a "big picture" appeal to many students, and they should use all the types of study strategies, from being told to firsthand experiencing. Reading and literature responses as well as writing strategies are usually reflective, anecdotal and/or self-exploratory.

In interconnected education, students are empowered with a healthy sense of wholeness because of emphasis on their micro-cultural identities, world views, integrated brain processes, learning styles and intelligences. On the other hand, they are empowered to work and play successfully with others who have diverse identities, views, cognitive processes, styles and intelligences.

We are all related. All things are connected.

# Chapter 2:

## Creative Planning for Interconnected Curriculum

> "As we listen to the female voice, gain greater understanding of the perspectives of indigenous peoples and become more global, our curriculum will need to reflect richer views of how humans construct meaning...[including] the beauty, the interconnectedness and spirituality in the world."
>
> —Arthur L. Costa and Rosemarie Liebmann,
> "Process Is as Important as Content"

C urrent educational theories that have the most meaning for creative teachers are those that restructure education as interconnected teaching and learning rather than as acquisition of fragmented, core knowledge and skills. Reviewed in this chapter are crucial ideas from theorists who name what is important in creative planning for an interconnected curriculum—a balanced approach between academics and the whole of children's lives along with teaching for the understanding of big ideas.

### Balanced Curriculum

As discussed in the introduction, traditional 19th century core academics—English, math, science and social studies—were initially targeted for content standards during educational reform in the 1990s. This narrow approach was described by Diane Ravitch (1995) as a backlash against the outcome-based movement of the 1980s that included some "interdisciplinary or nondisciplinary topics such as communications, environment and ecology, self-worth and adaptability to change" (p. 163).

This ironically back-to-basics attitude by a reform spokesperson met with an angry reception by many teachers, parents and community members who asked, if the topics mentioned by Ravitch did not have their place in restructuring, how could children be prepared to solve complex problems and function successfully as global leaders in the 21st century?

Arguments raged over what constituted "core" disciplines for today's world, and the result was that more than four subject areas were eventually included at the national level. States and school districts wrote—and continue today to implement and refine—as many as ten interdisciplinary standards for broad-based, student-oriented learning areas, rather than for territorially narrow, content-oriented disciplines.

The embedding of thinking skills into the context of meaningful curricular experiences became apparent in many state standards. Anne Lewis (1995) observed, "Judging by the new content standards now showing up, the emphasis is apt to be on learning content more through critical-thinking and problem-solving strategies than through rote learning of discrete facts. The groups producing standards so far have been politically savvy enough to balance knowledge with process, but the critics haven't often seen that" (p. 746).

In addition, business leaders did not overwhelmingly favor a total return to basics. When corporate executives of Fortune 500 companies were surveyed about the ideal education for children of the 21st century, they emphasized the need for "analytical, logical, higher-order, conceptual and problem-solving skills in addition to proficiencies in writing, reading and interpersonal communication" (Nidds and McGerald, 1995, p. 22). One businessman said, "What we look for are people who know how to ask questions, to evaluate situations, to solve problems," and another described desirable employee characteristics as "Curiosity. Good communication skills. Diligence. Self-direction" (Fitzgerald, 1996).

Former Education Secretary Richard Riley was rendered speechless in 1995 during a televised Goals 2000: Town Meeting, when a manager of the Ford Motor Company was asked to list the most essential job skills for the 21st century and he replied, not with the three R's, but with one word—teamwork.

An academics-only reform movement also ignored some of the most basic needs learners have today, when "all across the country schools are trying to cope with their students' ravaged lives by bringing in teams of social workers, by setting up programs for teenage mothers or drug abusers, and by offering limited dental and medical services. The Educate America Act doesn't even mention such programs, let alone provide them with the funding and public attention they so desperately need" (O'Connor, 1993, p. 704). Theodore Sizer (1995b) added, "While recognizing and appreciating the good will behind all that work, most of us who have taught a long time look at the standards and sag. This is particularly true of those who are teaching high school kids living under terrible conditions...So you read these lists, and you look at the kid who has just watched his brother get shot, and you say, 'Where is the country going?'" (p. 7).

An old model of teaching that sees students as merely empty vessels to be filled with academics has been replaced by child-centered schools, in which no conflict exists for creative teachers between knowledge and well-being. Teamwork as well as self-esteem, interconnectedness with one's environment and the ability to successfully adapt and communicate with others are recognized as important to be developed. The curriculum model described below embraces not only a balanced approach for the academic disciplines but also includes such interdisciplinary areas as personal development, multicultural education and media/technology literacy.

## Academic Disciplines

An interconnected academic curriculum includes the fields of mathematics, natural sciences, applied sciences, social sciences, physical education and the humanities. Generally accepted in a definition of the humanities are the areas of dance, drama, history, language, literature, music, philosophy and visual arts. Katz (1993) elaborates, "One can say that the fields of the humanities are those which study human experience, past and present, by means other than those of precise measurement" (p. 4). He also includes from the social sciences the "humanistic aspects" of economics, political science, psychology and sociology.

Humanities as a term has never been used much in preK-12 schools (except in Paideia), and Katz points out:

> "What we need to do is to determine how the new, inclusive and innovative humanities can increase the range of knowledge necessary to the intellectual development—that is, the liberal education—and social acculturation of young Americans, and how some of the new humanities research and teaching techniques can be made to work for school teachers. We must all, pre-collegiate and post-secondary teachers, work out not only new teaching materials and routines, but also strategies for establishing them...[Students] must be taught to read with discrimination, reason in complicated ways, appreciate the arts and distinguish values. These things they will learn primarily from the humanities, and they are not frills. They are indispensable" (p. 10).

Matthew Lipman (1984) adds that the discipline of philosophy in the humanities, and its subdiscipline logic, is the basic subject, because its content is thinking itself and it "provides the criteria that makes it possible to distinguish better reasoning from worse. Philosophy has long been concerned with the improvement of reasoning proficiencies, clarification of concepts, analysis of meanings, and fostering of attitudes that dispose us to wonder, inquire and seek meaning and truth" (p. 51).

*Integration:* single-discipline studies at their best are summarized by leading educators such as Heidi Hayes Jacobs (1986, 1989, 1992) as systematic, straightforward and focused; necessary for knowledge acquisition; efficient learning of closely related concepts and patterns of reasoning; and necessary examinations of ways professionals approach problems using methodologies unique to their fields. Kathleen Roth (1994) suggests, "We best develop our students' understanding of the world and its connectedness by giving them access to a variety of powerful lenses through which to view it, and the best way to craft those lenses is to immerse our students deeply (though perhaps not solely) in disciplinary studies" (p. 48). Howard Gardner and Veronica Boix-Mansilla (1994) explain, "Different disciplines call on different analytic styles and approaches to problem solving...Disciplines are not the same as subjects...[which] are devices for organizing schedules and catalogues" (p. 16–18).

On the other hand, interdisciplinary education is based on the principle that the ideas in any field have not occurred in isolation, and a comprehensive analysis of those ideas need not be limited to any single discipline. As Jerome Friedman (1999) points out, a continuum exists between the humanities and sciences because "creativity is similar throughout the entire curriculum. The same kinds of insight in terms of understanding something that come in the sciences come in the humanities, making relationships between various fields of study" (p. 63).

Interdisciplinary studies are championed by a great many educators (Beane, 1991; Krogh, 1992; Ebersole, 1992; Tanner, 1992; Perkins, 1992; Wiggins, 1992) because they mirror the real world; imply wholeness and unity rather than separation and fragmentation; give a broader view of the subject matter of each discipline; foster collaboration among teachers; offer young people opportunities to confront personally meaningful questions and engage in experiences related to those questions; capture students' interest and increase their levels of concentration; require students to do more higher-level thinking; yield more long-term learning; foster more creativity and thoughtfulness; and create conditions for students to see connections spontaneously.

Integrating the curriculum takes a variety of forms, "from better coordination between disciplines to a total blending of them into major conceptual themes, strategic processes or problem-based pursuits that cross disciplines" (Willis, 1992, p. 2). Some creative teachers integrate subject areas not only for educationally sound reasons but as a practical answer to the problem of an overcrowded curriculum.

Another form of interdisciplinary study is the self-contained core model found in typical American elementary schools, in which one teacher with multiple subject credentials integrates all skills, content and learning experiences in two or more subject areas, using a connecting topic to plan instruction in each area. The classroom teacher may also organize a topic with teachers in art, music, media, physical education and/or other specialist areas so that learners apply information and skills from these areas to a project that connects the topic to the areas.

For middle and high schools, a sampling of models that prove successful are the following (Ross and Olsen, 1993):

- Single-subject integration: the content and skills of one subject area are applied to real life.
- Coordinated model: two or more teachers integrate single subject areas to the same students, separately but cooperatively.
- Integrated core model: one teacher integrates two or three subject areas with the same students over two or three periods.
- Integrated double core model: two teachers join their integrated core models with the same students (i.e., math in context of science, language in context of social studies).

Robin Fogarty in *The Mindful School: How to Integrate the Curriculum* (1991a) identifies ten integrative models, and as editor of *Integrating the Curricula: A Collection* (1993), she presents articles that have more practical examples.

*Balanced approach:* capitalizing on strengths of both single-disciplinary and interdisciplinary studies is a better offering to students of diverse ways of learning, according to many experts (Willis, 1992; Jacobs, 1989; Jacobs, 1992; Perkins, 1992; Wiggins, 1992; Ackerman, 1992). Jacobs (1989) explains that students cannot fully benefit from interdisciplinary studies until they acquire solid grounding in various disciplines (p. 8), and creative teachers argue that a balance between interdisciplinary and single-discipline studies is needed because both approaches are found in the real world. Jacobs (1992) elaborates, "Let's get away from the rigidity of the disciplines but let's not backlash and go to the other extreme. I don't think it's a good idea to drop the power of what each discipline can offer. The most effective schools deliberately provide students with a variety of experiences" (p. 6).

David Perkins (1992) advises, "Teachers must first decide whether they value disciplinary expertise or flexible eclecticism more highly—an issue not easy to resolve...It's not clear which approach would serve the learner best in the long run. I could trump up arguments on both sides" (p. 6). Grant Wiggins (1992) suggests, "What is needed is better teaching of all subjects, including the finding of meaningful connections between them...Any thoughtful approach to curriculum is going to make things more contextualized and interesting" (p. 4). David Ackerman (1992) sums up, "Educators need to first and foremost consider carefully which approach will best serve student needs" (p. 6).

To achieve a balanced approach, Jacobs and James Borland (1986) suggest that "once students acquire a familiarity with the dimensions of the disciplines, it becomes feasible to develop carefully structured interdisciplinary study using a four-step method" (p. 161). The method is adapted as follows to reflect interconnectedness of curriculum, as discussed in this chapter and instruction, assessment, learning groups, resources and strategies in subsequent chapters:

- Step 1: Select a topic (such as a "Fundamental concept" or a "Generative topic" below).
- Step 2: Brainstorm associations (such as connections among disciplines and the real world).
- Step 3: Formulate guiding questions for inquiry (such as "Essential questions" and "Sub-essential questions" below).
- Step 4: Design and implement activities (such as "Exhibitions" and "Performances of understanding" below; see also Chapters 3, 4, 5, 6 and 7).

## Personal Development

Creative teachers recognize that affective and cognitive growth go hand in hand. The two rely on each other, because learners "acquire a sense of significance from doing significant things and positive self-concept can not be divorced from accomplishment. The curriculum for a course can not effectively exclude a non-academic concept such as values, for instance, since values themselves are represented and modeled by what is on a course syllabus" (Wynne and Ryan, 1993, p. 21).

Concepts of responsibility, teamwork, tolerance and honesty remain a part of day-by-day, hour-by-hour real life in schools. Interconnected education includes the nurturing of student competencies in knowledge about themselves (emotional intelligence), about other people (social intelligence), about school itself (practical intelligence) and about self-directed learning (student empowerment). A teacher's adage, "I take children where they are and bring them forward—socially and emotionally as well as intellectually" is part of interconnected education.

*Emotional intelligence* (McCown et al., 1998): understanding one's emotions and relationships, including the following:

- Self-awareness: recognizing and evaluating one's thoughts, feelings and behaviors
- Managing emotions: realizing what is behind one's feelings; channeling emotions in positive ways; recognizing the best thing to do in a situation; decreasing impulsivity
- Empathy: understanding feelings and perspectives of others
- Communicating: expressing personal opinions, concerns and ideas positively; active listening
- Cooperation: effectively working with others on common goals; following through on commitments
- Resolving conflicts: using the above emotional skills for problem-solving to help solve differences of opinion

*Practical intelligence* (Williams et al., 1997): understanding the context of school and its tacit expectations. Robert Sternberg (1990) explains, "Teachers have a wide array of expectations for students, many of which are never explicitly verbalized. Students who cannot meet these implicit expectations may suffer through year after year of poor school performance without knowing quite what is wrong" (p. 135).

Sternberg and a Yale team of investigators joined efforts with Project Zero at Harvard to develop the curriculum in *Practical Intelligence for School* (Williams et al., 1997), four dozen lessons based on the following kinds of tacit knowledge:

- Managing yourself: recognizing kinds of intelligences, learning styles and ways to improve one's own learning
- Managing tasks: using problem-solving strategies and study skills to get work done on time
- Cooperating with others: communicating effectively and analyzing social networks at school

*Social intelligence:* abiding by universal, non-negotiable and timeless standards of conduct that apply to everyone in society, regardless of micro-cultural identities. By the mid-1990s virtually every state education department had issued recommendations that schools include social development. Edward Wynne and Kevin Ryan (1993) elaborate, "Moral education and character formation in schools aim to transmit to pupils the community's best values and ethical ideals. An anthropologist might describe this effort as socializing the young into tribal morality...To do less is beyond being foolish. It is irresponsible" (p. 21). The authors concluded that an important part of education, then, is regularly posing to students the question, "What is the right thing to do?" Many public and private programs adopted in schools are based on classical values, such as the following:

- Caring/compassion/charity
- Cooperation/self-restraint
- Ethics/citizenship
- Honesty/trustworthiness/integrity
- Justice/fairness
- Perseverance/fortitude/persistence
- Respect/tolerance/flexibility
- Responsibility/duty

*Student empowerment:* a learner-generated design for curriculum involving inquiry that comes from the interests of learners themselves. Student empowerment requires not only sharing of the initial decision-making with students but also an opening up of the entire curriculum all the way through to allow for more choices, challenges and control for self-directed learning. Learners and teachers generate questions and plan collaborative learning strategies together. Learners are also encouraged to pursue their own personal path of inquiry when one question generates another or a new interest emerges.

Two teachers who base instruction on a learner-generated design describe their experience (Fisher and Cordeiro, 1994): "In our early days as teachers, curriculum was segregated...Our next step was connecting subjects thematically across subject areas, but teachers still did the planning...Currently, teachers give their students input into what will be learned and to collaborate with them on curriculum," drawing on interests of children and teachers in addition to the prescribed curriculum (p. 3). Another example is the Coalition of Essential Schools' philosophy of student-as-worker rather than teacher-as-deliverer-of instruction. Learners are encouraged to participate in the choice and implementation of concepts, essential questions, texts, objectives, strategies and exhibitions (Shannon, 1991, p. 32).

Jacobs and Borland (1986) argue that "students can, and in many cases should, be involved in development of interdisciplinary units" (p. 162), and Wiggins (1987) says that "there is no good reason why students can't have some say in designing essential questions" (p. 12). In planning a theme, Scott Willis (1992, p. 4–5) offers the following questions to foster student empowerment:

- Has it been planned from scratch with kids?
- Does it arise from students' own questions and concerns?
- Does it have substance and application to students' real life?
- Is it meaningful and age-appropriate?
- Does it fascinate students once they get immersed in it?
- Does it have major significance for students and society?
- Does it offer opportunities for students to create their own learning tasks?

An eloquent advocate for student empowerment is Ruthanne Kurth-Schai (1988), who calls for a total "reconstructed conceptualization of childhood" (p. 114). Rather than "children as victims of adult society...as threats to adult society...as learners of adult society [in which] the types of tasks assigned to youth indicate that young people are not expected to contribute to the welfare of the family nor the community...(we need instead) children as social inventors...contributors in society" (p. 115–116).

Kurth-Schai typifies youth-oriented educational innovations as conceived, directed and controlled by adults' perceptions of children's needs rather than by children's perceptions of their needs. She describes instead students from diverse backgrounds deciding together areas of responsibility in which they participate, assuming administrative control and receiving recognition for the work they do (p. 125–126).

She calls for a reconceptualization of the role of school as "agent of cultural transformation rather than cultural transmission," changing from museums where knowledge and values are preserved to laboratories where students design, simulate and evaluate alternative forms of the future (p. 127). She explains that this transformation is accomplished by providing opportunities for young people to act upon their thoughts in real-life settings.

### Multiculturalism

When the 2000 census revealed a higher-than-expected number of people—nearly seven million black and Hispanic Americans—who said they belonged to more than one race, Levonne Gaddy (2001) described the data "as the beginning of our having to redefine this social myth that we call race" (p. A14).

The census group in question was largely dominated by young people, "the most culturally, racially, ethnically mixed group of Americans ever. They do not see the world in a polarizing black-white construct...They aren't wed to a particular definition of who they are, who they should be, who they have to be...Even when they do confront racial barriers, they navigate them better than we did" (Smiley, 2001, p. 10).

Tavis Smiley further suggests that the richness of ethnic life in public schools today demands and deserves creative teachers who harness the power of culture to draw people together across racial and ethnic divides and provide a platform on which to relate. His ideas are to have dialogues, not monologues; embrace the essence of diversity; not to take rumors, statistics or stereotypes at face value; and "spend some time talking to kids—see how rational and reasonable they are about race matters" (p. 10).

Pewewardy (1998) explains that being a culturally responsive teacher means "being sensitive, aware and capable of employing cultural learning patterns, perspectives, family structure, multiple world views and languages in the teaching, learning and mental ecology of the classroom" (p. 31). Joseph Bruchac (2000) adds: "Our children come from an incredibly wide range of backgrounds and have many different ways of experiencing the world. We need to read and experience, with authenticity, things from their point of view to be a fully rounded human being" (p. 29).

Interconnected teaching and learning is rigorously multicultural across the curriculum, contrary to an argument by some educators that mathematics, natural sciences and physical education are pure disciplines and are thus exempt from multicultural reform and innovation. Instructional materials in these subjects, however, are no more neutral and culture-free than they are in the social sciences and humanities (Hamer, 1994b, p. 2). Irving Hamer (1994a) explains: "Multiculturalism affirms the tradition of the United States: in each of us there is a piece of all the rest of us. Cross-cultural studies compare cultures...Multiculturalism is to know and understand a context beyond the superficial"(p. 2).

Katz (1993) adds that a principal challenge to educators is "the clarification of pedagogically and intellectually responsible approaches to multiculturalism at all levels of education" (p. 8). Gardner (1998) calls for a melding of progressive and traditional perspectives in education that results in a return to "the purpose of K-12 education, which is to enhance students' deep understanding of truth (and falsity), beauty (and ugliness) and goodness (and evil) as defined by their various cultures" (p. B4).

However, a study by Pewewardy and Donald Willower (1993) found that views and values of Native American high school students were "shaped less by ethnicity or even reflective choice than by prevailing imagery of the mass media" (p. 55). An appreciation for the richness of cultures is important to counteract television's "frame and filter through which we see the world and its people (in) gloom, doom, famine, flood and disaster...Teachers must help students explore the ways media construct our window on the world and evaluate this representation in terms of its fairness and accuracy" (Considine, 1995, p. 5). Award-winning artist and author of over a dozen picture books, Gail E. Haley "forges cultural links by showing how children from different countries and backgrounds often share the same stories, myths and legends" (Considine and Haley, 1994, p. 147).

*Multicultural curriculum* (Cortes, 1990): "A continuous, integrated, multiethnic, multidisciplinary process for educating all American students about diversity, a curricular basic that is oriented toward preparing young people to live with pride and understanding in our multiethnic present and increasingly multiethnic future" (p. 3). Cortes offers the following seven student objectives for increasing awareness of diversity and decreasing social distance among groups:

- Understanding of groupness
- Understanding of both objective and subjective culture
- Ability to see the perspectives of others
- Understanding of our *E Pluribus Unum* heritage, both for the nation as a whole and for individual groups
- Understanding of the potential contribution that *Pluribus* can make to our society
- Ability to use, and not be used by, the media
- Deeper civic commitment

*Multicultural education* (Banks, 1994): "The total school environment reflects the diversity of groups in the classrooms, schools and the society as a whole...One of multicultural education's important goals is to help students acquire the knowledge and commitment needed to think, decide and take personal, social and civic action" (Banks, 1991, p. 4). Banks offers the following five dimensions (1994, p. 48) that help educators implement and assess programs that respond to student diversity:

- Content integration: "recognizing contributions from diverse groups (contributions approach), adding units on topics dealing with diverse groups (additive approach) or changing the curriculum so that subject matter is viewed from the perspectives and experiences of a range of groups (transformation approach)" (p. 48)
- Knowledge construction: "extent to which teachers help students understand how perspectives of people within a discipline influence the conclusions reached within that discipline" (p. 48)
- Prejudice reduction: "extent to which teachers help students develop positive attitudes about different groups" (p. 48)

- Equitable pedagogy: "extent to which teachers modify teaching so as to facilitate academic achievement among students from diverse groups" (p. 48)
- An empowering school culture and social structure: "extent to which grouping practices, social climate, assessments, participation in extracurricular activities, staff expectations and responses to diversity ensure educational equality and cultural empowerment for students from diverse groups" (p. 48)

## Media/Technology Literacy

Interconnected curriculum is in part a result of the fact that information media and technology is making connections for us. Lewis (1995) explains how technology is breaking up the educational system as we know it: "Up to now, schools have largely determined when students learn material and how much of it they learn...today they can soar past any assignment using the tools that the schools have given them...Making sense and creating understanding will become the dominant task of schools" (p. 750).

By October 1999, a four-year study reported in NEA Today revealed that America's 109,000 elementary and secondary schools have eight million computers for use in instruction, about one computer for every six students, and more and more teachers are using technology to transform their teaching (p. 29). The National Center for Education Statistics reported that the number of classrooms connected to the Internet skyrocketed from 3 percent to 63 percent between 1994 and 1999 (Nelson, 2001, p. 10).

The superintendent of a California school district (Thome, 1996) says that these new technologies are challenging us to change our approach in schools: "Our dreams of classrooms without walls are now attainable...Our classrooms need to become research laboratories. Most traditional lessons would then be beginning points, not ends in themselves" (p. 58). Katz (1993) also points out the dramatic impact of today's technology that allows the user to manipulate information in ways "it would have taken a hundred 19th-century scholars a century to accomplish" (p. 7).

In *Visual Messages: Integrating Imagery into Instruction* (1999), David M. Considine and Gail E. Haley caution that simply accessing information "can not be automatically equated with success in understanding or evaluating the words and images at the disposal of web browsers...What is needed is a broader, wider definition of literacy...expanded to include the ability to access, analyze, evaluate and communicate information in all its forms" (p. xvi). The definition of literacy must include not only the meaningful understanding and production of printed text and illustration but also of digital and electronic images, words and sounds in our media-saturated society.

Television and advertising define and reflect popular culture, which is today part of a subject-matter inclusiveness in education that Katz (1998) calls "a remarkable expansion of the idea of the 'text'...We 'read' styles of dress, patterns of sexual behavior, sports, photographs, buildings, popular songs. And to do so we have developed a great variety of new research techniques, since the old modes of reading traditional literary texts do not work for our new universe of subjects" (p. 8). Bringing popular culture into the classroom does more than connect with students' real lives; it also offers opportunities to connect to universal themes and ideas.

*Visual education* (Lacy, 2000, p. 243): a familiar strategy for "reading" both content and design of visual media employs a sequential framework from fine arts that is adapted to the well-known questioning strategies from Benjamin Bloom's 1956 *Taxonomy of Educational Objectives: Cognitive Domain*. The following questions— and each one is important, although time spent on them varies widely, perhaps taking a whole semester—encourage learners to examine closely what they see and hear and to respond in the same or another form (see also Still Visual Resources in Chapter 5):

- What do you see? (identification)
- How is it put together? (analysis)
- Why is it as it is? (interpretation)
- How successful is it? (evaluation)
- Can you make one? (production)

*Media and technology analysis* (Considine, 2000a, p. 23): Considine and Haley offer innovative strategies to analyze and evaluate television, advertising, movies and the news media. Considine states online (1995) that media literacy "addresses the skills students need to be taught in school, the competencies citizens must have as we consume information in our homes and living rooms, the abilities workers must have in the 21st century and the challenges of a global economy" (p. 3). He offers the following questions for teachers and students to discuss about the media, tools and technologies (see also Film/Video Resources in Chapter 5):

- Whose interests do they operate in?
- What are their values?
- What are the outcomes or effects?
- Who are their audiences?
- What are their unique characteristics or attributes?
- How can we best use them at school and in our personal lives?

Considine leads the way for educators to integrate media literacy across the curriculum in the same way that reading and writing are integrated. What he describes as "both evolutionary and revolutionary," media literacy supports traditional comprehension and production skills and is compatible with the aims of public education, goals and missions of schools and curriculum objectives already in place (2000b, p. 309). He describes mass media's place in the school reform movement, outlining academic subjects in which media literacy objectives are making an appearance in curriculum frameworks and state standards documents.

In *Imagine That: Developing Critical Thinking and Critical Viewing Through Children's Literature* (1994), Considine, Haley and Lacy also "provide opportunities to learn to read pictures as well as words, ideology as well as narrative" and to transfer that learning to "the wider world of iconic information that characterizes the information age...Picture books and the visual language they use can serve as media literacy primers, building bridges to the electronic, rapid-paced visual messages that come to us from our television and movie screens" by examining the common process of skills necessary to read stories in both print and nonprint (p. xviii).

## Concepts and Big Ideas

In addition to a balanced curriculum, a second creative endeavor of constructivist planners is to design teaching and learning with a focus on content as conceptual. In interconnected education, a task is seen within the context in which it is embedded, which stems from a style of learning that is holistic and divergent rather than linear and convergent.

The foundation for this focus on context can be found in Sizer's book, *Horace's School: Redesigning the American High School* (1992), in which the author presents the educational philosophy of "less is more," a theory borrowed from the theory of design by the German Bauhaus school and made famous in the United States by architect Mies van der Rohe. Sizer advocates for the covering of fewer things in the classroom so that learners spend more time discovering how basic ideas and tools are derived and used (p. 76). He encourages focusing on depth of understanding for concepts rather than feeding learners broad information. This creates a curriculum that he calls more valuable and more likely to be grasped and retained (p. 81).

Less is more was also the philosophy featured at a 1993 ASCD Pre-Conference Institute in which an institute staff representing the Harvard Graduate School of Education explained the Teaching for Understanding Project, a six-year collaborative effort between school teachers and Harvard researchers. In the project, a few key generative topics are recommended to be the core of any curriculum, forming a new pedagogy of understanding (Perrone, 1998). In the session's handout (Harvard Graduate School of Education, 1993b) is the explanation: "By delving deeply into a few well-chosen themes, by working toward a few important goals, by engaging in a few complex performances, students will learn and retain far more than if they had to work on many things in the same time period."

Richard Elmore (1992) adds, "Learning means the development of understanding [and] requires more than the simple recall of facts; for example, it might require drawing inferences from facts, applying existing knowledge to unfamiliar problems, and constructing explanations for why one approaches a problem in a particular way" (p. 45).

The Harvard team (Perkins, 1993) posits that what is needed is "a connected rather than a disconnected curriculum...a curriculum full of knowledge of the right kinds to connect richly to future insights and applications...Dewey had something like this in mind when he wrote of 'generative knowledge.' He wanted education to emphasize knowledge with rich ramifications in the lives of learners" (p. 32). A leader of the team (Perrone, 1994) added, "Understanding is about making connections among and between things, about deep rather than surface knowledge and about greater complexity, not simplicity" (p. 13).

From these two distinguished teams of educators at Brown and Harvard Universities come "new visions of teaching" (Cohen, 1993) that offer theoretical support for teachers and learners to base their studies on the big picture, which was discussed in Pewewardy's "Holistic Circle" in Chapter 1.

**Coalition of Essential Schools** (Brown University, 1983): the Coalition of Essential Schools, founded and chaired by Sizer, recommends that teachers identify a unifying, thematic concept and an Essential Question focused on that concept to create a climate of student inquiry rather than a teacher-oriented presentation of material. A common principle of the Coalition is that students will master a limited number of essential skills and areas of knowledge. This emphasizes "quality of work rather than quantity and uncovering knowledge rather than covering material" (Kamii, 1996, p. 7).

*Fundamental concepts:* general and powerful categories of significant ideas, phenomena or persistent problems that are abstract, broad, universal and timeless. The Rochester City School District (1995) in New York presents the following examples: Commitment, Pollution, Machines, Power, Symmetry, Humor.

*Essential questions:* the big picture questions that learners are to address after they have thought deeply about a concept. Coalition leader Wiggins (1987) states, "To present the student with a summary of someone else's inquiry...is to rob it of all engaging charm. The writer of textbooks is all too often like the boorish friend who wants to reveal how the mystery movie turns out before one has seen it" (p. 11).

*Sub-essential questions:* "additional questions that are tied to the Essential question, helping to maintain focus and clarify thinking by forcing students to come to terms with their logic" (Central Park East Secondary School, 1995).

*Exhibitions:* see Authentic Tasks and Assessments in Chapter 3.


**Teaching for Understanding** (Harvard Graduate School of Education, online, 2002): Harvard's program has the following five dimensions which work together as a framework for this highly successful constructivist process in which "understanding is more than acquisition of knowledge and skills but rather a demonstration of critical and creative thought" (Blythe, 1998):

*Throughlines:* overarching goals that describe the most important understandings students should develop during a course or entire schoolyear

*Generative topics:* powerful and engaging concepts, key ideas, goals or complexities at the core of any curriculum that yield insight and implications in many circumstances

*Understanding goals:* frameworks for specifying the most important understandings learners should gain about the central aspects of generative topics

*Performances of understanding:* several thought-demanding activities distributed throughout a lesson, unit or course of study that encourage connection-making and offer students a variety of ways to demonstrate understanding

*Ongoing assessments:* continual and useful evaluations and feedback

## Impact on Creative Planning

A most dynamic and positive impact of interconnected curriculum on the classroom is that more types of intelligences and learning styles are engaged. A positive transformation occurs in learners' attitudes and on-task behaviors when they interact with material related to their backgrounds, personal development and the popular culture in addition to academics. The very nature of the integration results in curriculum that is more creative, interdisciplinary and exploratory, with the teacher as conversational facilitator, coinvestigator and collaborator with the children (Considine and Haley, 2000b, p. 319–320).

Creative teachers maintain that success in school is determined by social and emotional well-being as well as by language skills, thinking skills and general knowledge about the world. Grouping arrangements in Chapter 4 offer students a variety of ways to interact with others as a foundation for interactions that are expected of them in society. Learning resources in Chapter 5 are used by teachers and students alike not only for information but often for enrichment, clarification of values and examples of appropriate behavior in a democratic society.

Lynn Weber Cannon (1990) elaborates that her broadest goal as a teacher is "to assist students in developing a framework to evaluate the social system, to question it, to understand how their own perspectives, life chances, options and opportunities as well as those of others are shaped by it. I want them to be the smartest social analysts they can be, because these skills will serve them well for the rest of their lives in a way that knowing the latest findings in a specific area of research will not" (p. 127).

Creative teachers recognize that they are taking risks when they create a customized environment in which students are empowered to build and maintain curriculum based on their prior knowledge and experiences, sometimes experiences that have occurred outside school. Teachers learn time-intensive team-building techniques and try innovative strategies involving real-life, hands-on peripheral learning. Learner-generated design changes the dynamics of the classroom, because communication equalizes students and teachers as coinvestigators.

Successful multicultural education requires that students, teachers and principals suspend their own world views long enough to appreciate, absorb and participate in someone else's. Teachers in interconnected education listen, learn information that enriches their lives and pass on to students that true multicultural commitment involves treating people of diverse cultures the way they ask to be treated. They also point out that the world view represented by the Medicine Wheel provides a valuable foundation itself for interconnectedness in curriculum and instruction.

While subject content clearly provides the focus and forum for a class, "events from the real world, both macro and micro, somehow have a way of intruding into the instruction, providing what educators refer to as teachable moments" (Considine, 1999a, p. 322). A more spontaneous and open atmosphere helps to empower young learners not only to maintain a healthy balance in their lives among books, computers, television, movies and video games but also to grow up with a healthy critical awareness of ways in which these resources impact their values and influence our society. This expands not only what students learn but helps them achieve deeper understanding of how they learn it, whether it is quality learning and why other people produced it in the first place.

Creative teachers (Brennan, 1999) help students "understand the big picture—for instance, how themes such as economy, migration and geography influence patterns in history…Kids should understand history, not just know history" (p. 1). Harvard's Teaching for Understanding program likewise helps "motivate students by assigning work that is meaningful and substantive...helps students understand the difference between correct work and good work...judges student work by real-world standards...and prepares students to manage the ambiguous and complex problems of real life" (Cronin, 1996, p. 73–74).

# Chapter 3:

## Creative Planning for Interconnected Teaching and Learning

> "In reality, this is my approach to teaching—to teach through my capacity to learn. Through this approach, I hope to demonstrate that teaching has little to do with transfer of information or test scores and much to do with the continuous discussion of the question, 'How do we wish to live together?'"
> —Patrick Shannon,
> "How Long Has It Been Since You Taught?"

The saying is that we give a name to something to organize it. That is one of the things educational theorists do—they name for teachers what we do or what we need to do, making us more efficient and effective in plans and actions with children.

As teachers develop, implement and refine a curricular scope and sequence for what learners need to know and be able to do, they use instructional designs with assessment tools for measuring how well learners can demonstrate understandings and apply skills. In this chapter, research about instructional design, authentic tasks and assessment is presented to aid in planning. My new instructional design system brings all the theories, including those in Chapters 1 and 2, into a plan that reflects interconnectedness.

I have given attention to those writers whose ideas have proven to connect with the classroom, naming honestly what goes on there and suggesting persuasively how things can be improved. They generally use language that is easy to understand and transferable to the preK-12 classroom. None offers a quick-fix approach to better teaching and all are learner-centered, pay homage to wisdom of earlier theorists, continue to update their research and, taken together, complement each other.

### Authentic Tasks and Assessments

Public preK-12 schools are periodically required to use large-scale standardized tests that are predetermined at the state, district and/or school level as part of a review and update of curriculum.

These traditional tests generally ask low-level, multiple-choice questions designed to test minimum competencies. They are often culturally biased, rarely require students to apply information or exhibit complex reasoning skills, provide grades but no meaningful feedback and often reward seat time rather than demonstrated competence.

As David Lazear (1994) points out, standardized testing practices "tend to be biased toward verbal-linguistic and logical-mathematical intelligence, with a smattering of visual-spatial thrown in for interest...[which is] unfortunately prejudiced against alternative (but nonetheless valid) ways of knowing" (p. 11). Standardized testing is acknowledged as the single largest obstacle to public school reform because of its reliance on numbers that do not adequately evaluate real student progress.

When additional evaluations are devised by individual teachers, students or collaborative teams of site-based educators, assessment better influences meaningful teaching and learning. Once creative teachers determine what knowledge and/or skills need to be addressed, types of tasks and assessments are chosen that are aligned to teaching and learning but are wide-ranging enough to take into account varied levels of knowledge and personal development as well as the diverse micro-cultures, world views, learning styles and multiple intelligences of learners.

**Tasks**

Coalition of Essential Schools and the Teaching for Understanding program place thinking and thought-demanding performances of student understanding as the foundation for meaningful instruction. The programs validate a curricular focus for today's educators of teaching for, of and about skillful thinking. The following strategy instruction for a variety of tasks involves modeling thinking for students (Rosenshine, 1986):

- Show learners a detailed step-by-step breakdown.
- Offer extensive practice with a range of examples.
- Talk out loud as you solve the problem.
- Discriminate distracting from relevant information.
- Identify a rule.
- Maintain a correct focus and preempt errors.
- Detect potentially faulty arguments.

- Gradually withdraw guidance until students can apply the strategy independently.

The following taxonomies are the most commonly used among teachers to describe types of tasks:

*Tasks for declarative knowledge* (Bloom, 1974): "learning that"; understanding demonstrates learning at level 1 and involves some or all of levels 2–6 in the following:

- Level 1: basic knowledge (ability to recall information)
- Level 2: comprehension (ability to understand an idea, concept or situation)
- Level 3: application (ability to apply understanding of concept)
- Level 4: analysis (ability to break down an item into its parts, forms or components and describe relationships of components to each other and to the whole)
- Level 5: synthesis (ability to arrange and combine pieces, parts or elements from different sources to create something new)
- Level 6: evaluation (ability to make judgments about value and state why)

*Tasks for metacognition* (Minnesota Department of Education, 1986): "learning how" a thinking process works; being aware of the mind's activity while learning; learning to monitor and control thinking for independent, self-regulated learning; learning how to learn using the following eight levels of discrete skills for processing information:

- Level 1: determining issues/needs
- Level 2: acquiring information
- Level 3: organizing information
- Level 4: interpreting information
- Level 5: validating information
- Level 6: producing new information
- Level 7: communicating information
- Level 8: evaluating outcomes

*Tasks for procedural knowledge:* "learning how"; learning physical or mental steps performed in a specific order using strategies, tactics or algorithms defined by a discipline; may be experienced directly or indirectly; learning the way to perform a process as a "set" or the same way every time

*Tasks for procedural transfer:* "learning how"; learning underlying principles that may be transferable to many tasks with a variety of results; learning rationale behind steps so as to flexibly perform processes in different ways at different times for different purposes

*Tasks for conditional knowledge:* "learning when"; learning contexts for strategies; learning the circumstances under which to use either procedural or declarative knowledge to elucidate a situation

*Tasks for integrated thinking processes:* combinations of all the above result in the following six special types of tasks:

- Concept development: differentiating among examples and non-examples of a concept; generalizing characteristics
- Problem-solving: recognizing and defining a problem and the conditions needed for a solution; devising and implementing a plan for its solution; evaluating the solution
- Decision-making: defining a goal and obstacles in its path; identifying, analyzing, ranking and choosing the best among alternative decisions for reaching the goal; implementing, assessing and modifying the decision
- Valuing: identifying value preferences and their consequences; committing to, internalizing and acting on the preference; making judgments based on the criteria
- Creative thinking: demonstrating originality, flexibility, inventiveness, elaboration and ability to generate and combine ideas into new ways of thinking; verifying and solidifying the idea
- Critical thinking: determining an issue to be addressed; recognizing patterns; analyzing and evaluating the patterns; accepting, rejecting or modifying the issue

## Assessments

In alternative forms of assessment (Perrone, 1988), *process*-based assessments evaluate how learners learn in addition to what they know and are able to do. *Progress*-based assessments show how much learners have improved, with scoring for gains in learning in addition to what learners know and are able to do. *Product*-based assessments involve tangible evidence of acquisition of knowledge and/or procedures, such as those listed below. Some assessments may involve all three aspects.

Grant Wiggins (1993b) describes how frequent and ongoing authentic assessment is embedded in classwork and offers students many tasks and many times to demonstrate learning. It focuses on the elements of instruction that are critical and transferable to the real world, is an impartial judgment that does not label students and uses language that is familiar and appropriate. It provides constructive feedback that helps learners understand their misconceptions and is used by teachers to drive subsequent instruction. Wiggins (1993a) explains further: "Assessment, especially testing, should be designed to improve performance, not just monitor it...Students should justify their understanding and craft, not merely recite orthodox views or mindlessly employ techniques in a vacuum...The student is an apprentice [and] authentic education makes self-assessment central" (p. 3).

Measuring student performance is conducted at intervals throughout instruction, with an on-demand performance of understanding required of students as well as an exhibition or project that may be completed over an extended period of time. Record-keeping is not the sole responsibility of teachers but may also be conducted by students in portfolios, checklists or logs.

Marshall Smith and Ramon Cortines (1993) say that learners are made aware of the interconnectedness of assessment in the learning process, and they play a role in evaluating their own progress. Students are given the assessment tool as a road map before they begin a task, know from the beginning of instruction what will be required of them, and compare exemplary work to lower-rated work to analyze what distinguishes them. The authors explain, "We have a history of not training students in the material they will be tested on. Other countries don't hide the test from students. That doesn't mean particulars are revealed to students. It means that teachers are able to gear when and how they teach towards the kind of things that will appear on examinations" (p. 767).

Vito Perrone (1994) describes meaningful assessments as a vital part of restructuring, but they become meaningless if they are created as a tag-on to an existing textbook-based curriculum. He explains that "without a growing discourse about curriculum purposes, student understandings and ways teachers can foster student learning, the assessment measures such as portfolios and exhibitions will not have a very long or inspiring history" (p. 13).

*Types of assessments*

- Case study: application of knowledge and skills to a specific situation and writing about the experience as a description, personal analysis and interpretation
- Checklist/documentation: learner's task assignment sheet; teacher's record for learner's classroom participation, task completion, etc., with dates, times and other notations
- Computer-based test: computer program that gives learner feedback, assesses how well he/she incorporates it into subsequent work, records the processes used, and offers simulations of real-world problem-solving situations
- Constructed-response: open-ended statement with which learner is asked to agree (listing examples to justify the answer) or disagree (explaining what an alternative answer is and why it was chosen)
- Cooperative-groupwork: group project only is assessed; contributions by individuals are assessed as well as the group's result; bonus points are given when certain members or when all members achieve; or individual points are added to form a total group score (Garmston and Wellman, 1992, p. 74–87)
- Demonstration: illustration of a procedure with performance of necessary steps and explanation of the results
- Discussion: evaluating using a group process; peer evaluation
- Display: poster, photo, chart, graph, etc., about a project, accompanied by verbal and written explanations
- Draw-and-tell test: picture or diagram drawn as a model (accompanied by written explanation) to represent concept in math story problem, geometry or science problem-solving exercise
- Essay exam: organization for points to be made and subjective writing about a topic or opinion
- Exhibition: see below
- Experiment: trial or procedure to discover or test a principle or supposition
- Individualized Learning Plan (ILP): measurement of a student's individual strengths and weaknesses; used by teacher, parents and learner to chart a plan of action to address the student's needs

- Inventory: record of literature, resources and evaluations used in a project; book list
- Journal: blank notebook for learner's reflections on processes, goals, thoughts, actions, targeting new aspects to study in detail; writing or drawing as record-keeping on a regular basis of experiences, knowledge, lessons or data; record of responses from others; description of ways in which an experience was helpful; personal release for inner self; expanded thinking or stimulation; see also Log
- Learner-generated assessment: exam question, evaluation method and/or grading standard set up by student
- Log: blank notebook in which learner writes down events or activities chronologically, as in a science logbook; "learning log" is response at the end of a lesson; anecdotal record; see also Journal
- Multimedia product: combined uses of nonprint resources, such as computer, photography, audio, video
- Parent response: communication from home that evaluates learner's work
- Performance standard: see below
- Portfolio/process folio: see below
- Problem-solving: staging of hands-on problem to solve, accompanied by verbal and written explanation
- Profile: composite demonstration of skills in different areas, such as technical reading, public speaking, written evaluation of information, communicating ideas using various media, showing steps in solving a problem or making an informed decision
- Project: production, presentation or display created by a team
- Reading-writing response: variety of responses to reading in writing (i.e., as critic, as one of the characters, as author)
- Retelling: relating main idea or details in a text
- Selection-item test: multiple-choice, true-false, matching on standardized test or pop quiz
- Self-assessment: journal, log, portfolio and/or interview in which learner reflects about what is learned or about processes used in learning; self-evaluation of stategies used, things to be changed, good and bad habits, uses of time; drawing or description of self; goal-setting; reflection on observations made by someone else; list of resources or help

needed; scoring one's own paper on a rubric before turning both in to the teacher

- Supply-item test: short-answer or essay on test or pop quiz
- Student conference/oral interview: discussion about activities, interests or experiences between student and teacher and/or other adults
- Survey/questionnaire: rating scale or yes/no to demonstrate preferences, evaluate activities, etc.
- Teacher-feedback: verbal, written or recorded response to learner's work and/or progress; narrative feedback form for conferences; comment form for student work might be limited to only a commendation (one thing done well) and a recommendation (one thing to focus on in future); anecdotal record for assessment of progress for report cards
- Teacher observation: documentation of student performance and behavior from a distance (observing from across the room), close-in (observing over the student's shoulder) and/or as participant (sitting down with the student to ask questions or discuss)
- Video/audio-based assessment: recording how well learner listens, questions, critiques and summarizes; performs task or experiment; cooperates in group projects; explains ideas and answer questions; makes oral presentations and responds to audience questioning
- Volunteer jury: community member(s) evaluate learner's presentation, oral report and/or answer to questions, using criteria established by teacher, and complete a written evaluation or rubric
- Writing sample: narrative, descriptive, persuasive or research paper

*Exhibitions:* assessment tools should be real-world demonstrations not only of what students know but also of what they are able to do with their knowledge (Sizer, 1992, p. 13). In the Coalition, educators "plan backward" by first considering "student destinations with integrity" for a course of study in order to better determine what the curriculum should be, how it should be taught and what learning students should be expected to demonstrate (p. 104).

"The student must Exhibit the products of his learning. If he does that well, he can convince himself that he can use knowledge and he can so convince others...The doing is the ultimate achievement. Just knowing stuff isn't enough...What is it precisely that a kid—any kid—should be able to show off to us?" (p. 20–25). Sizer's examples of Exhibitions for high-school students are rich and varied: filling out an IRS 1040 tax form for a fictitious family, extracting a constitutional principle from a Supreme Court decision, running a school recycling program, reciting from memory a compelling speech, troubleshooting the sabotaged engine of a 1983 Chevette. Some variations for successful Exhibitions are the following:

- Design characteristics: real-world activity, appealing, familiar, humanistic, reflective, personal, universal, sensible, serious, fun, interesting, demanding of respect, public, confidence-building, applicable, straightforward, relevant, practical, interdisciplinary, springboard to other studies, example of a larger issue, interconnected, theory combined with application, demanding, a completed entity, goes beyond a product, thoughtful, joyful
- How students may do their work: alone, in pairs, on a committee, in other groupings determined by task
- What may be given to students: time frames, specific criteria, selection list, choice of own subject, attached material, suggestions for gathering material, ascending-difficulty assignments, trial time, assistance by peers and/or adults, observation by adult, outside professional criticism
- What may be required of students: demonstration, use of information, research skills, descriptive skills, communication skills, imaginative skills, verbal explanation, defense of work, convincing arguments, fielding of questions, explanations of how and why, written report/essay/instructions, draw/design/devise using specific criteria, self-criticism, use of various languages/forms of expression/media, persuasive voice, persistence, organization, analysis, decision-making, speculating, going beyond data, extracting a principle, performing, troubleshooting, itemizing, supervising, surveying, establishing a pattern, developing new skills
- Judgment criteria: task completion, ability to do as well as know, display of intellectual habits, validity of overall idea and individual components, accuracy, consistency, precision, clarity, sophistication, coherence, orderliness, appropriateness,

enthusiasm, dependability, independence, attention to details, initiative, engagement, persistence, patience, usefulness of results

*Performance standards:* in standards-based reform, Matt Gandal (1996a) describes performance standards as those that "describe how well learners must know and do, specify how good is good enough and show how competent a student demonstration must be to indicate attainment of the content standards" (p. 33). The most dramatic change embedded in standards is that "performance tasks ask students to use their knowledge in situations that mimic real life; through demonstrations, and through the compilation of portfolios, students show how well they can apply what they have learned" (Lewis, 1995, p. 746).

Mieko Kamii (1996) adds that "interdisciplinary standards are difficult to write since the disciplines have their own methods of inquiry...It becomes incumbent on the faculty to share their curriculum with colleagues so as to ensure that students will have grappled with the major ideas and methods of the disciplines" (p. 2). Some standards from the Minnesota Department of Children, Families and Learning (1997a) are interdisciplinary in nature and lead to integration of subjects without neglecting skills and knowledge mastery unique to each discipline. However, implementation in schools proved problematic because performance packages of prescribed procedures were initially distributed, and teachers were allowed to adapt only the topic, product and/or rigor.

Robert Marzano and associates make a crucial distinction between performance standards for declarative knowledge (information) and procedural knowledge (fluency with which learner performs a process, strategy or skill). Their suggestion for turning declarative into procedural knowledge in order to create a procedural standard is to marry one or more of the complex reasoning processes—comparing, classifying, inducing, deducing, error analysis, constructing support, abstracting, analyzing perspective, decision-making, investigating, problem-solving, inquiry, inventing—to declarative knowledge and design the result as a procedural task (Marzano et al., 1993, p. 27). Questions to be answered when creating performance standards are:

- Which standards assess tasks for declarative knowledge and which assess tasks for procedural knowledge? Are expectations clear and appropriate to each?

- Are standards broken down into expectations during stages of development, such as ages 5–9, 9–14 and 14–18?
- What will the product of student work be?
- What criteria will be used to judge the work?
- How are different levels of performance to be described?

A rubric or grid of four scoring levels is usually used to describe performance based on evaluation criteria. It may have a list of all tasks required in a performance, but Marzano and Pickering (1997) recommend use of analytic rubrics for each task rather than holistic rubrics for an entire standard, since in the latter the lowest score on the profile is the student's final score (p. 67).

*Portfolios/process folios:* portfolios or process folios may be composites of many of the types of assessments above. They are folders, binders, scrapbooks or computer disks filled with carefully selected collections of learners' skill activities, writings, journals, drawings, research projects and math activities that represent effort, achievement, processes and progress over time. Each contribution should be labeled with the date it was written or created. Learners should evaluate their own work in a portfolio, analyze themselves as learners and set goals for improvement.

Younger students might include learning style information, writing samples, story retellings, oral reading audio tapes, invented spelling activities, sight word inventories, videotaped interviews with parents and other students, math skills sheets, self-portraits, anecdotes or summaries of classroom and playground activities, and comments about choices for the portfolio itself.

Older students might include book lists; tests; samples of writing (drafts as well as edited pieces); interdisciplinary essays; group projects; independent research; math and problem-solving work; learning style information; samples and rubrics for projects; teacher reflections; art work; video tapes of dramatic, musical or movement performances; photographs of science experiments; responses to reading or viewing assignments; diagrams, outlines or webs of written work; and one-page syntheses of self-discovery after assembling and reflecting on contents of the portfolio itself. Other options about portfolios are that they:

- May include notes by teachers and students about progress and anecdotes describing interactions and participation

- May be combination of print and multimedia
- May be all work in subjects for the year or selected pieces that learners want to include because they show progress
- May be reviewed to reflect on learning and processes
- May be used to evaluate work-in-progress or work-over-time
- May be work which students do well, was difficult, needs improvement, represents a learning experience, is typical of the student, and/or represents growth and development
- May be chosen by teacher, learner or by teacher and learner
- May provide opportunities for display or oral presentation
- May be shared with family members and other students
- May be compiled as an electronic/digital portfolio
- May be evaluated by a team of teachers, using a scoring rubric

### Instructional Designs

Two well-known and popular instructional models based on constructivism offer an excellent foundation for an interconnected design for teaching and learning. These models are Dimensions of Learning from *A Different Kind of Classroom: Teaching with Dimensions of Learning* by Robert J. Marzano (ASCD,1992) and 4MAT from *The 4MAT System: Teaching to Learning Styles with Right/Left Mode Techniques* by Bernice McCarthy (Excel, 1987). Both have been catalysts for organizational change and restructuring efforts around the country.

**Dimensions of Learning** (Marzano, 1998, online): a complex interaction of five dimensions that are not linear or hierarchical discrete steps operating in isolation; consequently, learners are often involved in more than one of the following Dimensions at the same time:

- Dimension 1 Attitudes and Perceptions
- Dimension 2 Acquire and Integrate Knowledge
- Dimension 3 Extend and Refine Knowledge
- Dimension 4 Use Knowledge Meaningfully
- Dimension 5 Productive Habits of Mind

Dimensions 1 and 5 are learner attributes that provide a backdrop for the other Dimensions and require reinforcing strategies in all phases of instruction. Marzano (1992) explains that decisions about Dimensions 2, 3 and 4 result in three instructional design models: Focus on Knowledge, which lends itself to mastery of knowledge and/or skills in specific content areas (Dimensions 2 and 3); Focus on Issues, which lends itself to application of knowledge (Dimension 4) to large interdisciplinary topics; and Focus on Exploration, which lends itself to individualized learning and enhancement of self-directed learning (Dimension 4).

Marzano and his associates (1993) also identify five lifelong learning standards that are "specific to no one discipline and can be used in many situations throughout a person's lifetime—complex thinking, information processing, effectively communicating, collaborating/cooperating, and exhibiting habits of mind" (p. 10). Costa and Kallick (1998) call similar lifelong skills "intelligent behaviors" (p. 2).

**4MAT System**(McCarthy, 1987): teaching methods, roles for teachers and student tasks given for each of four major learning styles the author calls Imaginative, Analytic, Common Sense and Dynamic. As teachers move clockwise around the four quadrants in the circle of McCarthy's model, the following progression for learners is developed:

- Quadrant 1 Integrating Experience with Self (Experiencing)
- Quadrant 2 Concept Formulation (Conceptualizing)
- Quadrant 3 Practice and Personalization (Applying)
- Quadrant 4 Integrating Application and Experience (Creating)

McCarthy's system is based on Sperry's theory of brain processing (see Chapter 1). The author of *4MAT* defines four combinations of perceiving and processing experience and information as learning styles for students, each with its own quadrant. Appropriate activities are constructed for each of the quadrants which are preferred by each of the four styles.

McCarthy also bases *4MAT* on development and integration of left- and right-brain processing, in which students of all four styles experience flexible use of the whole brain. She explains (1987), "It is time to teach to the whole brain, intellectual and intuitive, mind and heart, content centered and student centered" (p. 75).

The best of what Marzano's *Dimensions of Learning* and McCarthy's *4MAT* offer teachers is also what they have in common—the language is easily understood and the designs are commonsense methods of teaching and learning. Although Marzano's Dimensions are not intended to function in discrete steps, they can easily be seen to represent many of the same ideas as those found in McCarthy's progressive design, such as the following examples:

- Marzano's Dimension 1 Attitudes and Perceptions for valuing the climate and task can be thought of as a predictable result of teachers' successful interactions with students in McCarthy's Quadrant 1 Integrating Experience with the Self.
- Marzano's Dimension 2 Acquire and Integrate Knowledge is similar to McCarthy's Quadrant 2 Concept Formulation.
- Marzano's Dimension 3 Extend and Refine Knowledge is similar to McCarthy's Quadrant 3 Practice and Personalize.
- Marzano's Dimension 4 Use Knowledge Meaningfully is similar to McCarthy's Quadrant 4 Integrating Application and Experience.
- McCarthy does not go much beyond her instructional design to imply the development of lifelong learning skills; however, Marzano's Dimension 5 is focused on developing Productive Habits of Mind.
- Marzano barely mentions the need to adapt to learning styles in *A Different Kind of Classroom*; however, McCarthy's premise behind the entire focus in *4MAT* is to appeal to learning styles.
- McCarthy does not differentiate among types of knowledge; however, Marzano describes differences between declarative and procedural knowledge.
- Regarding *4MAT*, Lippitt (1996) describes the system as practical for teaching to wholeness and human diversity; regarding *Dimensions of Learning*, Michael Boucher (1994) adds his own idea for a Dimension 6 Valuing Diversity (resolving conflicts and demonstrating community leadership).

### Impact on Creative Planning

To common ideas in the two instructional designs by Marzano and McCarthy are now added earlier ideas from the equally exemplary works of Sizer, Perrone and their colleagues, as well as the important theories about holonomy discussed in Chapter 1 and balanced curriculum in Chapter 2. Creative teaching and learning is seen to come together in a new Interconnected Design that may be used in any way teachers choose.

For over two decades, the renowned theorists and designers whose ideas are reviewed here have contributed to the successful education of children, and their works are guiding lights for creative preK-12 teachers and administrators across the country. As a synergetic endeavor, my new Design reflects my research into their ideas, and I convey my profound respect and admiration for each of them.

### Interconnected Design

My Design uses language that is familiar to those in the preK-12 setting, but the graphic organizer has eight components that require explanation. Once all components have been explained, the resulting spiral is presented as an appropriate icon for the theory of interconnectedness and symbolizes the progression of interconnected teaching and learning over time. First, a look at the core of the Design:

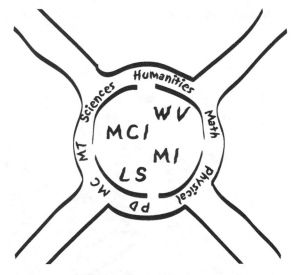

Figure 5: Inner Core

*Learner:* in a close-up view of the Design's core (Figure 5) is the whole child, profiled by micro-cultural identities (MCI), world views (WV), learning styles (LS) and multiple intelligences (MI), described in Chapter 1 by Gollnick and Chinn, Clark, Nelson, Pewewardy, Gardner and over a dozen learning-style theorists. Planning for interconnected teaching and learning revolves around the learner, fostering holonomy, or self-awareness combined with global awareness. The creative teacher recognizes that knowing as much as possible about each student and recognizing how best to address learners' individual needs is a step that must be taken before instruction begins. The core is drawn with a noncontinuous line, indicating that the learner is empowered as an interactive participant, open to influences around him/her and responsible for his/her own learning.

*Curriculum:* in a ring around the student in Figure 5 is the interconnected curriculum of the sciences, humanities, math, physical education and cross-disciplinary areas of personal development (PD), multiculturalism (MC) and media/technology literacy (MT). These aspects of a holistic, balanced curriculum are described earlier in Chapter 2 by Katz, Fogarty, Jacobs, Perkins, Wiggins, Sizer, Perrone, Kurth-Schai, Sternberg, Banks, Cortes, Considine and Haley. Spokes extend from this ring, indicating that the curriculum is both influenced by and reflective of the Design, which is now shown in full:

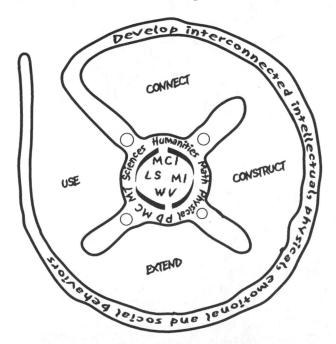

Figure 6: Interconnected Design

*Goal:* a full view of the Design (Figure 6) is a spiral with the ultimate goal of holistic education in the outer ring—"Develop interconnected intellectual, physical, emotional and social behaviors." Learning tasks are directed toward this goal, and they establish the positive climate of interconnectedness within the classroom. The goal is similar to learner attributes that other theorists have provided as backdrops for their designs: Marzano's Productive Habits of Mind (critical and creative thinking and regulating behavior), Perrone's Understanding Goals (central aspects of generative topics), McCarthy's approach to the whole brain and Sizer's Intellectual Habits (perspective, analysis, imagination, empathy, communication, humility and joy). My Design is directed at education for the whole person and emphasizes interconnected physical, emotional and social behaviors in addition to intellectual ones. This outer ring leads back to the core, where reside the child and the balanced curriculum, and it strengthens ties between creative planning for curriculum, interactive instruction and learners' own needs, abilities and interests.

Within the spiral in Figure 6 are also four kinds of teaching and learning events—connecting, constructing, extending and using understandings and skills—that are planned creatively for part of a lesson, entire lesson, unit or course of study. These four events are based on research into the similarities among instructional designs of Marzano, McCarthy, Sizer, Perrone and their colleagues, and they will be examined separately here.

Figure 7: Fourth Event

*Use*: as indicated in a close-up of the fourth event (Figure 7), creatively planning backward means that decisions are made *first* about types of assessment discussed earlier in this chapter. In this last event of my Design, plans are made for students to independently demonstrate how they can use their understandings and skills concerning a generative topic; perform a high level of active practice that integrates and synthesizes what they understand and can do; apply understandings to similar situations or transfer skills to different situations; gauge effectiveness of their processes and products; reach closure, including self-evaluation and a review of the significance of their accomplishments for themselves and others; and connect to lessons that have come before and to the next related lesson, series of lessons or unit.

Authentic assessments resemble real learning tasks, assess the abilities essential to daily life, stretch the learner's ability to understand concepts and to apply them in practical situations, appeal to diverse learning styles, and measure more complex mental processes in meaningful contexts than do current standardized tests. Authentic assessments may reflect meaningful aspects of the world outside of school, aspects of a particular discipline, or aspects of ideas and meanings valued in themselves as part of the school culture.

The three learning events that precede this one lead up to these final tasks, and students have been made fully aware of what is expected of them here. In addition to assessments in this chapter, Chapter 7 also offers types of learning strategies for students to produce and evaluate their understandings. This type of event is found in Marzano's Use Knowledge Meaningfully, Sizer's Exhibitions, McCarthy's Integrate Application and Experience and Perrone's final Performance(s) of Understanding.

Figure 8: Third Event

*Extend*: for the third learning event (Figure 8), plans are made about how learners are to practice their understandings and skills with monitoring and feedback. Practice takes the same general form as in the fourth event, and learners use the same learning processes, but in some cases the topic, product or rigor is different from the final demonstrations of use. Guided practice, scaffolding and independent practice are discussed as bridging strategies in Chapter 6. This type of event is described as Marzano's Extend and Refine Knowledge, Sizer's Exhibitions (practices or rehearsals), McCarthy's Practice and Personalize and Perrone's Performance(s) of Understanding (middle-level or progressively-complex).

Figure 9: Second Event

*Construct*: for the second learning event (Figure 9), decisions are made about how learners are to interact, with explanation and clarification of new material that is embedded in authentic tasks. A creative plan includes the design of simple-to-complex sequences in which skills are broken down into simplest components and taught individually when necessary, or students interact with discipline-specific content in small chunks and with examples. Teachers plan for modeling, demonstrating, initial guided practicing and checking for understanding. Chapter 6 offers learning strategies for accessing and processing information and skills.

The interconnected nature of this constructing event and the sub-sequent extending and using events also require that teachers present new material as closely as is reasonable in the same ways that learn-ers themselves will be expected to practice and perform their understandings of the material. Creative planning not only implies teaching from the onset using meaningful assessments but also teach-ing to types of assessments themselves. For instance, the form and processes of student Exhibitions or Performances of Understanding in the third and fourth events should connect to the form and pro-cesses modeled by the teacher in this second event. This type of event is patterned after Marzano's Acquire and Integrate Knowledge, Sizer's Exhibitions (as modeled by the teacher), McCarthy's Concept Formu-lation and Perrone's initial Performance(s) of Understanding (guided by the teacher, with monitoring and feedback).

Figure 10: First Event

*Connect*: for the first learning event (Figure 10), plans are made about how learners are to be introduced to a generative topic, concept or big idea that will be the focus for constructing, extending and using their understandings and skills. Creative teachers formulate or gen-erate with students a line of inquiry in which less is more; connect a topic to other topics and to the real world of learners; provide moti-vational and stimulating introductory activities; and begin to model as well as explain assessment tools that will be used. Chapter 6 offers examples of bridging/connecting and focusing/attending strategies. This type of event relates to Marzano's Attitudes and Per-ceptions (valuing climate and task), Sizer's Exhibitions (informa-tion about which is given from the beginning, with initial modeling by the teacher to give students examples of correct work), McCarthy's Integrate Experience with Self and Perrone's Generative Topic (the focus from the beginning, often presented as inquiry).

**Interconnected Design for Creative Planning**

*Discipline(s):* _____

*Standard(s)/Objective(s):* _____

*Assessment(s): Understand* _____

*Do* _____

*Past/future lesson, unit or course of study:* _____

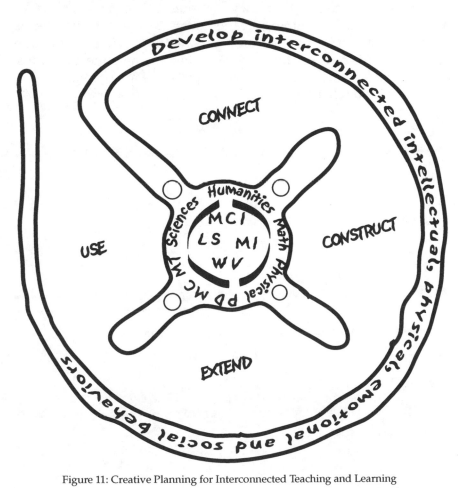

Figure 11: Creative Planning for Interconnected Teaching and Learning

*Interconnected Design for Creative Planning* (Figure 11): as seen in its entirety, the Design is open at the top, which is both entrance and exit since it points not only to discipline(s), standard(s) and assessment(s) addressed in this plan but also to past and future lessons, units or courses of study. Each of the learners' achievements is thus interconnected, building on and leading to others in which students apply understandings to new arenas.

The eighth component in the Design is a small circle imposed on each of the four spokes extending from the core. These represent four practical areas of teaching and learning that turn instructional design theory into practice. They are four basic considerations for teachers of student grouping arrangements, forms of media used as learning resources, strategies for accessing/processing information and skills and strategies for producing/evaluating understandings.

The choices creative teachers make in these areas are the topics of the next four chapters.

# Chapter 4

## Learning Groups:
## Arrangements for Teachers and Learners

"Q: What's the right size for a class?
A: I wish we had only five to ten kids in a class. First, it wouldn't be wild.
Second, maybe our teacher would take us places in her car."

—Tony Jackson (grade 5),
"What's the Right Size for a Class?"

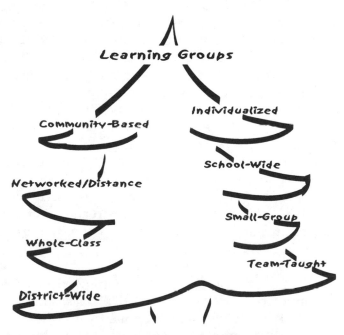

Figure 12: Arrangements for Teachers and Learners

Described in Chapter 1 is holonomy, which requires that learners of all micro-cultures, world views, learning styles and intelligences experience working alone as well as working with others in groups of varying sizes. Holonomy, some cultures agree, results in inner intelligence about (as well as for) one's self and outer intelligence about (as well as for) one's group.

Not all of the categories above lend themselves to every school's structure. Some schools may not philosophically embrace team-teaching or a school-wide thematic learning plan, or they may be financially unable to fully implement networked/distance learning. Creative teachers interested in incorporating such ideas into their teaching continue to vigorously advocate for them, as these arrangements prepare learners for life outside of school, for their future in the workplace and for participation in a global community.

Grouping learners to work together productively in various arrangements has become a crucial part of the restructuring of American education, as shown in the professional literature for over a decade. "Schools must be re-organized to allow more activity settings with fewer children, more interaction, more conversation, more joint activity" (Tharp and Gallimore, 1989, p. 23). Using groups is recognized by creative teachers as being more than "an occasional break from standard operating procedure... a mere teaching technique for a slow day" (Herreman, 1988, p. 5). Instead, the group process is like the real world, in which people are often involved in group settings. As such, teachers have a responsibility to teach the democratic process of working successfully with others.

As with learning strategies and resources, more than one grouping arrangement is often used during a single lesson and no one arrangement suits all learners or subject areas. "Although some educational gurus try to sell *the* way in their books and lectures, experienced teachers know that a *variety* of practices is a sounder policy" (Whitworth, 1988, p. 19). The content of instruction, not the desire to maintain control over students, should determine group size (Kierstead, 1993, p. 46).

An example of the ways in which the needs of learners and curricular objectives determine the mix of grouping arrangements is a three-group approach in Mortimer J. Adler's *Paideia Proposal* (1982), an instructional design which may be applied across the curriculum and transferred by learners into their lives outside the classroom. Patricia Weiss (1992) briefly describes Paideia, in which didactic teaching is suggested for a large class size when the goal is facts and the outcome is recall; using textbook and notes; using teacher strategies of brevity, clarity, variety in voice and movement; using learner strategies of listening, writing, discussing and memorizing.

During Paideia workable ability groupings, the suggested goal is skills and the outcome is performance; using focused activities; using teacher strategies of giving directions, modeling, observing, motivating; using learner strategies of practicing, discussing, self-assessment and critiquing. Seminar discussions are suggested for groups of 15–25 when the goal is ideas and the outcome is understanding; using Socratic teaching; using teacher strategies of listening, waiting, facilitating, empowering; using learner strategies of discussing, listening, writing and thinking critically.

On the following pages are presented a wide variety of grouping arrangements, with a list of suggested activities. Activities in this chapter are from the learner's perspective in whatever grouping arrangement has been chosen. Creative teachers are the best ones to choose how and when to use different arrangements.

To evaluate the work of any group, learners benefit from discussing the following (Golub, 1988):

- How does this grouping arrangement for learning differ from others?
- Why might you and others have been asked to work in this arrangement?
- What was your involvement or your role in the arrangement?
- What role was demonstrated by others?
- What skills were needed to demonstrate these roles?
- How well did you and others demonstrate these skills? What needs improvement? How will you improve and help others to improve?
- What did you learn about yourself and others while working in this arrangement? What can you do with this knowledge or skill? When is that use appropriate?
- What could be done differently next time in a similar arrangement?
- Is this an arrangement you prefer? Why?
- Could you arrange to work this way on your own? What would you need? When would it be appropriate?
- Why is it important for you and others to learn this way?

## Community-Based Learning

In a community-based learning arrangement, Mary Nebgen and Kate McPherson (1990) explain that the school opens its doors to make connections with the world around it and shows learners the possibilities that exist outside the building (p. 90). People in the community are major participants in learning experiences conducted in and out of school, rather than serving as occasional visitors in the classroom. The community genuinely becomes the classroom as students participate in job shadowing, social activism and service learning. As learners engage with the outside world, facets of individual- as well as social-consciousness are developed and strengthened.

Beyond using the world outside as a curricular resource, in this arrangement with the community the authors describe students as being prepared for workplace success as they plan, conduct and share important school projects that empower them to apply classwork material to their own lives and the lives of others. They examine the usefulness of classroom material to themselves and those around them—to daily life at home, to the environment they live in and to the worlds of work and play—and learn that they can contribute to their community to make a difference now, not just in the future (p. 90).

"People tend to think of community service exclusively as volunteerism, which conjures up concerns about liability, transportation and convoluted schedules. But frequently schools can discover community needs that they can meet within the classroom… ways course content can help solve a community concern, and ways class products can help others" (p. 91). The authors further outline key elements for teachers to develop service learning—professional development, site leadership, district support, preparation, time, communication and accommodation for differences among adults as well as children.

## Types of Community-Based Learning
### Business/political outreach

- Community helper
- Revolving-door partnership
- School/business partnership
- Workplace learning

*Educational outreach*

- Cross-school exchange program
- Higher education program
- K-16 mentoring
- K-16 team-teaching
- School without walls

*Environmental outreach*

- Camp
- Service learning

*Social outreach*

- Community activism
- Cross-age/cross-generational coalition
- School-community partnership

## Types of Community-Based Activities

- Adopt a daycare center and create educational materials; visit the children.
- Adopt a senior citizen center; correspond, perform, socialize with elders.
- Apply what is learned at school to projects that benefit others in the community; arrange for after-school internships at local institutions.
- Build public relations; submit school news to neighborhood newsletter.
- Choose a theme that connects school to neighborhood.
- Circulate a petition, raise money, conduct a debate, prepare background testimony, conduct an exercise within the community about an issue requiring improvement.
- Conduct an art fair, band concert, flea market, car wash as fund raiser.
- Correspond with or visit students in a school with a different locale; organize a mentorship program with a school that has different age/grade levels.
- Create a problem workplace scenario that has many solutions.
- Devise solutions to problems, invent new work practices or workarounds to cope with unexpected developments.
- Invite families who live adjacent to school to attend events.

- Invite people of all ages to work on school projects.
- Learn what people in the community do to make a living; role-play or write about someone interviewed; sponsor a career day.
- Organize clubs and hold meetings open to the public.
- Organize, sponsor or adopt a local athletic team; raise funds for equipment.
- Prepare a presentation about school or community history.
- Routinely make classwork presentations to parent and community groups.
- Sponsor, advertise and participate in a neighborhood clean-up; beautify the community by planting flowers, painting over graffiti.
- Use tools of the workplace as part of everyday learning.
- Visit businesses and institutions within walking distance; take the bus to city hall, local college or university campus; can involve school-to-work.
- Volunteer to work at a community center or park.
- Work in collaboration with mentors in the community.
- Write to legislators with concerns; visit their offices; invite them to speak.
- Evaluate a community-based arrangement by discussing questions such as ones in the introduction to this chapter.

### District-Wide Learning

District-wide learning offers many students their first opportunities for interaction with a broader community than their own school, home or neighborhood. This grouping arrangement fosters in learners a sense of belonging to the school system that guides their learning, an appreciation for the diversity within that system and a respect for the procedures and expectations established by it for the common good of the larger community of learners.

Many creative school districts articulate their visions for every school in statements that include all or some of the following:

- Safe, secure and welcoming environment
- Learner enthusiasm, engagement and progress
- Multicultural education implemented in each classroom
- Integrated/interdisciplinary programs available for all

- Effective learning strategies delivered by every teacher
- Professional growth opportunities for all teachers
- Shared decision-making and site-based management at all levels
- Leadership from site administrator and building plan
- Business and organizational partnerships
- Communication with all segments of the community
- Variety of learning groups to meet needs of diverse learners
- Authentic assessments to measure student performance
- Genuine parent involvement that includes all families

Focus of the present-day standards-based system is not only to accelerate student achievement but also to bring together teachers, administrators and parents in a unified effort within a district. A major advance toward school restructuring occurs when staffs, students and families demonstrate their commitment to visions such as those above by collaborating in the writing of school improvement plans that state how and when some or all of the visions will be addressed. Although all are equally important, one may be selected as a yearlong theme or a few are sometimes chosen as primary objectives for improvement in a building's three- or five-year plan.

Students join with their teachers in district-wide learning, and together they fit their school into an institutional context that in most cases is fluid, evolving and changing direction at the turn of the century. As active participants in the ongoing story of the larger educational community, students learn strategies for effecting change that empower them in the reform movement today and in the future.

### Types of District-Wide Learning

*Competition*
*Cross-grade event*
*Mission/pledge*
*Partnership*

### Types of District-Wide Activities

- Annual inventors fair: participate in a noncompetitive event that showcases student inventions; think of a problem and apply a creative problem-solving process to solve it; display solution, explain the problem and solution and how it was achieved.

- Competition: participate in an athletic/academic game or contest periodically held among schools within a district.
- District- or state-wide yearly competition: showcase knowledge in a subject area, judged by a panel of experts or subject-area teachers.
- District, regional, state, national and international problem-solving competition: showcase expertise for long term, hands-on problems in subject-area categories.
- Evaluation: take a test or complete a questionnaire that is standardized for all learners across the district, with results published to demonstrate district-wide learner achievement or evaluation of learning climate.
- Fund-raising: participate in a program or event sponsored by the district to raise money for the district or for a targeted school.
- Network: contribute school information or special points of interest to a district newsletter, over district radio or cable television.
- Open house: invite families, other caregivers and members of the community to visit the school building after the school day.
- Pen pal: correspond with a learner in a different school within a district, sometimes meeting for enrichment activities.
- Special purpose: participate in a program or event sponsored by the district at a central location.
- Transition: visit a higher grade-level school.
- Evaluate a district-wide arrangement by discussing questions such as ones in the introduction to this chapter.

### Individualized Learning

In individualized learning arrangements the student may be entirely self-directed or may work alone after receiving initial or periodic direction, guidance and assistance by the teacher or a mentor outside the school. The learner's goal is to complete a project or otherwise reach an objective on his/her own. The objective and product may be a learner-, teacher- or mentor-initiated idea regarding content, sequence and pace.

Teachers plan individualized arrangements through conferences with other professionals and counseling sessions with learners themselves. They individualize learning every day when they help students with spelling words or when they guide individual learners in organized activities. During large-group learning activities, learners may raise their hands, sign up on the chalkboard or "take a number" to indicate their need for individualized help.

## Types of Individualized Learning

### Adult-assisted

- Apprenticeship/on-the-job education/also School-to-work
- Community/neighborhood adults
- Conference/periodic review and evaluation
- Contract/selection of objectives
- Counseling/guidance and assistance/problem-solving
- Dual enrollment: home-schooling with school activities
- Family learning, i.e., parents, guardians, adult caregivers
- Home schooling
- Homebound instruction
- Individual education (see School-Wide Learning: Thematic focus)
- Individual Education Plan (IEP)
- Individually Prescribed Instructional Program (Joyce, 1996, p. 301)/prepared curricular materials according to learner's level, style, needs
- Individualized instruction/one-on-one with an instructor
- Learner-teacher interactive/environment arranged for learner's needs
- Learning station/interest center
- Mentoring/coaching/mediating/also School-to-work
- "Networked"(Fogarty, 1991, p. 95)/communicating with experts
- School-to-work/job shadowing/internship
- Special Education/remediation by a qualified resource teacher

- Teacher-learner investigative/exploring within prescribed parameters
- Tutoring

*Computer-assisted*

- Computer-based instruction, review and practice
- Computer-based reading, writing and multimedia
- Electronic-mail conferencing/networking with adults and/or peers
- Integrated Learning Systems/computer-based sequential lessons
- Internet research and recreation

*Peer-assisted*

- Family learning, i.e., siblings, young relatives
- School peer teaching/tutoring/mentoring/conferencing/coaching

*Self-directed*

- Contest/individual competition
- Correspondence/telephoning/long-distance communication
- Homework
- "Immersed" (Fogarty, 1991, p. 85)/intense study of personal interest
- Independent study
- Internalizing/self-motivation/self-regulation
- Journaling/observation log/learning log/daybook/notes for research
- Learner-as-instructor/sharing of student's own expertise or skill
- Reflective thinking/verbalizing or writing about learning process
- Self-assessment/goal-setting
- Self-directed study/choosing and controlling content, pace, sequencing
- Self-instruction/virtual self-teaching using resources
- Self-talking/internal dialogue/rehearsal/reviewing
- Social activism/contributing for the good of others

## Types of Individualized Activities

- Create an activity for others to do.
- Gather and organize materials for others to use at a new or existing learning station.
- Gradually assume responsibility for increasingly more complex day-to-day classroom tasks and assignments.
- Help others find materials or information they need.
- Help the teacher with materials during a lesson.
- Initiate an appropriate remark or activity that helps everyone in a group to get organized, quieted down, on task, etc.
- Interview someone and share process as well as information with others.
- Plan, create and share a project based on personal interest and/or within teacher's prescribed parameters.
- Set a personal academic or social goal for each day.
- Try something new three times before asking for help.
- Use self-discipline to ignore distractions.
- Evaluate an individualized arrangement by discussing questions such as ones in the introduction to this chapter.

## Networked/Distance Learning

The world as a classroom is possible through networked/distance learning using computers, video, telephones and the postal service. Individual learners, small groups or entire classes may communicate with classrooms in other school districts or experts in specialized fields, regionally, nationally or internationally. This model of learning is not direct or face-to-face but with computers or telephones, it can be in real time and offer infinite resources for students.

The etiquette for each of these types of mediated learning is vital for young people to know. The student who contributes positively to the learning community practices ethical behavior in regard to technology. Just as children learn telephone etiquette, so must they learn procedures for sending and responding by voice phone or video in interactive television. Just as the postal service has protocol for sending a letter, so must the rules of the road be obeyed for electronic mail.

Online security is a concern in schools, and almost every district requires that staff, students and parents sign Acceptable Use Policy agreements that outline the uses of the Internet that are appropriate in the school setting. Vandalism in cyberspace can be expensive and just as criminal as mail fraud, and ethical issues concerning software piracy and online cheating are an integral part of the curriculum.

## Types of Networked/Distance Learning

*Computer*
*Interactive TV*
*Postal service*
*Telephone*

## Types of Networked/Distance Activities

- Audiovisual exchange: personally record an audio or video tape about cultural items or classroom projects to exchange with other students.
- Closed-circuit: videotape a classroom activity and transmit live to other rooms in the same building.
- Collaborative interviewing: pair up online with students in higher education.
- Computer conferencing: talk to others using an information satellite network system, computers and speakerphone.
- Disk exchange: key journals, essays, etc., onto a computer floppy disk to trade with students at another school for similar material.
- E-mail: correspond with teachers, mentors, other learners.
- Fax: send and receive correspondence using a telephone line and Fax machine.
- ITV: engage in live, real-time audio and video that provide combinations of one-way and two-way interactivity among teachers and learners at several sites at one time, using cameras, monitors, microphones and wiring for a distance-learning network system.
- Networking: communicate with adults and other learners in the same building through e-mail and file-sharing;

"networked"(Fogarty, 1991, p. 95) or communicating with experts online.
- Newsgroup: engage in projects with other students online.
- Post office: write and receive letters, postcards and greeting cards by using the postal service.
- Teleconferencing: use two or more connected telephone lines with a speakerphone to converse with an expert, mentor, etc.
- Video pal: trade personally produced videos with students in another school.
- Evaluate a networked/distance learning arrangement by discussing questions in the introduction to this chapter.

### School-Wide Learning

In school-wide learning, all students and adults in a building share the same experience or parallel experiences. Experiences may be of varying duration, from an hourlong assembly program to a yearlong theme. Some experiences are school-wide structural designs, such as alternative schools that may "represent our most definitive departure from the programmatic, organizational, and behavioral regularities that inhibit school reform. Moreover, many of the reforms currently pursued in traditional schools are practices that alternative schools pioneered" (Raywid, 1994, p. 26).

Twelve school-wide programs were analyzed as research-based, reform models by Margaret Wang, Geneva Haertel and Herbert Walberg (1998) and fall into two categories: those that concentrate on comprehensive improvement ("focusing on school governance, organization and also may include revised curriculum") and those that have curricular changes ("focusing on content in one or more academic disciplines...fitting into conventional schools with minimal change") (p. 66). Comprehensive programs include Accelerated Schools (Hopfenberg et al., 1993), Coalition of Essential Schools (MacMullen, 1996), Community for Learning (Wang, 1992, 1997) and School Development (Comer, 1996). Curricular models, often pull-out programs, are Core Knowledge (Hirsch, 1993), Different Ways of Knowing (Catterall, 1995), Foxfire (Foxfire Fund, Inc., 1992), Higher Order Thinking Skills (Pogrow, 1995), National Writing Project (Smith, 1996), Paideia (Adler, 1983), Reading Recovery (Pinnell, 1995) and Success for All (Slavin et al., 1996).

As many different types of school-wide learning situations exist as there are communities that form them, and many terms are applicable when discussing a specific school—such as magnets, interdisciplinary and thematic programs. Some are popular innovations, while others have a remedial focus. Variations on a theme are what individual school-wide structures are all about and with that in mind, the terms below are defined separately but some may be seen to describe the same school.

## Types of School-Wide Learning

*Alternative school*

- Charter school: independent, state-funded, outside regular school district constraints
- Extended-day school: year-around, night school, summer school, etc.
- Magnet school: program of choice with focus on curricular area
- Mini-school: special program housed in a mainstream school

*Disciplinary focus*
- Interdisciplinary: experiences overlap subject areas
- Multidisciplinary: separate subject areas but connected by theme
- Transdisciplinary: theme with no divisions into subject areas

*Information system*

- Assembly: congregation for a program, celebration, etc.
- Closed-circuit video: all spaces in a school wired to receive and transmit video
- Electronic mail: network for staff/students to transmit/receive e-mail
- Newsletter: school and/or district news delivered to all teachers, students, families and community members
- Public address system: information announced over a loud speaker

*Thematic focus*

- Immersion: rewritten curriculum to reflect school-wide focus
- Individual education: students maintain choice and control of learning

- School-wide program: participatory projects, i.e., recycling
- Side-by-side thematic: subject-area learning related to a theme
- Thematic: umbrella topic permeating all instruction

## Types of School-Wide Activities

- Begin each day in a common space with teachers and other students for celebration, announcements, enrichment, inspiration, etc.
- Celebrate, advertise and communicate success of the school.
- Participate in before- and/or after-school programs and club activities with other learners, families and members of the community.
- Select special classes during periodic option-days.
- Work toward accomplishing goals among all subject areas, while meeting the same specific objectives within subject areas.
- Create visual reminders of a slogan, theme, etc., around the school.
- Read, write and participate in interactive activities in all subject areas.
- Participate in periodic multi-aged groupings to concentrate on topics based on individual interest.
- Daily celebrate school-wide theme.
- Evaluate a school-wide arrangement by discussing questions such as ones in the introduction to this chapter.

## Small-Group Learning

In small-group arrangements, any number of students, from a pair to roughly half the class, may join together as a team, squad, family, etc., for a shared learning experience. Most groups need to be small enough so that everyone can participate without constant supervision of the teacher.

Small groups are generally used for activities such as implementing competitive- or collaborative-learning processes giving special instructions, playing games, practicing oral reading or working with different books. They may be formed for special reasons, such as to bring together learners from the same or different micro-cultures or learning styles. Common interests in tasks are more effective bases for forming small groups than ability or compatibility.

The classroom may be arranged with tables or desks turned to face each other, stations with visual dividers/sound barriers, or cushions on the floor. Small-group activities are not suitable for all instructional situations but should be used as one arrangement in combination with other grouping arrangements.

Cooperative/collaborative groups encourage meaningful knowledge construction by students, provide an opportunity to learn from peers and give students increasing responsibility for their own learning. Research by Jeff Golub in *Focus on Collaborative Learning* (1988) has shown that collaborative groups promote higher achievement than tracking or individual competitive learning, because when learners talk among themselves, their active involvement in their learning aids in understanding and retention. Furthermore, when teachers listen to learners talk, they can diagnose what they know, what they don't know, what they may have misunderstood and what skills they need for working with others.

Golub's suggestions are that students must be trained to develop specific skills that are needed for collaborative work, the task needs to require a group effort rather than an individual effort and roles of teacher and learners must be clearly defined. Robert Garmston and Bruce Wellman (1992) advise that assessment may be based on quality or quantity of group work only, individual contribution combined with group result, individual assessment with bonus marks if all members achieve, individual scores added to form a total group score, or different standards for individual success on a test versus score for the group task.

## Types of Small-Group Learning

*Ability group*

- Heterogeneous: different levels of cognitive abilities
- Homogeneous/tracking: similar levels of cognitive abilities

*Interest group*

- Club: similar levels of interests, enthusiasm or curiosity; also social group

- Extracurricular: similar levels of physical, artistic or academic expertise as well as interests, enthusiasm or curiosity

*Social group*

- Behavior group: interpersonal skills and socialization
- Counseling group: facilitation of problem-solving or goal-setting
- Cross-generational group: communication among age groups
- Friendship group: knowing, understanding and appreciating others
- Learning-style group: needs due to similar or different styles
- Micro-cultural group: needs due to similar or different micro-cultures

*Task group*

- Bilingual group: speaking/learning languages of group members
- Building project: making something, with members having different pieces
- Committee: planning an event or problem-solving about an issue
- Competitive group: review, improvement, fun or change of pace
- Cooperative group: collaborative work toward a common goal
- Integrated service: working with resource personnel in the classroom
- Preparation group: rehearsal, practice, studying for a test
- Pull-out group: special services outside the classroom
- Skill group: similar help with a specific skill
- Study group: writing, reading, solving problems, doing projects, etc.
- Workshop: short instruction by teacher, who rotates among groups

## Types of Small-Group Activities

- Applied learning: define how a topic will be studied and reported.

- Buddies: be responsible for another learner; learning partners.
- Buzz group: discuss a topic for 3–5 minutes and share ideas orally, visually or in writing with the large group; dynamic discussion.
- Class presentation: select different tasks for class production.
- Data group: gather raw data and communicate to base camp.
- Debate team: select, research and present opposing viewpoints.
- 5-3-1: generate five key words about a topic, share/compare with other learners, select three words and finally select only one word from all offered.
- Group investigation: take on specific role within a group and prepare projects, research or report to share with the class.
- Interviewing: form questions, interview someone, record answers and organize a report; paired interview: alternate roles of an interviewer and interviewee; three-step interview: interview a partner about a topic, then the pair reverses roles and repeats the interview, after which each pair joins another pair and learners tell what their partners had to say.
- Jigsaw: study different aspects of a topic, regroup, then each member is regarded as an expert on a subtopic to teach to other members; jigsaw acting: read aloud while others dramatize.
- List of concerns: generate a personal list of concerns, questions or ideas about a topic and share/compare with another learner.
- Networking: share information between computers; file-sharing.
- Numbered-heads together: generate answers to teacher's questions; number off within group, then teacher randomly selects a number to answer for each group; numbering off: after studying together, number off one to four, then teacher calls on members with same number to answer a question or calls on another number if no correct answer is given, repeating until all students have responded.
- Observer feedback: describe interactions of other members.
- 1-to-4: answer a question, then agree on an answer with a partner, then with another pair and share results with large group.

- Panel discussion: select a moderator and present a topic for the class; panel of experts: develop set of questions and answers about topic, then assume roles of moderator, quizzer, judge and recorder for their group, one group then acts as panel and its moderator calls for three questions from quizzers in other groups and judges determine if answers are correct; process is repeated until all groups have acted as panel.
- Pantomime: pass around imaginary object or pantomime story; tableau: form a frozen picture by posing to dramatize a significant scene or event with characters one at a time speaking in character.
- Peer tutoring: advise other learners; also cross-age.
- Personal picture: respond with personal solution to an open-ended problem by role-playing, writing, designing a poster, etc.
- Poster report: create poster about topic that includes title or main idea and combines words and pictures to express that idea.
- Round-robin: take turns responding to a question or offering ideas about a topic; paired-verbal-fluency: take turns responding orally to a topic for three rounds each of 45, 30 and 20 seconds.
- Round table 1: guide group discussion; round table 2: take a turn adding to a list of answers to a question.
- Self-directed coursework: complete a teacher-designed module before being reassigned to another topic with another partner; one day to evaluate and write reports and one day to demonstrate accomplishments to others.
- Student Teams-Achievement Divisions (Slavin, 1983): work in four-member groups to master material presented by teacher, then take individual tests, with assessment on the basis of each member's improvement over own past record.
- Team-Assisted Individualization (Slavin, 1983): work on materials at own level but four-member groups check each other's work and help each other with questions, individual tests.
- Teams-Games-Tournament (Slavin, 1983): work in four-member groups to master material presented by teacher, then

compete in weekly, three-person academic tournaments to add points to group's score, with regrouping of learners every week.

- Telephone line: work in rows to see which row learns facts quickest.
- Tell/retell: tell ideas to a partner, then tell another pair each other's idea, then join another four and retell only the ideas not previously told, ending with a group recap of all eight ideas.
- Think aloud: talk aloud as a problem-solver or thinking through a problem, while partner as a monitor asks questions about the process to describe the thinking going on; think-pair-share: first think alone, then share with a partner, sometimes creating one idea to share with class.
- Turn to your partner (or neighbor) and…: reflect on what was just said, identify key points from the last few minutes, generate practical examples of ideas presented so far, then share with another learner a time when examples of these ideas were encountered, any concerns regarding the topic or which of these options may be best and why.
- Methods to use for forming groups are the following:

    1. Corners: teacher posts signs labeled with the names of four aspects of a topic in corners of the room and learners choose which corner to go to, subdividing if groups become too large.
    2. Counting Off: learners number off around the room and form groups according to ones, twos, threes and fours.
    3. High Fives: learners stand and raise their hands as a signal to others that they are seeking partners.
    4. Humming: teacher distributes titles of familiar tunes (i.e., "Pop Goes the Weasel") and learners move around the room listening for others who are humming the same tune that they are humming.
    5. Interest: learners choose which group to join according to personal preference (i.e., writing groups for poetry, fable, diary, drama or journalism).
    6. Just Like Me: teacher makes a statement (i.e., "I was born in this state") and learners form a group when the statement applies to them.

7. Line-Ups: learners form groups according to birthdays, shirt colors, etc.
8. Playing Cards: teacher distributes cards from a deck and learners form groups with others who have the same suits or numbers.
9. Round the Clock: teacher distributes handouts with a large clock face on it and a line for names beside each hour; learners record each other's names on the lines until all the lines are filled; when group time arrives, the clock hours are called out and learners match up with partners.

• Evaluate small-group processing skills by asking such questions as the following (Golub, 1988):

1. Did all members fulfill their role descriptions? Share ideas?
2. Were ideas responded to even if not agreed with or used?
3. Were members praised when they gave good ideas?
4. What was the most helpful thing a member did?
5. What was the group really good at? What could be done better?
6. What is one word to describe how the group worked?
7. What happened when a member was not contributing?
8. What kind of help was really needed?
9. What did members do that made the group feel good?

## Team-Taught Learning

A wide variety of team-teaching arrangements offers students opportunities to relate to more than one adult and experience a broader spectrum of grouping arrangements for learning. Teaming by adults may be the result of job-sharing by two half-time teachers, double-class scheduling to accommodate time or space limitations in a school, collaboration among subject area teachers to integrate content and skills across disciplines or dividing responsibility among teachers so that each of them teaches a subject area to all classes in a team. The primary goal of teaming, however, is to meet student needs by using special abilities of more than one teacher. Teaming itself is part of the learning experience, as the adults involved model their own efforts for the learners and incorporate team activities into their instructional design.

Some kinds of team-taught learning, such as clustering of subject areas, do not adhere to traditional schedules. According to Linda Chion-Kenney (1987), clustering is team-teaching that allows "a school day in high school to be restructured so instructors can teach many fewer learners for much longer periods of time. In some cases, this is accomplished by having teachers teach two subjects each so they can see half the number of students for twice the amount of time… For example, the English and social studies teachers each teach two double periods of humanities" (p. 20).

Involving another adult in the classroom (i.e., educational assistant, volunteer) may not be team-teaching as such, but it might be for short-term academic reasons, such as sharing expertise, storytelling, reading with learners, tutoring, reinforcing ideas in a lesson or monitoring learning stations. Involvement may be for social reasons, such as leading educational games, accompanying students on a field trip, mentoring social development, or helping with special projects, parties and celebrations. Another adult may offer enrichment opportunities through mini-courses, information from a different point of view or exposure to a different language and culture, or they may act as helpers, preparing materials for learners, gathering resource materials or supervising small groups of learners.

## Types of Team-Taught Learning

*Team 2-1-1:* two teachers for one whole class in one space
*Team 2-2-1:* two teachers for two whole classes in one space
*Team 2-2-2:* two teachers for two whole classes in two spaces
*Team 2-2-2 Plus:* several teachers for many learners in several spaces

## Types of Team-Taught Activities

• Take an attitudinal pre-survey of teachers and other students to lay a foundation for teaming; recognize goals, understand terminology and reach agreement with teachers about expectations, plans and procedures.
• Take part in making rules and deciding what to do in teams.

- Periodically participate in cross-age or multi-age groupings.
- Keep a journal or take an attitudinal post-survey to assess teaming efforts.
- Work toward evaluation or grades based on group performance rather than on individual accomplishments.
- Celebrate learning through team exhibitions.
- Participate in team-building, motivational activities with teachers.
- Discuss teaming with the family; offer feedback to teachers.
- Observe modeling of teamwork by teachers that shows how teams work.
- Work on assignments with a partner or as part of a team, jointly devising problem-solving strategies.
- Within a large-group team, work with a smaller group for seminars or projects and an even smaller cooperative group for assignments and assessments.
- Evaluate a team-taught arrangement by discussing questions such as ones in the introduction to this chapter.

## Whole-Class Learning

In whole-class groups, all students are guided through the same learning experience at the same time by a teacher. Baron Rosenshine (1986) describes large-group instruction as an effective, very efficient and timesaving means of introducing concepts, establishing a common set of terms among learners, setting the stage for small-group or individual activities, consensus-building and conducting summary discussions (p. 63). It is useful for presenting interesting problems, posing provocative questions, probing and guiding, making thinking visible, generating multiple approaches to solutions and using a variety of approaches to allow students who do not understand material in one way to encounter it in other ways.

Since information-giving and -getting is with and for all the learners in a class, the arrangement also fosters group identity, a sense of cohesiveness or purpose and shared responsibility for group achievement, attitude and behavior. Additionally, in some cultures, learning with and for the group is considered more beneficial than learning by and for one's self.

Students in one classroom may be the same-age/grade level or cross-age/grade level, and teachers may instruct in isolation or collaborate with other teachers of similar age/grade levels in planning units and sharing the task of locating appropriate materials. Classwork may relate to a single discipline, as is found in secondary public schools or, as is common in elementary public schools, an integration of skills, content and learning experiences in several subject areas may be presented by a single teacher who uses a connecting topic to create a self-contained interdisciplinary approach.

The classroom's seating arrangement may be rows of desks or tables facing an instructor or a circle/horseshoe of chairs in which all those involved—learners and teacher alike—become equal participants in the experience. Interactive instruction with meaningful student participation is as important for interconnected teaching and learning in whole-class arrangements as it is in individualized or small-group arrangements.

### Types of Whole-Class Learning

*Drill and practice*

- Mastery learning
- Quick drill

*Instruction*

- Audiovisual experience
- Direct instruction
- Evaluating/assessing
- Field trip
- Large group/small group/large group
- Mini-lecture

*Meeting*

- Discussion
- Educational diagnostic
- Informational
- Open-ended
- Planning session
- Social problem-solving
- Socratic seminar
- Wrap-up

*Production*

- Performance by members of the whole class
- Performance by others for members of the whole class

## Types of Whole-Class Activities

- Dialogue: discuss a topic with which all students are familiar and in which inquiry-based questions invite elaboration rather than yes/no answers; take turns without the formality of raising hands and listen without interrupting.
- Direct questioning: answer a question when directly asked to do so.
- Directed listening-thinking: make and record predictions about what might happen next at stopping points teacher has marked in a text.
- Double circle: form an inner circle with half of the class and ask questions of other half that has formed an outer circle; outer circle then asks questions, moves one person to the right and process repeats until circle is completed.
- Gallery walk: form a stationary line with half of the class and hold up work while the other half walks past to look at the display.
- Mentoring: work with a group of mentors who has adopted the whole class.
- People search: move around the room and gather answers to questions from others learners.
- Sentence strip tea party: move around the room with sentences or dialogue quotations from a sequential story written on strips of paper, read sentences to all other learners and hear all the other sentences; write what might happen in sequential order.
- 10/2: share and compare notes in small groups and help each other clarify concepts for two minutes after the teacher has presented material for ten minutes.
- Total group response: vote or otherwise indicate approval/disapproval by raising hands, thumbs up or down, etc.
- Walk-around survey: move around the room collecting information from other learners about recall or observations

about a topic and share/compare the surveys to form generalizations about the large group.
- Wraparound/whip/snake: respond in turn around the room
or opt to pass.
- Evaluate a whole-class arrangement by discussing questions
such as ones in the introduction to this chapter.

# Chapter 5

## Learning Resources: Forms of Media

"We need to recognize that there is not a single path to literacy, but multiple paths."

—David Hartle-Schutte,
"Literacy Development in Navajo Homes"

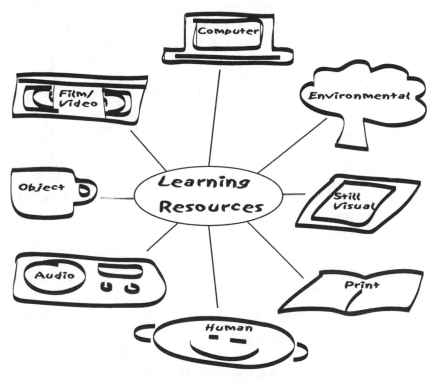

Figure 13: Forms of Media

S tudents in interconnected education learn from digital technologies as well as textbooks, from artwork as well as seatwork, from critically viewing as well as critically reading, from touching as well as observing, and from almost any and all persons, places and things. Some learn better when they utilize information from a certain person, place or thing rather than another because of differences in learning styles, intelligences, micro-cultural identities and world views.

Patricia M. Greenfield (1985) wrote that "each medium can be used to enhance the impact of the others...One medium's strength is another's weakness; thus the media are complementary, not opposites" (p. 18). Greenfield explained that a multimedia approach to learning can be more effective than using a single medium, can help children develop new skills that print alone may not develop and can motivate learners who are turned off by school. She and other media educators (Considine, 1999b; Tyner, 1998, 2000; Watts Pailliotet, 2000; Lacy, 2000; Silverblatt, 2001) urge that the pervasiveness of television, video games and computer technologies makes it crucial for teachers to discover how best to use them for educational value as well as entertainment value with young people.

Since Greenfield's book, more technological strides have been taken to make information accessible to the average person than had been taken in the previous five hundred years. Computers allow research activities to be more precise and up-to-date than ever before, giving learners access to electronic documents and high-powered word processing or multimedia authoring. Electronic media once implied one-way delivery of information, but today we have two-way, networked, interactive media that is improving at incredible speed. As Kathleen Tyner (1998) asks, "What educational media, used with what technologies, work with what students, under what conditions?" (p. 70).

Because of collapsed boundaries in our current technological world, the resulting interactivity has changed the way we must look at teaching and learning itself. According to Minnesota's Plan for Technology Education (1997b), "Technological literacy is being able to understand the relationships between technology today and social change...It is not sufficient to be literate only within specific technologies, but also to be literate in how these specific technologies change and impact our lives" (p. 1).

The obvious challenge for educators is to prepare young people for participation in an increasingly multimedia environment. At home as well as at work, their lives will continue to be shaped by dramatic advances in interactive formats under construction as fast lanes on the information superhighway. We are charged with the task of providing learners the necessary skills to find their way around in this information explosion, to know what they need, when to use which medium and how to use it ethically to communicate worthwhile ideas. Teachers and learners now expect technology-mediated education and call for funding, staffing and training to increase student motivation, foster basic skills, reduce dropout rates and better prepare learners for higher education and the workplace.

The colorful, high-tech world our youngsters live in means that they are often understandably more familiar with the new languages and unique ways of expression than are their elders. However, the young and not-so-young together form a community of learners with similar needs for new skills, and none of us must become blinded by the glitz of technologies in the classroom, forgetting what they are there for—as tools to enhance learning. Our task as educators, as it has always been, is to help children understand and use the best available tools, high-tech or low-, as effective guides for inquiry, exploration and discovery. These tools must be whatever works in the hands of individual students that enables them to construct contextual meaning. Creative teachers are the best ones to choose when and how to use them.

Tools such as books, films, computers and manipulatives are often called delivery systems by instructional designers. For our purposes here, they are called learning resources or forms of media used by teachers and students alike to access, process and report information. Opportunities are offered to experience all kinds of resources, and no one resource is used exclusively for an entire course of study. On the following pages are presented a wide variety of resources, with a list of suggested activities.

Multimedia productions, interactive learning stations and multisensory kits use combinations of these formats. Not all of the resources lend themselves to every topic or skill, but each of the eight may be used as follows:

- A primary resource, supplementary, enrichment or review
- A sole resource or combined with other types of resources
- At the beginning, middle or end of a lesson, unit or course of study
- For all or part of a lesson; use part or all of the resource
- By itself as a single example or with others of its same type
- Once or more than once to meet different objectives

- Straight through or stopping to discuss, explain, practice, review
- With or without students taking notes or reporting

Activities for each type of resource in this chapter are from the perspective of a creative teacher who is seeking better ways to use resources with students. The following guidelines for teachers apply to using all types of resources:

- Select the best from all available of the type, preview, and single out sections to emphasize.
- Gather and display any other supplementary materials.
- Arrange the classroom appropriately for use of each type of resource.
- Plan, share and evaluate a variety of activities similar to those listed for each resource.
- Call learners' attention to types of resources being used and reasons for their use.
- Contrast and compare benefits of the uses for different resources.
- Model the use, appreciation and enjoyment of micro-cultural points of view.
- Create age- and developmentally appropriate experiences using resources.
- Create real-life experiences using each type of resource.
- Use popular culture examples of each type of resource.

To evaluate the usefulness of any resource, learners benefit by examining such questions as:

- What type of resource was it? In what ways was it or was it not typical?
- Why did you use this type? Why was it the best resource to use for this information?
- How was the idea presented by the resource? Was the presentation successful for you? What else might have been done?
- What did you learn? What can you do with this knowledge or skill? When is that use appropriate?
- Could you create a similar presentation using this type of resource? What would you present? What would you need? Who would be your audience?

## Audio Resources

Storytellers and teachers who read aloud in the classroom notice with dismay that many students—and some adults as well—are poor listeners when visuals are not being shown. Most educators agree that young people have become seduced too easily by quick and clever imagery experienced elsewhere in the visual mass media. However, in the purest oral traditions of most ethnic groups, pictures or other props are not generally used. Rather, verbal skills of the tale-teller and auditory skills of the listener are solely relied on to create pictures in the mind's eye. Despite efforts to keep such pure traditions alive, simply listening for any length of time is in danger of becoming obsolete in the lives of our children.

One form of the mass media that young people really listen to—the recorded music industry—not only survives but thrives on the attention of each new generation. The popular music our students enjoy presents us with a most promising opportunity for interconnected learning of listening skills with those in reading and writing. A creative history, social studies or language arts teacher may play a recording of a familiar teen song in the classroom. Suppositions are made about the context for words and emotions conveyed in the lyrics until backgrounds are written and perhaps illustrated by students about fictitious characters involved. The lyrics appear—as a poem, a dream or a lament—in the students' stories and then are changed to reflect other stories the students invent. New songs, poems and stories continue to evolve and are recorded, inspiring other learners to listen, read and write their own.

Recorded music and other audio based resources such as environmental sounds, talk radio and audio-books are thought of as faceless or disembodied learning that is instructive even with one's eyes closed. For our purposes here, recorded music or story on tape are audio-based, whereas the same music at a concert or a story on stage are considered human-based because of interaction of performers among themselves and with the audience.

## Types of Audio Resources
### Interactive device

- Audio tape
- Compact disc

- Intercom/public address system
- Language master
- Telephone/cellular phone

*Radio*

- Call-in
- Commentary
- Commercial
- Community events
- Dramatization
- Drive-time
- Music
- News (on-the-spot or summary)
- Public service announcement
- Round table/forum
- Special report
- Speech
- Sports event
- Talk show/interview
- Variety show
- Weather report

*Recording*

- Audio tape
- Digital recording
- Phonograph record

*Sound*

- Human environment
- Natural environment
- Synthesized

## Types of Audio-Based Learning

- Listening to learn rather than reading or watching
- Reading aloud or reading along
- Mental imaging
- Attending to announcements, directions or instructions
- Listening to a simplified version of a difficult written text

- Moving to a rhythm or beat for dance, calisthenics or an exercise routine
- Responding to sound that establishes a mood
- Recording a personal journal, data report or daily observation log
- Simulating a famous radio broadcast
- Narrating a story, biography or historical event
- Presenting information before or after a field trip
- Interviewing
- Communicating on audio tape with a "talk pal"
- Independently studying
- Using audio alone as a story- or picture-starter
- Using audio as evidence or proof of an event
- Reviewing a lesson
- Updating information

## Types of Audio-Based Activities

- Contrast and compare types of aural learning, such as:
  1. Spoken words: were they live or recorded, narration or instruction, etc.?
  2. Music: was a piece classical, popular, folk, etc.?
  3. Sound: was it animal, human, a special effect?

- Contrast and compare types of audio recordings for quality of sound and ease of use.
- Discuss sounds that diverse micro-cultures and learning styles love or hate as well as possible reasons for their reactions and what might be done inside and outside school to accommodate differences.
- Play chapters from an audio-book daily in the classroom as if the story were serialized on the radio.
- Devise a note-taking tool for an audio-based resource, such as:

  1. An outline of key words for pertinent verbal information, musical elements or special effects to listen for
  2. Paper and pencil for responding artistically to music or for jotting down key points to remember in a discussion afterward

- Use different techniques to enhance an audio recording, such as adjusting the volume to achieve a desired effect or using headphones to individualize learning.
- Agree beforehand on a silent-response signal if you desire learners' feedback to your prompts or questions while they are listening, such as hand raised, thumb up or thumb down.
- Assign different tasks or roles for learners, such as information-gatherer, critic, technical analyzer to appeal to different learning styles or intelligences.
- Preface the audio by allowing time for learners to get comfortable, explaining why listening only is helpful in this situation to meet a specified objective, announcing certain elements they are to listen for and describing any pertinent background for the audio-based resource.
- Listen to the same audio more than once to gather exact quotes or details (different tasks or roles may be assigned for each experience).
- Discuss how some sounds, voices and music make you feel or how they influence your behavior; analyze reasons found in micro-cultural identities.
- Evaluate audio-based learning by examining such questions as the following:

   1. What type of audio-based resource was this? Who or what was heard?
   2. Why did you listen? What was the main idea?
   3. How was the idea presented? Was the presentation successful for you? What else might have been done? Why would that be more successful?
   4. What did you learn from this resource? What can you do with this knowledge?
   5. Could you make a similar audio experience? What would you present? What would you need? Who would be your audience?

### Computer Resources

The basic advantages of computer resources are that they are interactive, individualized, self-paced and highly motivational for most young people. Effective educational computer programs also have easily used on-screen instructions and good printed documentation, offer a range of skills levels, are age-appropriate, develop higher-level thinking and support and extend specific objectives in an existing curriculum. In addition, by offering a variety of options for explorations and demonstrations of learning, computer-driven telecommunications and multimedia productions open the way for teachers and learners to work and learn together, making any course of study more democratic, up-to-date, interdisciplinary, multi layered, fluid and open-ended.

Computer-based learning is uniquely determined by brands and capabilities of whatever hardware and software is being used, both of which are evolving so fast that descriptions here are very basic. The majority of teachers and learners are not interested in highly technical aspects of computers and programs but want to know instead how the technology meets their needs and enhances interconnected teaching and learning. Well-trained computer users, just like their novice colleagues and classmates, still have to learn how to use each new product that comes along. Whether experienced or inexperienced, the following suggestions from "Teaching Effectively with Technology" (Dyrli and Kinnaman, 1995) are useful for computer instruction as well as most other types of teaching and learning:

- Relate technology to personal experience.
- Provide unstructured time.
- Introduce new terms in writing.
- Make instructions concrete.
- Give instructions different ways.
- Separate talk time and work time.
- Give instructions in bite-sized chunks.
- Avoid making conclusions for students.
- Announce the approaching end of each activity.
- Make links to the next activity.

## Types of Computer Resources

### Hardware

- Digital camera
- Digitizer/scanner
- Driver

- Input device
- Microcomputer
- Modem
- Output device
- Storage device

## *Multimedia*

- Compact disc
- Fixed-sequence multimedia
- Hypermedia/hypertext

## *Software*

- Commercially produced
- Online resources
- Personally programmed
- Pre-installed operating system

## *Telecommunication*

- Electronic mail
- World Wide Web

## Types of Computer-Based Learning

- Calculating using a database-managing program, record-keeping program, spreadsheet program
- Communicating using an online telecommunication system
- Creating graphics using a design program, clip art program, multimedia system
- Individualizing instruction using a drill-and-practice program, tutorial program, Integrated Learning System
- Recreating using an action-arcade, entertainment or game-like program; graphic-adventure program; text-adventure program
- Researching using a computer-customized textbook, problem-solving program, quiz-designer program, simulation program, spatial visualization program
- Word processing using an authoring system; presentation program; desktop-publishing program; electronic-publishing system; prewriting program; spell-, grammar- and style-checking program

## Types of Computer-Based Activities

- Compare and contrast types of computer programs and systems, their uses and purposes.
- Use computer programs in a variety of ways:

  1. By individuals, pairs or small groups of learners
  2. By large groups with demonstrations on a large screen
  3. With or without sound
  4. With headphones to individualize learning
  5. With or without printouts or note-taking

- Agree on a visual signal (hand raised, styrofoam cup placed on top of the monitor) to use for individual learner response and/or request for feedback/assistance during the computer experience.
- Design on a clipboard a note-taking tool, written instructions, an outline of content or graphic helpers.
- Vary the same assignment according to learners' different levels of computer literacy.
- Use programs more than once, repeating skills and employing increasing levels of difficulty.
- Evaluate computer-based learning by examining questions such as the following:

  1. What type of program was it? What learning activities did it involve? In what ways were these typical for the type of program?
  2. Why did you see it? What was the main purpose?
  3. How was the idea presented? Was the presentation successful for you? What else might have been done?
  4. What did you learn from this resource? What can you do with this knowledge?
  5. Could you make a similar program? What would you present? What would you need? Who would be your audience?

### Environmental Resources

Students often need guidance in how to learn standing up. From a very young age, they are so conditioned to sitting down for lessons that when they get up and walk around somewhere—for instance, on a guided tour of a museum—they can become disoriented, unfocused and unruly. A few basic rules for "Learning Standing Up" (Lacy, 1986b) are:

- Standing together requires leaving each other alone.
- Staying together means we all learn the same things.
- Place, host and purpose deserve our respect.
- Looking and listening is learning.
- Talking, taking or touching (without permission) is trouble.

A sense of how to interact in a place defines environment-based learning. It involves the differences among places, an awareness of kinds of information to be derived from them and an understanding of how to act and react in them. Teachers introduce a sense of place for students initially by their own classroom design, by types of learning activities they orchestrate there and by the respect for purpose, rules and procedures which reinforce that spatial design and those activities.

Another important aspect of environment-based teaching and learning is to raise awareness of ecological interdependence. Planners and preservationists have begun to reflect a "new urbanism" that encourages city designs that highlight natural features of the terrain and connecting, gathering spaces for people to better interact. Interviews in the community can give students insights into people's interaction with the spaces around them. How does the environment determine the activities and culture of the people in a place? How have they adapted to and in many cases changed the natural environment? What are the positive and negative effects? What can students do to improve their own environment?

### Types of Environmental Resources

*Indoor space* (large): i.e., museum, auditorium, government center
*Indoor space* (small): i.e., house, classroom, community center
*Outdoor space* (natural): i.e., nature preserve, woods, ocean
*Outdoor space* (human-made): i.e., stadium, playground, zoo

### Types of Environment-Based Learning

- Recognizing places that are indoors or outdoors with natural attributes, human-made attributes or a combination of attributes

- Identifying what a place is for (i.e., entertainment, business, formal learning, governing) and who it is for (i.e., children, young people, adults, elders, everyone)
- Analyzing how to use a place (i.e., alone or shared with others, quietly or noisily)
- Interpreting whether a place is private or public, static or ever-changing, for display or interactivity and for observation or participation
- Analyzing how to move around in a place and how to take care of it

## Types of Environment-Based Activities

- Agree on a response signal (learners raise one hand if they have something to say and raise both hands if they can not see or hear).
- Devise a note-taking tool on a clipboard (with pencil tied to the clip), such as an outline or graphic organizer for learners to fill in information.
- Assign small-group work, with each group looking or listening for something different or performing a different task.
- Preface the experience by explaining to learners its purposes, structure, expectations, rules and procedures; research or conduct activities about the objective of the experience, including brainstorming kinds of learning that may take place and questions learners may want to ask; rehearse appropriate behavior if needed.
- Visit the same place more than once to observe natural or human-made changes; different roles may be assigned for each visit.
- Arrange far in advance for necessary parental permissions, adult volunteer helpers, transportation, refreshments, etc.
- Compile an emergency bag to take along (writing materials, Band-Aids, coins, tissues, safety pins, etc.).
- Conduct learning activities while waiting, walking or on the bus.
- Discuss all aspects of the experience afterward in the classroom and follow through with related activities.
- If the experience involves an exhibit or display:

1. Do not try to see everything available.
2. Concentrate on selected items for study.
3. Read and use materials provided by exhibitors.
4. Arrange for a tour guide who works well with students.
5. With young children, organize experience as a scavenger hunt, mystery to solve, fantasy adventure, etc.
6. Model and encourage respect for exhibits that reflect opinions or viewpoints that may be unfamiliar to students.
7. Wear comfortable clothes; check coats and bags.
8. A one-hour experience is best; two hours should be maximum.

• If the experience involves outdoor learning, *Teaching in the Outdoors* by Donald and William Hammerman (1983, p. 13) advises:

1. Relate the experience to sensory awareness, seasonal changes, environmental quality, survival checks and balances, adaptation, problem-solving and/or the philosophy of interconnectedness.
2. Be prepared for unforeseen incidents; take advantage of teachable moments.
3. Relate abstract knowledge to the world of reality.
4. Bring compasses, tape measures, calculators and log books to solve live word-problems.
5. Distribute a guide sheet for self-guided experiences or for posing questions, pointing out specific items of interest, clarifying terminology, provoking thought and opening discussions.

• If the experience involves animals, *The Science Teacher* (1990) recommends the following guidelines:

1. Handling of animals by students must be gentle or in some cases forbidden, as with baby birds.
2. Live organisms must be free from transmittable diseases or other problems that may endanger human health.
3. Learners are encouraged to develop a strong commitment to responsible, quiet and gentle care of living

creatures, including knowledge about the life habits and physical needs for a species.

4. Laboratory-bred or non native species must not be released into the wild to disturb the normal ecosystem or become pests.

- Evaluate environment-based learning by examining such questions as the following:

    1. Where did you go? What type of place was is? What was its purpose?
    2. Why did you go there? What was the main idea?
    3. How was the place? Was it a successful experience for you? What else might have been one? Where else might you have gone to experience the same idea?
    4. What did you learn from this resource? What can you do with this knowledge?
    5. Could you plan a similar experience in a place you know? What would you do there? What would you need? Who would go?

### Film/Video Resources

Movies, television and video have the strongest effect on our emotions of any of the mass media. Film/video resources inform and entertain in unique ways by showing us other people, places, things and events in motion and in color that may be impossible or dangerous for us to see for ourselves. Film/video collapses (speeds up) or expands (slows down) real time for processes or sequences of events. However, the past, present or future (here or elsewhere, real or fictitious) still seems to come to life. Creative educators in the National Council of Teachers of English (1996) recognize that the early definition of literacy as an ability to read and write must now be expanded to include viewing and visually representing as a result of our growing consciousness of how people gather and share information in a global society.

As similar in many ways as they appear to be, Fred Camper in an article "Film Is Not Video/Video Is Not Film" (1986) explains that important exhibition differences exist among moving film

(16mm, 8mm), television (broadcast, cable-cast or closed-circuit) and videos (tape, disc, DVD):

- Movie projectors can show images as large or small; television and video playback is limited to size of the television set, unless a video projector is used.
- Movies are impractical to pause, fast-forward or rewind; television is impossible; video is easy.
- Movies are intended for flat and rectangular projection; television screens are convex and do not have the same dimensions as movie film.
- Movie film has firm edges as borders; a television set's borders are indistinct and curved.
- Movie film is clear and sharp; a television set has a narrower range for focusing and color intensity.
- Movies are viewed as if their images hover in darkness; video and television images emanate from a box and have lighted distractions.
- Movies and videos are not paced to fit schedules or commercial breaks; television productions collapse or expand real time to fit a schedule.
- Movie film must be developed; television and video can be live.
- Film is special; television is familiar.

Preparation is important if film/video is to be used appropriately in the classroom. Selection of the best available production for study requires checking copyright date for timeliness and analyzing credit credentials to determine credibility, authority and viewpoint of the creators. Film/video resources must be previewed by the teacher, once straight through to determine suitability and lack of micro-cultural biases and a second time to take notes about content, language, vocabulary, characters, visual highlights, special features, recall questions, sequencing and pacing to pause for discussion.

Materials to be gathered might be an outline or visual organizer of the content, activities for pre-teaching difficult concepts and other resources to study before or after viewing. Room-darkening is necessary for film. If an Interactive TV system has been installed, monitors, cameras and microphones must be arranged. To participate in an electronic field trip, support materials may be requested and an orientation broadcast should be viewed before learners interact with presenters during live broadcast.

## Types of Film/Video Resources

### *Movie*

- Adventure/disaster/gangster/horror/western
- Animation/fantasy/science fiction
- Comedy/musical
- Docudrama/historical
- Experimental/independent/foreign
- Instructional/cultural/natural
- Propaganda/war

### *Television*

- Animation/fantasy
- Commercial/home shopping
- Docudrama/documentary/instructional
- Episodic/hourlong drama/soap opera
- Game show
- Movie of the week/theatrical performance
- Music/music video/variety
- News/news magazine/weather
- Political/special report/essay
- Religious
- Sports event
- Stand-up comedy
- Tabloid/talk show/interview

### *Video tape/video disc/DVD*

- Commercially recorded
- Personally recorded

### *Video interactive*

- Electronic field trip
- Interactive TV
- Video game
- Videoconference

**Types of Film/Video-Based Learning**

- Appreciating/expressing
- Categorizing/comparing/contrasting
- Defining/describing
- Directing/instructing
- Documenting/exploring/informing
- Entertaining/storytelling
- Idealizing/persuading
- Interacting/communicating

**Types of Film/Video-Based Activities**

*Before film/video*

- Announce whether the film/video has any features that are problematic and the reasons why (i.e., if it is old, is in black and white, has no story line, has a bad soundtrack, has difficult vocabulary).
- Explain why all (or parts) will be shown, why it will be shown once (or twice), why audio will be used (or the instructor will narrate), why it will (or will not) be stopped, rewound or fast-forwarded and why interruptions for questions or discussion will (or will not) be included.
- List some questions to be answered by the film/video and/or list new words, phrases or major concepts.
- Make a K-T-W-L chart or ask for prior knowledge about the topic.
- List pertinent names, dates, places or objects in the film/video.
- Play a segment without sound as a background for an introduction.
- Agree on a silent-response signal (hands raised, thumbs up or down) for learner responses while a non-interactive film/video is on.
- Devise a note-taking tool, such as:
    1. An outline with abundant white space to take notes
    2. A visual organizer with large sections to fill in
    3. Blank paper marked or folded into sections that are easier to see if the room is darkened
    4. Several note cards for jotting down ideas or pictographs

- Assign different roles for film/video critics, with responsibilities to report on any or all of the following:
  1. Applicability of visual/aural content to topic of study
  2. Positive and negative aspects of the film/video
  3. Unusual or eye-opening aspects of the film/video
  4. Typical genre aspects of the film/video or aspects that are combined
  5. Visual/aural techniques used to convey content
  6. Visual/aural clues for place, time, mood

### During film/video

- View a non-interactive film/video uninterrupted with full discussion afterward or view segments with pauses for short discussions.
- View more than once for reinforcement, to reach different objectives or to review if learners misunderstood something. (If students concentrate so hard on assignments, encourage watching for overview during the first showing and watching for details during the second).
- During pauses, ask for reports from different critics listed above or ask what just happened, what feelings were provoked, what will happen next, what new words or key ideas were introduced and/or what visual/verbal details learners noticed.
- If viewing segments over time, introduce other activities (reading, writing, researching, experimenting) related to the topic.
- Turn off audio if a segment is viewed as introductory motivator, if teacher will narrate because the audio is either too simple or too sophisticated for learners, if key points require emphasis, if learners are to use skills in visual observation only or if learners are to narrate or interpret as the segment proceeds.
- Turn off visual for reinforcement of important concepts or appreciation of narration/soundtrack.
- Fast-forward to personally edit material.

### After film/video

- Share reports from film/video critics assigned beforehand.
- Discuss additional aspects as might warrant attention, such as character development, new facts or ideas, issues not

adequately covered, ease of understanding, how diverse micro-cultures might interpret content, how unique elements of film/video were used and how to use the film/video as springboard for further study.

- Conduct an image/sound skim: "When you close your eyes and think of what we viewed, what images do you see? What sounds do you hear?"; encourage discussion about what was seen and heard; distinguish between specific criticism and personal reaction; point to specialness of production.
- Evaluate film/video-based learning by examining such questions as the following:

    1. What type of film/video was it? What were the creators' credentials? In what ways was it typical of its genre?
    2. Why did you watch it? What was the main idea?
    3. How did the film/video present the idea? Was the production successful for you? What else might have been done? What might have been left out?
    4. What did you learn? What can you do with this knowledge?
    5. Could you make a similar film/video? What would you present? What would you need? Who would be your audience?

### Human Resources

In live, face-to-face, real-time interactions, people communicate not only verbally through words and sounds but also visually through body language, postures, movements, facial expressions and clothing. Objects or other visuals are props to support verbal information rather than primary resources for this type of learning.

Gail E. Haley, who writes about her frequent experiences as a visiting author/illustrator in *Imagine That: Developing Critical Thinking and Critical Viewing Through Children's Literature* (Considine, Haley and Lacy, 1994), offers the following suggestions for having a guest in the classroom (p. 185):

- Find out whether the person has prior positive experiences working with students.

- Contact the person through correct channels (i.e., publisher, resource catalog).
- Invite the person far in advance.
- Offer alternative dates/times.
- Have another person in mind if the first one is unavailable.
- Ask what the person prefers to do and plan around that.
- Find out if an honorarium is expected and when it is due.
- Determine whether there are expenses and who will pay them.
- Arrange for transportation and/or lodging if needed.
- Establish a clear understanding with the person about the following:

  1. What will be done with students
  2. Ages and number of students
  3. Anything special about students (i.e., bilingual class)
  4. What kind of interactivity is expected
  5. What the person needs (i.e., space, equipment)          .
  6. Where the person is to go upon arrival
  7. Who the coordinator is for the person's visit
  8. Schedule, including break(s) and/or lunch arrangement
  9. Whether the person is available after the classroom visit for meeting with teachers, autographing, book sales, etc.
  10. Whether audio or video recording is allowed

- Arrange in advance for equipment, space, book sales, etc.
- Prepare students by studying about the topic or the person beforehand and discussing behavioral expectations for the visit, including information about any cultural-specific courtesies and communication styles involving a guest who is a member of a micro-culture other than that of the learners.
- Meet the guest in the school office.
- Introduce the guest to the class.
- Remain in the classroom and participate in discussions or question period.
- Assure student behavior is respectful and attentive.
- Act as time keeper for the guest and help with closure and exit.
- Return an evaluation if the guest left one behind.
- Follow up the visit with a thank-you note to the guest.

## Types of Human Resources

- *Classroom teacher/subject specialist:* professional in a subject area who is held accountable for student progress
- *Other adult at school:* administrator, another teacher, support or resource personnel, guest, volunteer, others with expertise to share
- *Person outside school:* parent, sibling, guardian, caregiver, guide, helper, host, performer, others with expertise to share
- *Student:* learner in the class, another class or another school with expertise to share

## Types of Human-Based Learning

- Informing/explaining/demonstrating/modeling
- Interacting/discussing/interviewing/problem-finding
- Expressing/reflecting/praising/describing
- Imagining/role-playing/fantasizing/dramatizing
- Influencing/suggesting/facilitating/guiding/coaching
- Socializing/playing/getting acquainted

## Types of Human-Based Activities

- Compare and contrast the purposes, learner expectations, presentation styles, and expected behaviors for different types of human-based learning.
- Agree beforehand whether students may:
  1. Raise hands to interrupt with questions or responses
  2. Participate in a question-and-answer session immediately following the speaker
  3. Submit questions or responses in writing to the speaker or teacher

- If notes are to be taken by learners, determine beforehand what points or ideas will be covered by the speaker and whether a note-taking tool (outline, visual organizer, etc.) will be distributed.
- For best appreciation of some human resources (i.e., a live performance or field trip), give different assignments to different small groups of learners, for which instructions might be to note details of various aspects of the experience.

- Prefacing human-based learning may be done differently, such as the following:

    1. Informing is best begun with an anticipatory set which includes a focusing strategy, bridging strategy and overview or general idea about expectations and objectives.
    2. Interacting may in addition include brainstorming or list-creation by learners themselves.
    3. Expressing often effectively begins with a simple title of what is to follow.
    4. Imagining usually relies on the elements of surprise, wonderment, fantasy or the outrageous as prefatory action.
    5. Influencing requires thoughtful articulation of a statement of position at the beginning.
    6. Socializing demands informality, spontaneity and the ability to change direction entirely.

- Introduce a guest or unfamiliar instructor, explain task or reason for visit and suggest ideas to listen for; demonstrate cultural-specific courtesies and an appropriate communication style for guests who are members of micro-cultures that may be different from those of the learners.

- When learners are expected to attend over an extended length of time, use a variety of presentation styles such as the following:

    1. Speaking from different places around the room
    2. Walking around or sitting down with the learners
    3. Using visual aids of various kinds
    4. Pacing instruction by changing voice, pausing to discuss and acknowledging feedback
    5. Reciprocal teaching: actively involving learners by asking them to summarize, clarify, ask key questions, state key ideas, predict, etc.
    6. Engaged lecturing: incorporating proverbs, riddles, puns, metaphors, slogans
    7. Being inventive: "becoming" a character, a machine, an emotion, etc.; re-creating an historical event as a story and involving learners in re-creating the scene; role-playing famous person; reciting or role-playing a poem,

speech, famous quotation or song lyrics and asking
learners to respond as if they lived in the historically
appropriate time and place

- Use effective speaking skills, such as appropriate vocabulary, style of expression, presentation format, quantity and
quality of ideas, with a minimum of distractions. According
to Patrick Miller in *Nonverbal Communication* (1988), clothes,
facial expressions, body postures and movements are cues
to a speaker's emotions, self-esteem, definition of beauty and
micro-cultural identification. Eyes, voice and touch are channels of communication that also provide information, regu-
late interaction and express emotion. Use of "public space"
(distance of 12–25 feet) is for one-way communication, as in
assemblies; "social space" (4–12 feet) is for interaction among
instructors and large groups of learners; "personal space"
(2–4 feet) is for conversation among instructors with small
groups or individual learners; "close space" is reserved for
sharing confidences, protecting someone or aiding in a crisis
(p. 10).
- Evaluate human-based learning by examining such questions
as the following:
  1. Who was the person? What were his/her credentials?
  2. Why was the person making a presentation? What was
     his/her main idea?
  3. How did the person present the idea? Was the presen-
     tation successful for you? What else might he/she have
     done?
  4. What did you learn? What can you do with this knowl-
     edge?
  5. Could you make a similar presentation? What would
     you have to say? What would you need? Who would
     be your audience?

## Object Resources

A variety of objects from the sublime to the ridiculous can be
studied as subjects in themselves (i.e., sculpture, architecture and
other works of three-dimensional fine art) or as metaphors for

something else (i.e., "How is this sponge like your baby sister?"). A perspective on abstract thinking is that indeed all metaphors are rooted in physical sensation, such as the tactile experiences with concrete, object-based resources discussed here.

In addition to the usual math manipulatives or laboratory science apparatus brought into the classroom, many other objects from bicycle handlebars to freezer bags may serve as metaphors or to attract learners' attention, enhance memory and elucidate verbalized concepts. Common household, school and office supplies may also be recycled as raw materials for inventive object-based project constructions in any discipline, enabling learners of all ages to express themselves creatively and look at familiar things in new ways.

A study of objects from diverse micro-cultures offers insights as well as practical information about the ways people are alike and different, such as the following:

- What people value
- What people do for fun
- What daily life is like
- What the natural environment is like
- What materials are common or rare
- What level of technological sophistication has been achieved
- What the social structure is like
- What kinds of work people do
- What homes, clothes, food and tools are like
- What people use to communicate
- What people use for transportation
- What kinds of industry, government and religion people have
- What people make at home and what they buy
- What children play with
- What artistic style is favored
- What people use to celebrate

## Types of Object Resources

### Antique—Curtain

- Antique, collectible, memorabilia, souvenir
- Arts and crafts supplies, brush, crayon
- Audio and video cassette box, film can
- Automotive and cycle parts, handle bar, pedal

- Balloon, kite, paper or model airplane
- Bead, marble, gum ball, checker, poker chip
- Bottle cap, lid, six-pack holder, can tab
- Box, basket, bottle, can, barrel, bucket, milk carton, tube
- Button, emblem,  badge, decal, patch
- Candy, cereal, pasta, seed, nut, vegetable, fruit
- Cane, crutch, walker, wheelchair
- Card game, board game, playground game
- Cellophane, clear acetate, aluminum foil
- Clock, watch, sundial, compass
- Clothes, shoe, hat, glove, jewelry
- Coin, bill, token, play money
- Computer disk and envelope, mouse, joystick
- Construction tools, hardware
- Costume, prop, makeup, mask, scenery
- Curtain, window shade, blind, screen

*Envelope—Model*

- Envelope, folder, tablet, card, stamp, post-it note, marker top
- Eyeglasses, goggles,  binoculars, telescope
- Fabric, rug, wall hanging
- Flag, banner, pennant, insignia
- Game piece, domino, dice, spinner, poker chip
- Horn, bell, chimes, whistle
- Household furniture, broom, clothespin, hanger, kitchen utensils
- Hygiene and beauty supplies, toothbrush, comb
- Lawn and garden furniture and supplies
- Light fixture, candle, flashlight, lamp shade
- Linens, towel, blanket, pillow, tablecloth
- Lock, latch, key
- Luggage, backpack, briefcase, purse, wallet
- Lumber and other building materials
- Math manipulative, calculator, abacus, ruler
- Measuring, weighing and mapping tools, globe, scales
- Medical and dental supplies, Band-Aid, toothbrush
- Mobile, sun catcher, ceramic figure
- Model, miniature, model piece

*Packing—Sponge*

- Packing bits, molded packing piece, bubble-wrap
- Paper sack, plastic shopping bag, freezer bag
- Paper, plastic and styrofoam plate, cup, tableware
- Party supplies and decorations
- Pet and wild animal supplies, feather, fur, claw, tooth, bone
- Photographic equipment and supplies, tripod, flashbulb
- Physical fitness and sports equipment
- Picture frame, photo album, scrapbook
- Plant, tree limb, leaf, fresh or dried flower
- Plumbing and electrical supplies
- Puppet, marionette, ventriloquist's dummy
- Ribbon, wrapping paper, bow, gift bag
- Rock, minerals, soil, sand, fossil, shell
- Rope, string, chain, tape, wire, cable, shoelace
- Rubber band, paper clip, rubber stamp and pad
- Safety equipment and clothing
- Sandpaper, contact paper, tracing paper
- Science equipment and supplies
- Sewing and needlework supplies
- Sponge, paper towel, scrubber

*Tent—Wheel*

- Tent, tarpaulin, awning, net
- Thermometer, rain gauge, weather vane, fan, umbrella, snow shovel, barometer, wind sock
- Three-dimensional fine art, sculpture, architecture, assemblage, mixed media, folk art, stitchery, ceramics, glassware, jewelry, furniture as art
- Toothpick, popsicle stick, tongue depressor, dowel, straw, pipe cleaner, twist tie
- Toy, dollhouse, building block, plastic figure
- Trophy, plaque, award ribbon
- Uniform, tools and accessories
- Wallpaper and carpet samples, floor or ceramic tile
- Water, beverage, semisolid or frozen liquid
- Wheel, gear, pulley, weight

**Types of Object-Based Learning**

- Recognizing an object as a thing to be studied in itself or as a metaphor
- Identifying an object as animate or inanimate, natural or human-made, manipulative or stable and multisensory or appealing to only one of the senses
- Analyzing an object as physically similar to or different from other objects
- Interpreting an object as useful or not useful in a field of endeavor
- Appreciating an object as unique or as typical of a kind, as utilitarian or decoration or both, as common or precious, as a thing that is or is not useful, needed, creative or fanciful
- Analyzing an object as primitive or sophisticated; from the past, present or both; and as accurately or inaccurately constructed
- Interpreting an object as nutritionally, economically or symbolically valuable and helpful or harmful to someone or some thing

**Types of Object-Based Activities**

- Compare and contrast physical characteristics and uses for types of objects or different examples of the same type (i.e., clocks, toys).
- Record and attempt to define an unusual object by the spontaneous responses of learners upon first seeing it.
- Take notes as a list of attributes, a drawing, a list of adjectives describing the object, etc.
- Vary assignments according to the type of object-based learning desired.
- Introduce unusual objects with who, what, when, where, why and how questions.
- Offer more than one experience with an object to become proficient or appreciative of its use, operation or existence as a work of art.
- Determine an object's use by one culture or many cultures.
- Name and number specific features or elements of an object.

- If an animate object, describe its growth pattern or life cycle.
- Note an object's decoration, pattern, proportion of parts.
- Describe, sort, order, compare attributes of an object.
- Note mechanics (if any) that make an object work.
- Define or conjecture purpose or function of an object.
- Note difference or similarity of an object to other objects.
- Classify objects according to size, shape, color, texture, weight.
- Describe what an object is made of and how you can tell.
- Describe a type of object in the past, present, future.
- Measure an object and draw to scale.
- Describe the utilitarian or aesthetic appeal of an object.
- Use the same manipulative objects in a variety of learning experiences within the same discipline or across disciplines.
- Recycle common household or office objects when making board games, shoebox dioramas, art projects, inventions, etc.
- Improve visual skills by laying out objects, covering them and asking learners to name what is there or to identify an object after it has been removed or to describe the specific order in which objects have been placed.
- Evaluate object-based learning by examining such questions as the following:

    1. What was the object called? How can it be defined?
    2. Why was it instructive (in itself or as a metaphor)?
    3. In what ways was it studied? Were those ways successful for you? What else might have been done?
    4. What did you learn from this resource? What can you do with this knowledge?
    5. Could you make a similar object? What would you make? What would you need? Could you use it to make something else? What else would you need? What would be its purpose? Who would it be for? Why would it be worth making?

## Print Resources

Second only to human resources, use of print is the most widely used educational resource in American schools. Learners typically use only a narrow scope of print materials in the classroom (i.e., textbooks, handouts) which do not reflect the day-to-day reading experiences they have in real life. Effective instructors create print-rich environments in the classroom that mirror society's full range of authentic literacy functions, needs and uses.

Print materials come in a variety of forms, are widely available or easily reproducible for learners' use and can be easily interrupted for discussion purposes and returned to again and again if needed for personal perusal. Instead of reading a textbook, try one or more of the following: advice columns, beauty tips, calorie charts, directions, editorials, fashion articles, game rules, horoscopes, invitations, job applications, ketchup bottles, lyrics, menus, obituaries, postcards, questionnaires, record covers, schedules, telephone books and want ads.

Print-based learning as described here is about reading to learn rather than learning to read. It often involves the use not only of printed words but also of the printed images that may illustrate those words.

### Types of Print Resources

*Book/booklet*

- Activity book, almanac, atlas
- Brochure
- Catalog
- Diary/journal, dictionary
- Encyclopedia
- Fiction book
- Guidebook
- Handbook
- Manual
- Nonfiction book, nontraditional book (i.e., pop-up)
- Scrapbook
- Workbook
- Yearbook

*Miscellaneous print*

- Banner
- Label
- Puzzle

- Sign
- Ticket
- Words on a T-shirt, balloon, etc.

## *Periodical*

- Calendar
- Magazine
- Journal
- Newspaper

## *Single-sheet*

- Announcement
- Card, certificate
- Document
- Fax/computer printout, flyer, form
- Handout
- Letter, list
- Note, notice
- Pamphlet
- Recipe
- Script
- Worksheet

## Types of Print-Based Learning

- Comparing
- Decoding
- Defining
- Describing
- Explaining
- Expressing
- Information-gathering
- Instructing
- Narrating
- Persuading
- Sequencing
- Storytelling

## Types of Print-Based Activities

- Compare and contrast different types, purposes, formats of print resources.
- Agree on a silent-response signal if desired (hands raised, thumbs up or down) to use for individual learner responses or requests for help during reading.
- Take notes in a journal or on note cards; a list of questions, an outline or visual organizer of ideas may be distributed to facilitate note-taking.
- Give assignments to different groups of learners (i.e., reading for character motivation, reading for setting details).
- Contrast texts and illustrations of the past with today.
- Visit a publishing house or invite a writer to speak.
- Establish criteria for selection of different types of print resources.
- Contrast and compare intended audiences of different types of print.
- Determine what a writer was trying to say and whether the print resource was the best medium to express it.
- Produce a variety of types of original print resources using different technologies, i.e., desktop publishing with clip art, shrinking or enlarging text and images on a photocopy machine.
- Research how technology has changed and continues to change the ways we communicate in print.
- Relate a text to learners' lives, motivations and needs.
- Compare information about the same topic in a variety of print resources.
- See also Chapter 7 for strategies in reading and writing.
- Evaluate print-based learning by examining such questions as the following:
    1. What type of print resource was it? Who created it? What were their credentials? What was their viewpoint?
    2. Why did you read it? What was the main idea?
    3. How was it organized? How was this helpful? What else might have been done?
    4. What did you learn from this resource? What can you do with this knowledge?

5. Could you create a similar print resource? What would you write about? What would you need? Who would be your audience?

### Still Visual Resources

American education has historically favored verbalizers in the classroom and has tended to relegate the use of still pictures to instruction for the very young. However, many learners of all ages are visualizers who learn best if presented with pictures, as compared with verbalizers who respond better to verbal or written information. For verbalizers as well as visualizers, the interpretation, appreciation and creation of diagrams, drawings, photographs and other visuals is increasingly seen as a basic literacy skill required in today's visually oriented society. Two-dimensional still visuals often play an important part in both print- and computer-based learning; discrimination among three-dimensional, still or moving visuals is a vital skill in object- and human-based learning; mental imagery is a part of audio-based learning.

Tom Crockett (1994) in a Polaroid Education Program brochure describes six "Modes of Visual Learning" (expressing, communicating, exploring, recording, motivating and imagining) that serve as a framework for visual information handling skills, such as the following:

- Ability to organize images for display
- Ability to establish visual criteria and a visual language
- Ability to substitute images for words
- Ability to combine images with text
- Ability to integrate images with live presentations
- Ability to alter, manipulate or transform existing images

### Types of Still Visual Resources

*Art print—Cartoon*

- Art print, assemblage
- Billboard, bulletin board
- Cartoon, chart, comic strip, comic book, computer graphic

## *Diagram—Hologram*

- Diagram, drawing
- Graph, graphic
- Hologram

## *Logo—Map*

- Logo
- Map, microform, mural

## *Painting—X-ray*

- Painting, photograph, poster, projection
- Rebus
- Sign, storyboard
- Stereogram, optical illusion, overhead transparency
- Visual aid (i.e., flip chart)
- Visual miscellany (i.e., postage stamp)
- X-ray

## Types of Still Visual-Based Learning

- Categorizing, comparing, labeling
- Defining, describing, documenting, explaining, illustrating, instructing
- Decorating, expressing, displaying
- Promoting, idealizing, symbolizing
- Re-formatting, exploring
- Sequencing, directing

## Types of Still Visual-Based Activities

- Compare and discuss differences among still visual-based resources, such as a photograph, drawing and/or x-ray diagram of the same subject.
- Respond to a visual verbally, by creating a visual, by describing in writing what can be learned from it.
- Take notes by drawing or listing attributes.
- Show a visual using revelation method of one section at a time, adding or subtracting sequentially, chronologically or by relationships of parts to the whole.

- Take photographs or videos of activities and behaviors by this year's students to use as examples for next year's students.
- Use principles of composition (balance, contrast, dominance, harmony or unity, proportion, repetition, rhythm, variety) to analyze the artistic elements (color, line, shape, space, texture, light and dark).
- Create visuals based on a theme, such as an event, an idea, a place, a thing, people, a feeling, a mood or in combinations.
- Look for clues for the meaning behind a representational picture, such as:
    1. What are people, animals or things doing?
    2. What kinds of costumes, clothes and jewelry are worn?
    3. What objects are included?
    4. What does the background look like?
    5. What relationships do things in the picture have with each other?
    6. What artistic style has been used?
    7. What and how have the artistic elements been used?

- Identify, analyze and evaluate the impact of visual biases, such as ageism, caricature, cultural racism, elitism, ethnocentrism, Eurocentrism, handicapism, prejudice, propaganda, religious defamation, scapegoatism, sexism, stereotype and tokenism.
- Evaluate still visual-based learning by examining such questions as the following from an inquiry strategy used in fine art appreciation that offers guidelines for studying visuals of all kinds:
    1. Identifying, inventorying, observing, labeling, listing: "What do you see? Who, what, where is the image? What are the colors, shapes, lines? What is this type of visual called?"
    2. Analyzing, categorizing, comparing: "How is the visual put together? What are the details of visual composition? What is a summary of the content? How are segments of the medium used? What and where are the most or least, largest or smallest, closest or farthest artistic elements?"

3. Interpreting, synthesizing, inferring, predicting: "Why is the visual as it is? What is the main idea? How is use of this medium different from use of another? What is the mood, feeling or intent conveyed? Who made the visual? What is the visualmaker's philosophical, political, social or personal viewpoint?"

4. Evaluating, judging, rating, concluding: "How successful is the visual? Does the content have validity? Was use of the medium effective? What is your response? What else might have been done? What did you learn? What can you do with this knowledge?"

5. Producing, applying, translating, constructing: "Can you make a visual like it or different from it? What will you show? Who will be your audience? What will you need? What are the steps you will follow?"

# Chapter 6

## Learning Strategies 1–6: Interactions for Accessing/Processing Information and Skills

"The teacher's role is to set up a workplace that persuades students to say, 'Aha! I see that, if I work in this place, it's going to satisfy me. I see, in this place, that knowledge is power.' Teachers can't make students learn, but they can certainly set things up so that students want to learn."
—William Glasser,
"The Key to Improving Schools"

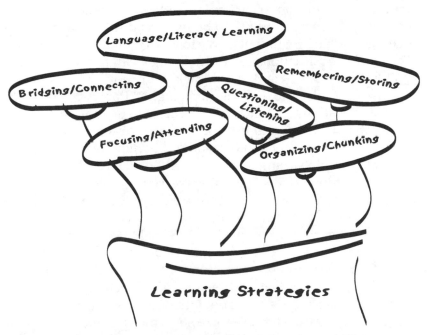

Figure 14: Interactions for Accessing/Processing Information and Skills

Teaching and learning strategies are so numerous and varied that they occupy two chapters—this chapter about interactions for accessing and processing information and skills and Chapter 7 about interactions for producing and evaluating understandings. Two chapters of reasonable lengths rather than one extremely long one is a preferred organization for the reader's ease of use, but teaching and learning is meant to be recognized as an interconnected process in which strategies from both chapters are interdependent.

Accessing and processing information and skills involves acquiring and organizing data, defining problems and generating solutions, developing concepts and the language needed to convey them. Meaningful strategies of all kinds are whatever a creative teacher and student *do together* during a lesson, unit or course of study in order to accomplish these tasks. The main premise is that every strategy employed to achieve outcomes in creative classrooms should be a *positive interaction* among teachers and learners.

Another premise is that students themselves should also be actively engaged in learning how and when to use whatever strategy is employed in addition to curricular content. Students must learn where and when strategies are to be used as different ways of approaching problems. "Students have to learn that different methods work in different situations. If you're fixing a car, the same wrench doesn't fit every part. You have to pick your tools. What students learn most often relates to how they are taught" (Roberts, 1994, p. 7B).

Some educational theorists find it useful to include such things as cooperative learning and uses of media as strategies, but in this book they have been included in other chapters about grouping arrangements and learning resources. Others devise a taxonomy of strategies according to type (i.e., affective, self-monitoring, information-organizing). Still others assign specific strategies and grouping arrangements for models of teaching, divided according to what type of task they attempt to accomplish (i.e., Social Interaction for group skills, Information Processing for knowledge acquisition and processing). Still others define instructional design as either deductive/inductive, explicit/implicit or directive/nondirective.

In this chapter these educational theories have been very helpful in deciding how best to organize strategies for optimum use in the classroom and are best left up to creative teachers to use when they see fit. Many such models or strategic systems (i.e., mastery learning, direct instruction) "have been employed successfully in a wide variety of areas involving academic, physical and mental development" (Joyce, 1996, p. 183). "When these models and strategies are combined, they have even greater potential for improving student learning" (Joyce, 1987, p. 13). Creative teachers will add other strategies that are familiar to them to the lists in this chapter and in Chapter 7.

Creative uses of strategies may be for part of a lesson, an entire lesson, unit or course of study. Strategies may often be combined, but not all strategies lend themselves to all topics or all students. Learners themselves should not only be made aware of the strategy used but also participate in its selection, be guided in its use and practice using it for other topics and in other areas of their lives. During implementation of most strategies, creative teachers interact as facilitator or guide-on-the-side with students, frequently monitoring their progress, checking for understanding, providing immediate feedback or corrections and encouraging transfer to new situations.

Some of the strategies in this chapter and in Chapter 7 are initiated by teachers (but are often added to students' repertoire during strategy instruction), and some are specifically for students. Sections for teachers are noted at the beginning with a *(T)*, sections for students are noted with an *(S)* and sections for both teachers and students are noted with a *(TS)*. Student questions for evaluating strategies are included in Chapter 7, when the remaining types of strategies for producing and evaluating understandings are discussed. However, the following general suggestions for teachers are helpful now before discussing specific types of strategies:

- Include real-world as well as subject-specific tasks; include coursework that has intrinsic interest and develop basic skills as a means to an end for real-life purposes; as often as possible, involve learners themselves as partners in determining what will be learned and how, so that instruction emanates from needs and interests; make use of strategies already successfully in use in learners' micro-cultures or in other subject areas.
- Provide positive reinforcement, encouragement and praise; involve all learners affirmatively, helping each of them to participate; demonstrate empathy, support and acceptance of all involved; treat a variety of competencies with respect, courtesy, sensitivity and dignity; develop individual as well as group processing skills; demonstrate a dynamic, enthusiastic teaching style which varies the rhythm or pacing of

instruction; include affirmations of answers and feedback; reward effort as well as success.

- Include strategy instruction as well as subject-area instruction; have smooth transitions; alternate a longer wait time with a quicker pace when needed; periodically halt to check for understanding; use effective nonverbal communication; create a dynamic tension between challenge and comfort for learners.

- Monitor, modify, refine and reestablish expectations if needed; involve learners in self-monitoring, self-control, goal-setting, self-verbalizing and self-recording techniques; incorporate any applicable special talents learners have; consistently give learners practice in making good choices; provide a sense of order by mutually agreeing upon expectations and reasons for those expectations.

## Bridging/Connecting Strategies

A most meaningful motivation to learn comes from curiosity or a need to know. This requires that teachers involve learners in determining reasons for learning. Transitional bridging and connecting strategies offer opportunities to anchor and build on prior learning, to apply a task to individual interests or to make personal connections. Bridging is also a way to connect or transfer information or skills to the information or skills in other subject areas, offering a method for seeing and understanding patterns everywhere.

Bridging might mean reviewing to stimulate recall of prerequisite knowledge or skills, practicing skills that will be needed for new learning or synthesizing to uncover what students think something would be like if it were reorganized differently. Bridging has also been described as a problem-finding strategy or simply asking the question, "Why are we doing this?" In interconnected education, bridging is vitally important because it can provide learners with a big picture in which to place their learning. It can be seen as stretching a subject out to see all its parts and how or where they relate within a context to other subjects. Some learning styles, intelligences and micro-cultural ways of knowing are deeply rooted in this need to see the big picture.

Practicing depends on the amount of time allotted to a task. Billie Jo Smith (1990) explains that intense or massed practicing requires many periods to be scheduled close together, whereas retention over time requires distributed practice or periods scheduled farther and farther apart. She adds that practice often involves imitation of a skill modeled by an expert and may also lead to transfer of that skills to another situation, being careful that errors do not occur when context-specific skills are applied elsewhere. Linda Hazard Hughes (1991) adds, "In bread baking you can't separate the skills, one by one, to practice them; it's the whole process that counts. So, too, with learning. The steps are all there, to be sure, and each learner needs to experience them over and over again" (p. 33).

## Types of Bridging/Connecting Strategies

*(TS) Bridging from:* teachers and students make connections by considering the following questions to determine the kinds of bridges to make from something else:

- Entry-level skills: What skills does the learner already have that would help in learning this new topic? How and why did the learner develop skills about another topic? How can those reasons and processes be useful for this new topic? For a future topic?
- K-W-L-W: "Know or think I know" to "Want to know" to "Learned" to "Want to know next" chart: What does the learner already know (or thinks she or he knows) about this topic? Is the knowledge a result of scholarship, personal thoughts, experiences or assumptions? What does the learner want to know about the topic? What is the new study material expected to tell? What did the learner find out? How does the information match what was already known? Which questions were answered? Which were not? Where does the learner go next? What are additional questions? How might the learner get answers?
- Learning styles: How can the learner apply the most comfortable learning style to the learning of this new topic? How and why is this approach the most useful for the learner? What can the learner gain by approaching this topic from a different learning style?

- Prior knowledge: What information or skills does the learner already have that relates to this new topic? What is known and unknown? How and why did the learner learn the previous information? How can those reasons and processes be useful for this new topic? For a future topic? Is there a need to reorganize the previous information to aid in the learning of this new topic? If so, why and how?
- Programs to patterns to goals: What useful program or chain of steps is needed to accomplish a goal related to this topic? How is it built? What pattern is involved in the program? Is it linear (repetitious, predictable) or chaotic (random, irregular)? How can it be extracted? How can this pattern be applied to another goal, either logically or intuitively?
- Simple to complex: What are simple examples of the topic? Complex examples? In what ways are the simple and complex examples alike and different? Which are useful in the short term? In the long term?
- Tools, patterns or methods for one topic to another topic: How alike/different are the tools, etc., for understanding two different topics? How might the tools, etc., used for one apply to another? What would stay the same, and what would have to be changed? Does it benefit or hinder the understanding of the topic? Is there yet a third way to understand both topics? Can the learner describe or make this third way?

*(TS) Bridging to/from:* teachers and students make connections by considering the following questions to determine the kinds of bridges to make either to something else or from something else:

- Cognitive/affective: How do feelings and attitudes influence and/or reflect the learner's thinking about the topic? How does thinking influence and/or reflect the learner's feelings and attitudes about the topic? How can the learner internalize and value what is thought and felt about the topic?
- Concrete/abstract: In what ways are aspects of this topic concrete or abstract? What are concrete examples of an abstract topic? What is an abstraction applied to a concrete topic? When and why do concrete examples help comprehension of an abstract topic? When and why does an abstraction help understanding of a concrete topic?

- Conditions for use: When and under what circumstances is understanding of this topic most useful for the learner? Least useful? When and under what circumstances might understanding of this topic be most/least useful for others who are different from the learner?
- Context within a discipline: When and where does this topic fit into larger topics within a subject area? How does this topic influence or reflect the content of the larger topics?
- Contexts within other disciplines: How does this topic relate to topics in other subject areas? How is it interdisciplinary? Cross-disciplinary? How might this topic be integrated with topics in other subject areas? How and why is awareness of connections, similarities, differences and analogies among topics within disciplines useful to the learner?
- Imagery: How is this topic like something else? What is an analogy, metaphor or simile for this topic? What would a visual image or symbol of this topic look like?
- Interconnected learning: How and when does a topic fit into the learner's need for balance among intellectual, physical, social/emotional and intuitive aspects of life? How and why does this topic make the learner stronger in one or more aspects?
- Micro-cultures: What is alike/different about how people in various micro-cultures interpret this topic? How might learning about this topic be useful to others who are different from the learner? How might it not be useful? How might one micro-culture's interpretation of a topic conflict with that from another micro-culture?
- Natural/human-built: How can the learner ascertain the difference between natural and human-built things? What are their properties? What is alike/different? How are they useful/desirable? What is a combination of both? Could the learner devise one?
- Other topics: What topics come before and after this topic? Why does this topic occur before or after other topics? How and why might this topic be sequenced differently in relation to other topics?
- Outside world: How is this topic relevant to real-life experiences of the learner beyond the classroom? How is this topic

useful to society/the environment? What impact does it have on society/environment? How and why does society/the environment have an impact on this topic?

- Parts/whole: What are the topic's parts (details, specifics, sections, portions, fragments, attributes, elements, properties)? How would you describe its wholeness? What does it take to bring all the parts together as a whole? To break a whole down into its parts? Why is this parts-to-whole relationship desirable or undesirable? When? For whom?
- Past/present/future: What were the understandings about this topic in the past? How did they influence or reflect a world that was different from today? What are the understandings about this topic today? How do they contribute to the world as we know it? What may be the understandings about this topic in the future? How might they change the world?
- Scientific observation/fantasy: What if one (real/unreal) were like the other (unreal/real)? What would it look like? What are the possibilities of this happening? Why?
- Self: What does the learner need to learn about this topic? What can the learner do with knowledge about this topic? How is learning about this topic helpful to the learner now? How may it be helpful or meet the learner's needs in the future? In daily life? At home? In the workplace? To beliefs? To fears? To pleasures? To play activities?
- Theory/practice: What is the wisdom or fallacy found in a theory or idea? How does it fit the learner's knowledge of real practice, way of thinking or value system? What is an opposing theory or idea? What are ways to put into practice a theory or idea? What happens when one does?

(S) *Practicing/applying* (Smith, 1990): teacher provides the following three-step approach to practicing that allows student to proceed from guidance to scaffolding to independence:

- Guided practice: usually for small tasks when the objective is for learners to do something in about the same way as the teacher. Short periods of instruction or modeling, followed by practicing small amounts of the task (broken down into its parts), followed by quick feedback and corrections, are more motivating than are longer sequences of instruction.

- Scaffolding: a form of support that is specific enough to the task but general enough to encourage students to transfer it to another context. Smith lists prompts, questions or modeling of a task in a different way to help the learner apply and transfer understandings to new situations.
- Independent practice: may require students to transfer learning to other tasks. Homework, outside projects, assignments and tests are Smith's examples of independent practice.

*(S) Synthesizing:* student reorganizes, combines or arranges parts or pieces into a whole to establish a pattern or product not clearly present before, as in the following:

- Controlled association: describe objects or thoughts as they come to mind, but restrict to a given context or subject area.
- Free association: describe objects or thoughts as they come to mind with no restrictions.
- Linked association: describe objects or thoughts as they come to mind, and each association becomes the stimulus word for the next association in a train of associations.
- Prompting new possibilities (Fredericks, 1991, p. 51): create new combinations of ideas, alter the way things happen, change the course of history or nature, apply a characteristic to every member of a group or magnify events or details.

### Focusing/Attending Strategies

Focusing strategies are defined as attention-getting, motivating, goal-setting, climate-setting, warming up, generating curiosity or probing in ways that are real and challenging to learners. Establishing rapport with learners and a positive climate are two important things teachers do to encourage high levels of cooperation and self-directed involvement in the classroom.

Focusing/attending strategies are the ways teachers initially capture students' interest and continue to maintain interest in the task at hand. The strategies take into account the whole learner and accommodate the affective and social needs of young people as well as their cognitive development.

For teachers to acclimate the classroom for successful learning requires that they know as much as possible about themselves as well as about their students. Then they must know how to use strategies and behaviors that respond to learning styles, intelligences and micro-cultural identities. Expectations for an orderly, safe and accepting environment must be defined. Teachers also must observe, interview or survey students to assess their present level of motivation about a task, because research shows that what motivates one learner may be a weak strategy to another and no motivation at all to others. An inappropriate focusing strategy can actually de-motivate learners.

Teacher commitment and enthusiasm are required to convince learners that an experience is relevant to their own lives and that they will benefit from attending to instruction. A clearly understood framework for learning is presented, i.e., purpose, overview and general idea of the lesson; bridge to prior lesson and subsequent lesson; ways to search for meaning; ways to record, remember and share information. Focusing/attending strategies are used at the beginning and all the way through a lesson, unit or course of study whenever they are necessary to refocus after an interruption. They may introduce a lesson or an idea within a lesson.

Specific focused behaviors are established that are age-appropriate, clearly explained and consistently expected. Positive behaviors are reinforced and unfocused behaviors are redirected when necessary. Consequences for unfocused behaviors should be clearly-explained beforehand and then carried out in a uniform, fair, consistent and non-debatable manner. Characteristics of successful interventions for inappropriate learning behaviors are that they fit the situation, create anxiety for the student, are boring, isolate the behavior as well as the learner and do not give unwarranted attention to either.

### Types of Focusing/Attending Strategies

*(T) Acclimating*

- Take a poll of students' attitudes or ideas about a topic; interview someone about what they know about the content.
- Reformat known facts about the content as a graphic organizer; present key points at the beginning, middle and end of a lesson.
- Pose a content-related problem and brainstorm solutions.
- Predict the content of textual material based on its title.
- Announce a skill for the day (i.e., seeing details).

- Note key people, places, things, ideas and events to watch or listen for.
- Conduct a think-along or brainstorming of questions and ideas; probe for learners' intuition, insights or new ideas.
- List new vocabulary words; introduce subject-specific terminology; list key words for learners to categorize afterward.
- Pose open-ended questions about the content; cite examples of relevance of the content to everyday life.
- Summarize present opinions of experts about a topic.
- Deliberately make a mistake, exaggerate a concept, perform a task incorrectly or create a chaotic situation; then straighten things out with help from students.
- Recite a riddle, idiom, slang expression, humorous verse or song; change the usual tone, volume or pace of your voice; use power words (i.e., "I wonder if," "Here's how to," "The best way to").
- Challenge an old way of thinking by describing a discrepant event; begin with a startling or dissonant statement.
- Relate a personal example, human-interest anecdote or bit of trivia.
- Create/describe some scenery/props that set the stage for a place/era to be studied.
- Present a topic as a novelty, puzzle, mystery or game; be provocative, theatrical, humorous or challenging.
- Pretend to talk into a walkie-talkie or telephone; set an egg timer and when it goes off, ask questions.
- Participate in breathing, stretching, rhythm or other relaxation exercises; guided imagery; vigorous physical activity; play-acting or role-playing.

*(T) Attention-getting*

- Ask for volunteers to repeat directions.
- Blow a whistle, kazoo or party noisemaker; bracket: push your hands to each side as indication that now is time to stop one thing and start another.
- Call for specific body movements (i.e., left arm up); clap a patterned rhythm that learners repeat; count backwards like a rocket blasting off, seconds left in a football game or dropping temperature.
- Flicker lights off and on.

- Hold up a curious, strange or unfamiliar object that everyone can see.
- Identify a specific thing for all learners to look at; instruct learners to sit on their hands for the count of ten; involve students in physical movement such as "do as I do."
- Keep your own hand raised until all students' hands are raised.
- Make team name tags to foster group pride; move around the room quickly and then freeze.
- Pantomime "Put your finger on your nose... ear... chin... etc."; pantomime "Putting on our manners" like clothes; play a rhythm instrument or specific piece of music; practice a listening-skill game.
- Repeat "Hello" until all students respond "Hello."
- Say a prearranged signal such as "Eyes on me" or "10-9-8"; shine a flashlight on whatever you want learners to pay attention to, show a prearranged visual cue such as a stop sign or a big plastic eye.
- Use thumbs up/down to indicate acceptable/unacceptable noise levels; use transitional phrases to announce a different task (i.e., "It's time to think," "Who's got an idea?").
- Vary the usual pattern of your voice (i.e., slower, softer).
- Write/draw on the chalkboard or overhead stage while giving directions.

## (T) *Multisensory*

- To appeal to auditory learners: ask students to repeat what you have said; describe how to do a task; use lists or outlines to represent information; depict a problem situation using colorful language; describe an intriguing object; use recordings, chants, dramatic music, sounds; speak as if you were someone else; relax with mental imagery, soothing music, environmental sounds; use aural-based words (i.e., "well said," "low key," "tune in").
- To appeal to tactual/kinesthetic learners: ask learners to demonstrate what you have said; have learners perform a task; use manipulatives to represent information; depict a problem situation using learners as participants; pass around an intriguing object to be touched; use actions, dramatic

movements, games, making and doing; have learners act like someone else; relax with aerobic exercises; use tactual-based words (i.e., "touchy," "handle," "relaxed").

- To appeal to visual learners: write or draw as you speak; show how to do a task rather than talk about it; use a visual organizer to represent information; depict a problem situation using pictures; display an intriguing object; use color, imagery, dramatic lighting; dress up as someone else; relax with a mental imagery exercise that encourages visualization; use visual-based words (i.e., "look," "watch," "viewpoint").

## (S) Reinforcing/intervening

- Activity: spend time with a favorite adult for special task or project.
- Brainstorming: list unfocused behaviors and examples of when, how and why they are disruptive; select one at a time to work on; write clear definitions with reinforcements, interventions and follow-through.
- Contract: write a plan telling how behavior will be corrected.
- Expert help: behavior is observed by another adult invited to the classroom; strategies being used are evaluated and behaviors are discussed.
- Interview: discuss a definition of an unfocused behavior with a teacher, explain why it exists, what to do about it and ideas for improvement; intrinsic reward: value a sense of achievement, personal success, increased self-respect, progress, a good day.
- Lengthening: attend for a specific time period, increasing the length of time gradually over several class sessions.
- One at a time: concentrate on one focusing behavior at a time (i.e., listening).
- Peer mentoring: as a focused learner, help an unfocused learner or define how a classmate's behavior disrupts learning; pledge: an adult promise to do something fun/outrageous if a goal is met; prize: concrete object given after an accomplishment.
- Questioning: repeat the assignment, the expected behavior and definition of the expectation.
- Recognition: receive private/public praise, certificate, positive note or telephone call home, Student of the Week award,

leadership job; refocusing: teacher restates instruction or changes pace of instruction; removal: remove yourself from a distraction or vice versa; restatement: teacher says aloud the learner's name, the unfocused behavior and the expected behavior, rejecting behavior rather than learner.

- Shadowing: behavior is observed by caregiver all day in the classroom.
- Time out: run an errand, do homework or help with a classroom task, after which focusing is expected; time wasted on unfocused behaviors is subtracted from time for other activities; token: item or activity using tickets, funny money or points.

### Language/Literacy Learning Strategies

Creative teachers and learners interact using meaningful language and literacy learning strategies in the reading process for decoding, comprehension and vocabulary development. Using narrative and expository texts, students are involved in constructing, communicating and transforming knowledge. Whether involved in a teacher-directed or self-regulated process, they are thinking about and understanding what is read and learning how to apply the strategies to new texts.

Encouragement to improve quality and quantity of reading appears as classroom, school-wide, district-wide or nation-wide strategies, such as the following:

- Appreciation day: celebration that emphasizes poetry, speeches and chapters chosen and read aloud in a large group
- Book club: small group that reads and responds to the same titles or genre
- Book fair/book swap: books brought from home to be traded with others
- Computerized incentive: points given for test-taking about books that are organized in a software program by reading levels
- Free reading time: silent reading session scheduled in a classroom or school
- Readathon: contest to see how much students can read in a specified amount of time

- Reading calendar: check marks for individual reading made on each day of a calendar, with monthly and yearly prizes
- Story hour: adult or student reading aloud for the enjoyment of others

## Types of Language/Literacy Learning Strategies

*(TS) Comprehension* (Watts Pailliotet, 2000): teacher and learners collaborate on the following:

- Advance organizer; anticipation guide
- Brainstorming
- Character analysis; cloze activity
- Discussion web; DRTA
- Inference
- K-W-L-W chart
- Macrocloze (i.e., deleting parts of a story); miscue analysis
- Pattern guide; previewing
- Question-and-answer
- Read-tell-retell; repeated reading; Re Quest
- Scrambled story; skimming; story impression (i.e., clue words); story mapping (i.e., intersected list, paragraph fill-in, story boarding, flowchart, model of action, time line); story summary; student-generated exam; student-generated question; student/teacher conference
- Teacher questioning; text structure (i.e., main idea and supporting ideas)
- What/why/when/how questions; whole language (reading, writing, speaking and listening skills are developed concurrently)

*(S) Reading*: learner participates in various reading strategies as the following:

- Choral reading: in a group of learners, read aloud different parts of the text.
- Cooperative integrated reading and composition (CIRC): in a four-member group, meet for reading, with group scores based on individual scores.
- Decomposition: study a complex text broken down into its parts.

- Dialogue read-aloud: choose a character in a story and read aloud the character's dialogue while a narrator reads aloud the expository sections of the story.
- Directed reading: establish a purpose for reading, read a segment of the text, answer mid-point questions, predict what comes next, continue until the text is finished, confer with teacher or partner.
- Jigsaw reading: with others, alternate reading aloud and asking questions.
- Memorizing: commit a text to memory and share the text with others, i.e., historical oratory, reciting poetry.
- Oral recitation.
- Paired mentoring: as an older student, read to younger ones.
- Paired/repeated-reading: with a partner, take turns reading aloud and helping each other; punctuation reading: read aloud only as far as a punctuation mark, then another reader continues until the next punctuation is reached and so on; paired/dyadic: share responsibility with another learner for reading together and receive the same evaluation.
- Questions-list: use questions to guide reading.
- Read alone: participate in independent silent reading.
- Read aloud/act out: as teacher reads aloud, pantomime action in the text; read aloud/listen: listen as teacher reads aloud; read aloud/read along: read along silently as teacher reads aloud; read aloud/read aloud or dual reading: read aloud simultaneously with teacher; read-aloud marathon: read from a book for five minutes before passing it on to next reader; read around or round robin: take turns reading aloud with others; reading to: read aloud to someone else.
- Reading groups: read to others in a group, tutor and talk to each other about what is read.
- Reading road map: read with strategies and questions provided by teacher.
- Repeated reading: reread material several times, varying the ways it is read aloud or establishing different reasons for reading the same text.
- SSR: simultaneously say what is read.
- Self-management reading: in a group of 4–7 homogeneous readers, elect a chairman, who each day writes reading assignments on chalkboard and calls on each member, and a

secretary, who collects papers and checks them off against members' names in notebook to report to teacher. Each member reads assignment and writes down the following: a sentence summary that answers who, what, when and where; two questions about how or why; a list of difficult words. At a 10–minute meeting, members read their summaries, ask the questions which other members take turns answering, present three of the difficult words which the group looks up, and may conclude by telling parts of the assignment they like best or discussing new, interesting things learned. Teacher moves from group to group to monitor meetings, check papers and follow up with remedial work as needed.

*(S) Study* (Fielding, 1994): learner engages in self-regulated reading:

- Ask yourself questions while reading: Do I understand all directions? What problems am I having? Is there anything further I should be doing?
- Decide on reading materials that are easiest, fastest, most accurate and most interesting.
- Develop a routine for reading (i.e., doing the most difficult assignment first, studying away from television, having a homework schedule).
- Develop a reading plan: choose a subject, jot down what you already know, find and read sources for more detailed facts, organize the information.
- Get help from others when you don't understand something; get the "big picture" by reading a book's table of contents.
- Get an overview of the assignment: What is important about this to me? What am I going to try to do? What do I already know or have? What do I need or want? Who can help me? How can I keep track of my learning and thinking?
- Identify major versus minor problems in an assignment, and choose among various ways to deal with them. Make focusing statements ("I need to concentrate only on this one thing right now"), self-rewarding statements ("I did a really good job with that") and coping statements ("I made a mistake, but I'll get it right next time").
- Keep a record of the time it takes for reading tasks (i.e., looking up words, using an index) and try to improve; keep a reading journal on a calendar.

- Make a list of what you don't know about a subject and study this material rather than wasting time rereading what you know.
- Mentally rehearse how research will proceed, which can be as important as conducting the study itself, often including procedures to follow and how you will ultimately assess the results.
- Use note-taking strategies (Watts Pailliotet, 2000): use SQ3R (survey, question, read, recite, review), SPRCS (survey, preview, read, construct, summarize), Three R's (read, record, recite) and PM2R (preview, map, measure how long it will take, read).
- Outline a text; list only essential words or phrases from a paragraph on a note card; use chapter headings, summaries, vocabulary lists and end-of-chapter material in textbooks to glean what's important; use good types of print material as models for your own writing; use picture clues to understand meanings of unfamiliar words.
- Read the same passage aloud and more than once; restate or summarize a difficult passage in your own words; listen to someone else read a passage; listen to other learners' plans for reports.
- Skim a section for the organization of main ideas; study with other people when you need help; summarize each paragraph to increase comprehension of a long text.

(S)*Vocabulary* (Watts Pailliotet, 2000): learner utilizes one or more vocabulary-building strategies, such as the following:

- Artistic/dramatic response
- Bio-poem; brainstorming; bulletin board with found words
- Caption; capsule vocabulary exercise; cloze passage; concept circle; concept ladder
- Definition-classification-categorization; delete/replace parts of speech to convey/change mood (i.e., verbs, nouns, adjectives in fairy tales or news stories)
- Exclusion brainstorming
- Free-form outline
- Game (i.e., Jeopardy, Trivial Pursuit); graphic organizer
- Hit list (i.e., words to avoid)
- Interest inventory

- Labeling classroom object; listing relative pairs
- Matching exercise
- Onomatopoeia; open and closed word sort
- Paired word and sentence; parody; peer editing; persuasion (i.e., commercial, propaganda, euphemism); Predict-O-Gram
- Reading log; retelling
- Semantic feature analysis (i.e., class, example, attribute relations); semantic map; show-and-tell word; small-group or paired worksheet; story creation (i.e., using target words, parts of speech); storytelling; student-generated lesson; structured overview; student-made recording for listening
- Text revision; themed instruction (i.e., alphabetical, conceptual); think aloud; treasure hunt (i.e., find the context clue)
- Using dictionary, picture dictionary and thesaurus
- Vocabulary computer software
- Word bank; word exploration; word game (i.e., homophones, synonyms, antonyms, analogies); word-knowledge rating; word map; word preview; word root; word search; writing goal; written imagery exercise

### Organizing/Chunking Strategies

Among many psychological needs is the need for order. Two rules of thumb from learning psychologists and instructional designers enable creative teachers to help students order, organize or chunk information in an integrated learning experience. One rule says that five to nine bits of information are all that human beings can usually absorb at one time before they reach overload. Some of us are able to stretch our capacity to process more information when sub-categories are formed for each of the bits. Each of the subcategories must also have no more than this average of seven additional bits.

Another rule is not to lose sight of the big picture. Bits of information that are understood as carved out of a larger topic are ultimately returned to their context. Some developmental levels, learning styles and micro-cultural identities learn best when pieces are seen to be part of a whole. Organizing backward by beginning with the present day and working back through history can also be a way for learners to better understand historical contexts and appreciate contemporary topics.

Organizing/chunking strategies are general ways to structure an average of seven bits of information for students to remember within a context. Researchers use many terms for these strategies: listing, grouping, labeling, sorting, patterning, ordering, categorizing, shaping, clustering, lumping, associating, coding and attribute listing. Information may be organized in an engaged lecture (i.e., direct instruction or mastery learning) and by use of inquiry or discovery methods (i.e., direct questioning, observing, experiencing and guidance). The strategies used may be deductive or inductive and learner-oriented or discipline-oriented.

### Types of Organizing/Chunking Strategies

*(T) Advance verbal/written organizer:* teacher orally delivers ideational anchors for a topic prior to the learning experience or distributes copies of written examples and clarification of discipline-based concepts which will govern information in the experience. In *Models of Teaching* (Joyce, Weil and Showers, 1996), the authors state, "The organizer is not just a brief, simple statement; it is as idea in itself and, like the learning material, must be explored intellectually. It must also be distinguished from introductory comments, which are useful to the lesson but are not advance organizers... The most effective organizers are those that use concepts, terms and propositions that are already familiar to the learners, as well as appropriate illustrations and analogies" (p. 183–187). The authors go on to describe the following two types of advance organizers:

- Expository: teacher represents an intellectual scaffold on which students will hang the new information (i.e., basic concepts of economics presented prior to study of the economic condition of a city).
- Comparative: teacher discriminates among old and new concepts in order to prevent confusion caused by their similarity (i.e., similarities and differences between division facts and multiplication facts).

*(TS) Chunking:* teacher and learner organize subject areas into topics, subtopics, mini-topics and specific details to be studied, such as the following:

- Comparison/contrast: How are two topics alike/different? Parts of the topic? What are reasons/consequences for these likenesses/differences? How can topics be changed to be more alike/different?

- Concept/issue: What issue is central to the topic's discipline? What is of interest to professionals in the field? What is a challenging concept about the topic? How does it relate to real life?
- Description: What are the parts of a topic? How are they related? What are traits, forms, functions? What are simple and complex examples?
- Micro-cultural perspective: What are similarities/differences in viewpoints about a topic among micro-cultures? In values, attitudes? How might someone different from you look at the topic? How do diverse groups of people usually learn about the topic?
- Needs of learner: How does an individual student learn? What does she or he need to learn? How does her/his learning style drive the teaching of the topic? What teaching strategies suit this learning style?
- Pro and con: What are advantages/disadvantages of a topic? What are cognitive/affective points of view? What is the criteria for evaluating/judging the topic?
- Structure of a discipline: How is an established structure in a discipline arranged? What are logical/law-like interrelationships about the topic? Where does a topic fit into a whole? What is the hierarchy? How can a topic be broken down into simpler parts?

*(TS) Closing organizer:* teacher and learners in a large group participate in a closure activity after study of a topic. Robert Garmston and Bruce Wellman (1992) advise that "closings, like openings, should be as powerful and as magical as you can make them... Closings that are too long lose energy. Be especially conscious of your voice and nonverbal messages. Answer questions and respond to individuals without needing to worry about cleaning up" (p. 32–34). Some types of closings are the following:

- Accomplishment: participate in a brief summary of understandings about a topic.
- Completion: predict or foreshadow what may be experienced next, assuring that closure for one experience leads to new experiences.

- Narration over time: list a sequence of events about a topic over time, with cause and effect or problem-action-results.
- Program of sequential steps: list a procedural order of activities that make a topic work, with patterns of stages/cycles and cause and effect.
- Stories, quotes and poems: review highlights of your study and/or add pertinent thoughts by others that best express your thoughts about the experience.
- Syllabus: write an explanation of purpose for a course of study, with objectives, strategies and ways to demonstrate learning.
- Web-In-Reverse: write or draw an aspect of a topic on post-it notes and stick them on the chalkboard; everyone participates in deciding how all notes should be moved and re-grouped in related clusters to create a web about the topic.
- Worthiness: share personal learning and validate others who made critical contributions to the experience.

*(TS) Graphic organizer:* teachers and learners visually illustrate verbal or written statements, reformatting information or ideas into simple or highly complex visual displays. They may be prepared in advance by the teacher or created during a lesson with students' input (i.e., parts of an object are labeled to provide visual relationships or ideas during a discussion). Kinesthetic organizers are also included here as visual representations of ideas, such as learners who perform physical actions (i.e., walking along a path of papers that have answers to questions written on them, stopping at the correct answer) or objects that move, which reformat verbal or written information into static or moving live-action visual displays. In spatial description, learners draw the relationship an object has to the space around it, draw a map of what a topic might look like or otherwise visualize a topic.

Some graphic organizers begin with a simple visual figure like a circle, with more circles added as the lesson progresses, and color coding, icons and additions or subtractions are used to enhance understanding. Some evolve into wildly complicated clusters, trees, chains, etc., which are indeed the names given to dozens of kinds of graphics. Often exacting uses are assigned to each kind, but such prescriptions are limiting and hard to remember. Many attributes suit several purposes and can be legitimately used for whatever purpose a creative teacher chooses. Mind maps, for instance, can be flowcharts, pyramids, feature charts, herringbones, semantic maps and clustering for analyzing and problem-solving. When broken down into basic kinds, graphic organizers can be seen to incorporate one of the following eight designs (see Figure 15):

• Lines and braces

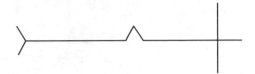

• Charts, matrixes and graphs

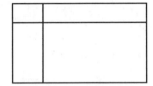

• Clusters, webs and bubbles

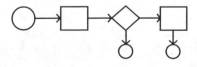

• Flowcharts and chains

• Trees and fishbones

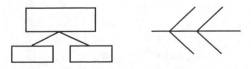

Figure 15: Types of Graphic Organizers

• Wheels, boxes and frames

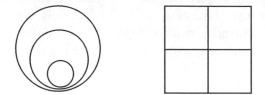

• Pictographs, schematics and figuratives

• Overlapping circles and rectangles

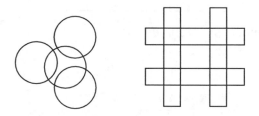

Figure 15: Types of Graphic Organizers (continued)

### Questioning/Listening Strategies

There is a saying that to question well is to teach well. Asking pertinent questions involves everyone directly in the learning process and demonstrates that teachers too are still studying and learning. Good questions stimulate thought, lend themselves to answers that will give a wide span of interesting information, present opportunities for originality, are challenging and require more than just short answers.

One type of corrective feedback, offered by Garmston and Wellman (1992), is called "Feel-Felt-Found." In this strategy, the teacher responds to a learner's answer by saying, "Many students feel the way you do about this, and I have felt that way too, but as I studied the topic more, I found that..." (p. 16).

Garmston and Wellman also explain that creative teachers achieve a balance between group-oriented questions and those directed to individual learners. They also weave questions and answers, piggybacking on answers to construct other answers or new questions. They do not stop after the first question because answers to good questions often provide fertile material for follow-up questions, i.e., eliciting evidence for opinions, asking for other learners' reactions, pushing a discussion to a next higher level or clarifying unclear thinking. Wait time is also given that allows learners to think through their answers before anyone is called on and to stress that thinking itself is what is expected of them.

Listening is the other half of talking and to encourage active listening, strategies must be used in which students listen to increasingly difficult material, to think, to remember and to respond. Effective listening skills are the abilities to concentrate on, organize and interpret what is heard, and teachers facilitate active listening by eliminating distractions, telling learners what to listen for, using supportive body language and visuals, clearly presenting material, restating main ideas or details and demonstrating active listening themselves. Learners should question and listen because they want to and developing, refining and sustaining questioning and active listening skills are crucial to interconnected teaching and learning.

## Types of Questioning/Listening Strategies

### (TS) *Differentiated questioning*

- Evaluation question: ask for agreement/disagreement about a viewpoint, offer opportunities to apply information to one's own life or personal experience.
- Fact question: ask who, what, when, where, why and how, as well as the evidence to support answers; recall.
- Inference question: ask for unstated ideas or integrated information gleaned from several sources; predict; leads to asking more questions.
- Interpretive question: explore meaning; offer possibilities for multiple opinions, all of which might be correct.
- Rhetorical: ask "What if?"
- Journalism: build from simple answers to complex statements.
- Summarizing: organize what has been done or said thus far.
- Synectics: respond to metaphorical questions or generate alternatives, new ideas or solutions to a difficult problem by

"guessing, wishing, taking mental excursions, using distant and loosely coupled analogies, improvising highly speculative and approximate connections, and freely employing any thought from any source that can be imagined—no matter how irrelevant it seems" (Weaver and Prince, 1990); four-box synectics: label each box of a grid with everyday objects and generate four to six ideas to compare a topic with the labels in each box.

*(T) Questioning framework* (Marzano, 1992, p. 71)

- Abstracting ("What pattern underlies this information?")
- Analyzing perspectives ("Why is this information considered good?")
- Classification ("Into what groups could you organize these things?")
- Comparison ("How are these things alike and different?")
- Constructing support ("What argument supports this claim?")
- Deduction ("Based on generalizations, what can you conclude?")
- Error analysis ("What is misleading about this information?")
- Induction ("Based on facts, what can you conclude?")

*(TS) Inquiry process*

- Authenticity: work on real-world problems that are self-motivating; use a puzzling or discrepant event; prepare six questions about a topic and read the first aloud; if other learners can not answer who or what the topic is, the second question is read aloud; proceed through questions until the correct answer is given.
- Metacognition: self-regulate the learning process to understand where you are in the process and to help know how to keep track of information; knowledge-transforming and knowledge-creating as well as knowledge-telling; ask yourself higher-order questions, such as "Why is this a good idea? What would make this better? Which do I like best? What does this remind me of? Does this agree with other information I have? Is this useful? How? Why?"
- Question-formulation: pose explicit questions related to the inquiry and communicate with outside world to find

answers; continually reform questions as new information is gathered; one learner in a pair is assigned questions related to a topic and another learner is assigned the task of finding answers.

*(TS) Thought-provoking curriculum* (Wiggins, 1987, p. 15)

- Reach consensus about which questions represent main points.
- Conduct a discussion based on shifts in perspectives, using strategies, such as clarifying (revisit your own statement or question that seems ambiguous; say things another way); probing (explain your responses and reach further into your thinking) and elaborating (respond in detail about a topic).
- Ask exploratory, in-depth or open-ended questions; generate test questions; question ideas that are incomplete, confusing or controversial; refine questions until they evolve into other questions; write down questions for each lesson, then in small groups decide which questions would be the best to bring to the whole class.
- Influence the direction of the course content with thought-provoking questions.
- When something goes wrong in a lesson, question what and why.

## Remembering/Storing Strategies

Researchers explain that the short-term memory bank is very limited in the amount of material it can store at one time. If knowledge is to be acquired, stored and retrieved, it must be organized efficiently. Long-term memory involves associations with words, visual imagery and sensory experiences that are stored for long periods of time. In working memory, information is temporarily stored until it is stored in the long-term memory or lost (usually in about twelve hours). Recall is that information stored at an unconscious level that is brought into the conscious mind and depends on how well material was stored in the working memory.

According to Susan C. Jones (1995), the following main components are considered in memory-enhancement strategies (p. 2):

- Teach to all the sensory modalities.
- Information is remembered best if it is interesting or useful.

- New information is easier to remember if it can be linked to something already stored in the memory bank.

## Types of Remembering/Storing Strategies

### (S) *Categorizing*

- Attribute listing: list everything about a topic according to the attributes that apply; change some or all of those attributes to enhance memory of the original attributes.
- Comparing: describe fully one or more specific objects or ideas, determine criteria needed to list similarities and differences among them, make lists and create key words for the lists; concept attainment: compare positive and negative examples of a concept to determine the attributes that define the concept and distinguish it from other concepts; concept formation (inductive thinking): gather and record bits of information relevant to a topic, then organize the bits into groups according to their common characteristics and label each group.
- Relationships: put items into categories that are related to one another.

### (S) *Mnemonic/metaphor association*

- ABC summary: generate topic-related words or short phrases that begin with each letter of the alphabet; acronym: use first letters of the bits of information to create a word that can be easily remembered and used to trigger recall of the bits; acrostic: use a series of words, phrases or verses in which the first letters in each line form the alphabet or spell out the word to be remembered.
- Concrete association: find concrete examples of an abstraction to associate with information to be remembered.
- Inside out: find a smaller word inside an unfamiliar word and make up a sentence using both to remember the unfamiliar word.
- Key word: identify one word that stands for an idea.
- Link word: connect a familiar word or phrase to an unfamiliar word; create a visual that uses the familiar word but can be associated with the meaning of the unfamiliar word.

- Metaphor, analogy and simile: make a direct analogy (compares two things or ideas); personal analogy (identifies with things or ideas); compressed conflict (compares a thing or idea from two or more frames of reference); algebraic analogy (creates equal relationships between two things); synectics (makes the strange familiar and the familiar strange); mind trick: use any other word-associative technique to remember (i.e., transforming a bit of information into another word that is easier to remember).
- Pegword: associate ordered information with numbers; find words that rhyme with numbers; personification: assign proper names, faces, even personalities for items to be remembered; phonetic link: identify a familiar word that is acoustically similar to a new word and create a picture of the familiar word to associate with the unfamiliar word; phrase: use words that start with the same letter as the bits of information and combine into a phrase.
- Rebus: draw a picture of the word; related-word: think of another word related to the one to be remembered; rhyme: use a familiar nursery rhyme to accompany the information.
- Substitute word: replace an abstraction with something that sounds like the abstraction and can be pictured in the mind; symbols: break an activity down into parts and assign symbols to the parts; use the symbols when writing or conversing about the activity.
- Word game: make up a crossword or word search using new words.

## (S) *Sensory association*

- Colors: color-code bits of information.
- Experiential activity: observe, directly experience and identify physical properties of an object or person.
- Feels like, smells like, tastes like: use different paper textures to record information; eat and/or smell different foods to associate with information.
- Mental imagery: visualize where bits of information are in a text; create a visual in the mind's eye to accompany information.

- Pictures: use a picture to bridge the gap between the concrete and the symbolic; place association: position signs around the room that have words or pictures of ideas.
- Rhythmic chanting: beat out a rhythm or a tune to accompany information.
- Song: use a familiar tune to accompany information; superlearning: breathe in rhythm with information that is delivered using an eight-second cycle for pacing out spoken data at slow intervals, using three different intonations (normal, soft and loud) and playing slow Baroque concertos as background music.
- Tactile association: tie a string around one finger, put a Band-Aid on another, a rubber band around another, a twist tie around another and associate bits of information with each.
- Visual imagery: use a simple picture or drawing that looks like the subject; may be literal, humorous, ridiculous, impossible or illogical; may be a picture that substitutes for a word, is out of proportion, is an exaggeration or implies action.

## (S) *Sequencing*

- Episodic connections: arrange information or steps to be remembered in chronological order on a time line, flowchart or series of flash cards.
- Location: arrange information to be remembered on a map or visual organizer.
- Mental walk: draw pictures of items on a list and place them in sequence along a familiar path or clockwise in a familiar room.
- Numbering off: present bits of information with other learners, using different tones of voice or standing in various parts of the room; associate bits with the learners who presented them and how they presented them.
- Quantity or quality: arrange information according to amount, size or degree of importance.
- Turnaround: with your back turned, give step-by-step directions to someone else for drawing a picture about a topic.
- Visual sequencing: use sequenced illustrations of familiar actions that represent known information but relabel the illustrations with new information.

# Chapter 7

## Learning Strategies 7–12: Interactions for Producing/Evaluating Understandings

Figure 16: Interactions for Producing/Evaluating Understandings

Creative teachers recognize that strategies for producing and evaluating information are connected with strategies for accessing and processing that information. Separation of strategies in this book into two chapters is solely an organizational device for the reader's ease of use. The introduction to Chapter 6 serves as preface for this chapter as well and, as in that chapter, *(T)* notes strategies for teachers, *(S)* notes strategies for students and *(TS)* notes strategies for both teachers and students.

Adding new strategies to a repertoire can require a good deal of time, creativity and thoughtfulness. However, habitually relying on a few ways of doing things denies students opportunities for learning in different styles and for practicing new skills themselves. Just as artists or car mechanics know that different tools are best for certain situations because they have used them, so do teachers become skillful by using a variety of strategies that meet their specific instructional needs. When the strategies don't seem to be working anymore, the creative teacher searches out new ones or thinks of alternative ways to achieve an outcome.

One approach to devising a repertoire of strategies is learner-oriented, in which are considered learners' intelligences, learning styles, world views and micro-cultural identities as well as what they can do, what they already know and what they need to do and know next. Another approach to strategy-building is discipline-oriented, in which are considered the uniqueness of a specific content area and/or whether a comparison exists with any other content area that might be useful. Drew Gitomer (1994) explains, "Disciplines pose different questions, engage different processes, have different rules of evidence and varying forms of communication...We must go beyond the surface activities and toward the cognitive goals of developing the knowledge, skills and understandings that permit students to reason and communicate within and across disciplines" (p. 35).

Students and teachers benefit from evaluation during and after use of the strategies mentioned in this chapter and in Chapter 6. This is an important part of strategy instruction itself. Evaluating includes asking the following kinds of questions:

- What type of strategy was it? What learning activities did it involve? How is it different from other strategies?
- Why did you use it? Why is it important for you and others to learn this way?
- What was your involvement or role? What was the involvement or role of others?
- What skills did you need? How well did you demonstrate these skills?
- How was your understanding of a topic made clear by use of this strategy? Was the presentation successful for you? What else might have been done?

- What did you learn? What can you do with this knowledge or skill? When is that use appropriate?
- What needs improvement? How can you improve and help others to improve?
- Is this a strategy you prefer? Why? Could you use this strategy for another purpose? Could you use this strategy on your own? What would you do? What would you need?

## Discussing/Reflecting Strategies

A discussion may be conducted in public (forum or panel) or in private (conversation or interview). It may be held for enlightenment (a literature study or political debate), problem-solving (a scientific/social inquiry or psychotherapy/encounter group), decision-making (a committee or ad hoc task force) or in combination. Whether it is formal and structured, informal and unstructured or a bit of both, an effective discussion is an interactive, cooperative effort and demonstrates an awareness of interpersonal skills and sense of groupness. A good discussion group relies primarily on oral interaction and has a sufficiently small number of people, with a sense of belonging and mutually accepted norms of behavior, rules and procedures. Its goal is "to achieve some interdependent goal, such as increased understanding, coordination of efforts, or a solution to a shared problem" (Brilhart and Galanes, 1997, p. 5).

Reflection is like a discussion with oneself. As such, it has many of the same traits as group discussions: goal-seeking, searching for understanding, problem-solving and decision-making. It is an inquiry-based mental processing of points of view. Reflecting strategies enable learners to focus on learning, manage their time well, stay on task, understand the need for help, accept criticism, be goal-directed, demonstrate respect for others, take responsibility for personal actions and keep trying.

## Types of Discussing/Reflecting Strategies

*(TS) Classroom discussion:* teacher leads a subject-mastery or issue-oriented conversation requiring learners to practice reasoning, articulating, persuading, disagreeing, negotiating and conceding, using the following strategies:

- Brainstorm what learners know about a topic before instruction begins.
- Encourage metacognition or analysis of the thinking processes involved in learning by thinking "out loud" to demonstrate processes at work, describe what goes on in your head when you think, listing the steps and missteps you took.
- Initiate a dialogue that requires contributions of complete sentences rather than one-word answers.
- Introduce and define new words which will be used.
- Probe to expand on and clarify answers, justify answers, refocus attention on key concepts, prompt further responses or enhance student interaction.
- Prompt for suggestions of synonyms for overused words.
- Prompt volunteers to periodically summarize main points.
- Reveal subtopics in intriguing ways, i.e., as steps in a flowchart, as a "fortunately/unfortunately" chain of events.
- Summarize essential information on an outline, visual organizer or questionnaire for students to take notes and organize main ideas.
- Some creative ideas for initiating learners into stimulating discussions are the following:
    1. Discuss what a common object (sneakers) implies about a culture.
    2. Discuss probability ("likely" versus "unlikely") and estimation ("when", "how much") in such real-life exercises as: "It will snow today," "Rabbits will fly" or "We will have cheese pizza for lunch tomorrow."
    3. Invite members of another class into your classroom and negotiate with them for use of space and degrees of comfort.

*(TS) Problem investigation:* teacher presents a topic as a problem in need of solution, as an open-ended situation for which many possible endings are discussed or as a problem encountered in a text to be analyzed in the following ways:

- Advocacy: Peter M. Senge in *The Fifth Discipline* (1990, p. 42–43) offers helpful suggestions for students in balancing advocacy and inquiry in discussions:
    1. When advocating your view, make reasons explicit, encourage others to analyze your view, encourage others

to provide different views or actively inquire into other views that differ from yours.

2. When inquiring into others' views, clearly state your assumptions about those views, state data on which your assumptions are based or ask questions only if you're genuinely interest in a response.

3. When you arrive at an impasse, ask what data or logic might change others' views or ask if there is any way you might together design an experiment that might provide new information.

4. When you or others are hesitant to express your views or to experiment with alternative ideas, encourage thinking aloud about what might be making it difficult or design ways to overcome these barriers.

- Classroom meeting (Glasser, 1969): "a nonjudgmental discussion about what is important and relevant; social prob-lem-solving meeting is concerned with the students' behav-ior; open-ended meeting is concerned with intellectually important subjects; educational-diagnostic meeting is con-cerned with how well students understand the concepts of the curriculum" (p. 122).
- Group investigation (Joyce and Weil, 1996): "students are or-ganized into democratic problem-solving groups who attack academic problems and are taught democratic procedures and scientific methods of inquiry as they proceed" (p. 38).
- Jurisprudential inquiry (Joyce and Weil, 1996): relying on learners' familiarity with values embedded in the principles of the Constitution and the Declaration of Independence, this inquiry model is a case-study method created especially for social problems involving public policy issues; learners ana-lyze cases, identify public policies and options for dealing with them; learners develop skills of clarifying and resolv-ing issues (value problems, factual problems and definitional problems) and an awareness of the political, social and eco-nomic problems facing society; involves the following phases (p. 38):

1. Orientation to a case, materials and facts
2. Identifying the issues, values, and questions

3. Taking positions in terms of value of consequences
4. Exploring the stance(s) and patterns of argumentation by establishing violation of values, clarifying with analogies and setting priorities
5. Refining and qualifying the positions
6. Testing factual assumptions behind qualified positions by determining relevance and predicted consequences

*(S) Self-regulation:* Marzano et al. (1993) has designed student rubrics for "Habits of Mind" standards from Dimensions of Learning that learners might use to assess their self-regulation, critical thinking and creative thinking. Penny Silvers (1994) has also written the following series of twelve "Reflective Questions That Span the Inquiry Process" (p. 26):

• Intent (why learner does something)

1. What's my intent?
2. What's important about this to me?
3. What am I trying to do?
4. How can I keep track of my learning and thinking?

• Engagement (experience doing something)

1. How is my learning going?
2. What if any adjustments do I need to make?
3. What new strategies am I using?
4. What risks am I taking?

• Artifact (result at the end of the process)

1. What growth and change can I see in myself?
2. What have I learned about myself from this experience?
3. How am I different now than I was before?
4. What do I know now that I didn't know before about writing (and about myself as a writer), about reading (and about myself as a reader) and about learning (and about myself as a learner)?

• "Self-talking": learners strengthen their reflective skills by affirming themselves, as in the following ways:

1. To foster self-esteem, repeat to yourself "I can do this" or "I will do this," picture yourself successfully accomplishing something, tell yourself how well you are

     doing so far or ask for feedback from others about how
     well you're doing.

2. To overcome negativism, repeat to yourself "I want to
   learn this" or mentally list ways that today's work is
   better than yesterday's.
3. To reflect: finish "I Learned" sentence stems (i.e., "I
   learned that I..., I noticed that I..., I discovered that I...,
   I was surprised that I...and I was pleased that I...") or
   finish "I Wonder" sentence stems (i.e., "I wonder if I...,
   I wonder why I..., I wonder whether or not I...and I
   wonder when I...").

*(TS) Socratic dialogue* (Paul, 1990): teacher or student leads a seminar or discussion limited to a text, which may be a written work,
work of art or piece of music that everyone is acquainted with. Learners talk and listen to one another as well as to the leader and support their statements with references to the text. Everyone's input
and thoughts are valued. Informal seating is arranged in a circle or
square, and participants take turns talking without raising their
hands for permission.

    The seminar leader prepares probing questions that elicit
examples, assumptions, implications and connections (not simply
answers) that will expand understandings of broad ideas or concepts in the selected text (not narrow facts) in order that learners
might better understand text by thinking (not by reviewing content). Questions are worded so that learners do not know what the
leader thinks answers should be. Questions do not assume everyone reached the same conclusions. Five open-ended questions are
usually sufficient.

    The leader does not state personal opinions or "right" answers
but draws as many learners as possible into the discussion and periodically summarizes what has and what has not been dealt with
regarding goals, objectives, nature of a problem or issue, relevance
of information, alternative interpretations, key concepts and ideas,
assumptions and alternative points of view. Seminar leaders listen
carefully, do not interrupt when participants are talking to each other,
and do not intervene if a conflict arises among them. Group silence
or wait time is given to allow participants to think about responses.
Types of questions that facilitate Socratic dialogues (Paul, 1990,
p. 147) are the following:

- For clarification: "Could you give an example?"
- For probing assumptions: "What is underlying what you say?"
- For probing reasons and evidence: "How do you know?"
- For viewpoints on perspectives: "What is an alternative?"
- For probing implications and consequences: "Because of that, what might happen?"

### Human-Based Communicating Strategies

Communicating strategies are divided in this book into the broadest of categories—human-based and media-based—but the types of skills involved are often combined and practiced together (i.e., research assignments that require learners to answer orally and in writing). "Understanding is more likely to occur when a student is required to explain, elaborate or defend his or her position to others; the burden of explanation is often the push needed to make him or her evaluate, integrate and elaborate knowledge in new ways" (Brown and Campione, 1986, p. 1059).

The acquisition and demonstration of human-based communicating strategies (i.e., use of oral, body language and movement skills) require creative as well as critical processing on the part of learners. Since communicating strategies lead ultimately to assessment, modeling by teachers and practice are as important for students as are modeling and practicing problem-solving. Using creative human-based communicating strategies, learners find the words to say what they mean and follow logical steps in talking about a topic. They learn to persuade, to negotiate and to explain a difference of opinion without threatening others. They learn to express themselves with eloquence, grace and humor.

### Types of Human-Based Communicating Strategies

*(S) Concluding:* learner conducts fieldwork reporting and/or manipulating of data by sight (i.e., poll, survey, counting "straw votes"), by pencil and paper calculations (i.e., checklists, graphs), by handheld tool (i.e., calculator, yardstick) and by computer (i.e., data-processing software). Strategies may be the following:

- Attribute analogy chains: add analogies to each category in an attribute list.

- Attribute list: categorize physical, psychological or social characteristics.
- Calendar stick: mark each month on a stick and use to remind the class of events over an entire school year (early First Nations People did this to record time, creating symbols for important events).
- Conceptualize: identify examples and non-examples of a topic, classify attributes of the examples and interrelate the classifications to conceptualize a structure of the topic.
- Databases: compile math or science observations, personal information or historical details.
- Forced field analysis: list forces working for and against a change; list factors that could reduce restricting forces and strengthen facilitating forces; determine the most promising action steps to take.
- Forced relationship: connect two or more normally unrelated topics.
- Griot: act as a traditional African record-keeper to interview other learners about major events for a class history.
- Human graph: line up with other students according to specific categories.
- Human time line: line up with other students to represent historic dates that are listed in a time line on the floor.
- Interviewing: ask questions and share experiences with subject experts.
- Post-it graph: place post-it notes with opinions in columns of a graph on large chart paper.
- Posting message: exchange information with other learners in online discussion groups.
- Reorganization: adjust procedures for a topic so that they reflect procedures found elsewhere for another topic.
- System management: measure, test and analyze materials to assess properties and composition.

(S) *Debating:* learner defends a position or convinces others of an opinion, such as the following:

- Debate: as learner or group A, present a two-minute argument about a topic followed by a thirty-second rebuttal by learner or group B; learner or group B argues its case for two minutes, followed by a thirty-second rebuttal from learner or group A; each of you submit thirty-second concluding statements; non-debaters take notes and report on which side was more convincing and why.

- Hot seat: assume the identity of historical figures and answer questions in character.
- Mock trial: assume the roles in a courtroom and conduct a trial about a topic.
- Panel: two or more learners represent different attitudes or viewpoints about a topic; teacher or another learner as moderator introduces them to the audience and gives them equal time to explain their views; questions are asked by audience, moderator or panelists themselves.
- Persuasive speech: recite an historic address; state a personal opinion and present a succinct and well-structured defense (present any data supporting the opinion; stick to a few, specific points; repeat important words or phrases for emphasis; begin or end key sentences in the same way to show how points are related; make smooth transitions).
- Theatrical: present a compelling argument through storytelling that attempts to convince an audience of the rightfulness of an idea, event or decision.
- Web site: present an opinion in a chat room on the Internet and share differing opinions from around the world.

*(S) Explaining:* learner relates information using sensory, comparative and superlative words; with/without use of hands, touching or seeing, such as the following:

- Describe (i.e., a procedure, an image, an object, a problem-solving strategy).
- Elaborate (i.e., on place names, definitions).
- Fantasize (i.e., use metaphors or expressive language, storytelling).
- Give directions (i.e., for a game, a maze, a destination, a scavenger hunt).
- Give details (i.e., about a process, a decision, a map).
- Teach-it-back (i.e., instruct the class in knowledge or skills that have just been imparted by the teacher) .

*(S) Performing:* learner relates or recites a literary, historical or original idea, such as the following:

- Act in a randomly selected role for a simulation within the context of a hypothetical situation.
- Adapt a contemporary or historical event.
- Create a tableau by reconstructing a frozen dramatic scene.
- Create improvised dramatics by performing an ending to a plot before the story is completely read aloud.
- Conduct a parade.
- Dance or play music to tell a story or express an emotion.
- Participate in dramatics, puppetry, a monologue, a dialogue, storytelling, a pantomime, an impersonation, shadowing or mirroring movements of a partner.
- Participate in interactive theater: perform with audience participation.
- Perform extemporaneous reading or speaking.
- Present a humorous/serious interpretation.
- Role-play or model a demonstration.

### Media-Based Communicating Strategies

Over fifty years ago, H. D. Lasswell (1948) offered five variables to consider for analysis of the mass media that ring as true today as they did then: "Who...says what...in which channel...to whom...with what effect?" (p. 37). In our subsequently networked, diverse society, the practice and application of media-based communicating strategies relate directly to achievement of the learning objectives and standards intended to prepare learners for the 21st century.

Human-based communicating strategies are described as those that involve learners' abilities to verbally reach conclusions, debate, explain and perform in face-to-face situations. On the other hand, media-based communicating strategies involve skills in word processing; creating graphics or multimedia (digitally); video- or audiotaping (electronically); and drawing, sculpting or otherwise expressing themselves three-dimensionally or two-dimensionally. Storytelling is an example of how the two types of communication are different (i.e., a teacher or learner may use human-based skills in the oral tradition or theatrically to tell a story and also use media-based skills to write, tape or artistically represent the same story).

## Types of Media-Based Communicating Strategies

*(S) Digital:* learner uses computer technologies to create media such as the following:

- Database construction: tabulate results in such fields as:

    1. Agricultural databases (i.e., states, crops, average temperatures)
    2. Career databases (i.e., interests, capabilities, skills required)
    3. Historical databases (i.e., years, places, events)
    4. Personal databases (i.e., family members, pets, favorite things)

- Desktop publishing: publish information, stories and visual as well as written ideas in a class newspaper, literary journal or magazine that is formatted, saved and printed.
- Graphic creation: create images, diagrams and photographs by designing, transforming, rotating, replicating (using clip art), scanning, saving and printing.
- Multimedia creation: combine still and moving images, sound, written text and interactivity using multimedia or hypertext software.
- Spreadsheets: tabulate numbers (i.e., surveys, grades, experiments).
- Telecommunication: contribute views, thoughts or stories to a chatroom dialogue on the Internet; communicate with an e-mail keypal.
- Word processing: key in information, stories and ideas that are then formatted, saved and printed.

*(S) Electronic:* learner uses audiovisual technologies to create media such as the following:

- Audio tape: simulate a radio program, panel discussion, speech, press conference, debate, music, narration for a slide/tape show, storytelling with dialogue and sound effects, self-guided tour or directions for a process.
- Miscellaneous: create 8mm-film animation; slide show; music synthesizing.
- Photograph: (see Two-dimensional below).
- Video tape: create a commercial, public service announcement, dramatization, infomercial, demonstration, TV

magazine, news, special effects, documentary, story, interview or talk show, quiz show using long shots, medium shots and close-ups to guide the viewer's attention to realistic content, somewhat realistic content or unrealistic content

*(S) Three-dimensional:* learner expressively or scientifically assembles and displays information or ideas in three dimensions, creating visual media such as the following:

- Art: make a collage, mosaic, sculpture, stitchery: use found objects and experimental art processes.
- Book: make special features such as pop-up pages, peek flaps, wheels.
- Environment: transform the classroom into interactive museum, gallery, zoo or store.
- Experiment: follow directions or diagram to put something together.
- Junk: analyze obsolete or common items as unsightly waste, recycled resource or art; implement an ad hocism exhibit that shows objects used in unusual ways.
- Miniature: make a clay figure, puppet, paper doll, shoebox diorama, origami.
- Object: collect micro-cultural or historical items for game, ritual, meal, storytelling, party, parade, play; may be aromatic, flavored, tactile; may have articulated designs (parts are shown) or closed (parts are hidden); may be standardized or individualized.
- Promotional material: convey ideas or decorations on class button, T-shirt, etc.

*(S) Two-dimensional:* learner expressively designs and illustrates information or ideas in two dimensions, creating visual media such as the following:

- Art: draw, paint, make prints.
- Book: make a nonfiction book cover and illustrations, coloring book, picture dictionary, wordless or topsy-turvy book.
- Game: make a jigsaw puzzle, board game, overhead projector or chalkboard game.
- Photograph: make a subject-driven, theme-driven or design-driven essay, collage or sequence of still-film images.
- Picture: draw or diagram an idea; illustrate a story problem; create a cartoon, comic strip, postcard.

- Promotional: create an ad, package, box, magazine, book, record cover, poster.
- Sketch-to-stretch: make a drawing for a quote, passage or entire text; create a visual for a verbal analogy.
- Symbol: make a sign, logo, crest, shield, flag, quilt square, rebus, flowchart.
- Visual organizer: make a calendar, map, sequence of pictures.

### Reading Response/Literature Response Strategies

Just as creative teachers model literate behaviors by sharing with students what they themselves are currently reading, so do they also model their own responses to texts. As they read a text aloud, they ask themselves questions and point out strategies they use for comprehension. When discussing a text, they may give examples of outside evidence that supports the points made, offer conflicting interpretations for the same information or give more recent information and new examples.

Side by side with their students, they also model reading/literature response strategies by writing about the words, phrases or parts of a text they personally relate to or question. They may compare two stories or coverage of the same topic in different resources, study two texts with opposing points of view, discuss how they were presented and whether they were based on information, emotion or belief. They may model the reformatting of a written text visually, aurally or kinesthetically.

**Types of Reading Response/Literature Response Strategies** (Watts Pailliotet, 1999)

*(S) Artistic*

- Adapt a story as dramatic reading, choral reading, dance, music lyrics, play, audio or video script.
- Create an advertising campaign (i.e., slogan, book cover, press release, poster, give-away contest, bumper sticker, promotional materials).
- Readers theater: read aloud from print material and play the roles of characters (primarily oral interpretations) with a narrator reading aloud the action; readers sit or stand in front

of the audience, may enter and exit by stepping forward, standing up or moving to a new position, may express thoughts and feelings as well as deliver dialogue or expository passage, convey emotions and characterizations through voice inflection, intonation, etc.; action or changes in setting are described by narrator(s) speaking directly to the audience; no props, scenery, costumes, lights or special effects are required; no memorization, acting or stage movements are required.

- Re-create a favorite scene as a drawing, painting, sculpture, mural, mobile, collage, diorama, comic strip; illustrate major scenes with captions.

## (S) *Oral*

- Accept or reject an idea based on evidence within a text; state plausible conclusions or inferences; explain reasons for liking or disliking a text.
- Compare a text with universal themes; describe how it reflects historical or social context in which it was written; compare it to your own experiences.
- Interpretive oral reading: read aloud with expression and little reliance on text; use appropriate inflection, intonation, phrasing, etc.; emphasize key words or phrases; create a mental picture of the action and communicate that action with voice and body language; practice until reliance on the text is minimal and eye contact with the audience is increased.
- Making connections: pretend to be a character in a text and explain how you fit into the plot; give examples from personal experience of ways in which a text affects life or lives of others, had an effect in the past or will in the future, is connected with another text, etc.
- Prediction: make predictions about the text before discussion begins; describe a hunch or an intuition about a text.
- Present a one-minute book-talk to large group; summarize with three details, two key points and one main idea; use sensory words to describe a text.

## (S) *Peer exchange*

- Battle of the books: create questions based on books commonly read and conduct a quiz show.

- Book study group: support other learners by reading together, exploring concepts, responding individually in journals, presenting insights to large group, reflecting on and evaluating study.
- Compare theme or character with a nonfiction article or current event.
- Conduct a book conference (Fiderer, 1988, p. 60): after reading a book, write questions on a card; another learner reads the same book and both learners answer questions; other learners read the same book and repeat the process.
- Conduct reading and response as a round-robin in a small group.
- Discuss with others how a difficult text might be changed for the better; discuss what an author does not mention or what a character does not consider and how these elements might change story or character development; discuss a paradox, discrepancy, ambiguity, provocative question, analogy about a text or ways it might be interpreted differently by members of various micro-cultures.
- Envelopes: discuss questions written on fronts of envelopes and work as a group to discover evidence in a text that supports answers to the questions, which are written down and placed inside the envelopes and rotated to other groups for evaluation before a class discussion.
- Group reading: read individual copies of a text silently and write a brief response; read responses by other learners and write a second response; one volunteer then reads the text aloud; group discusses how understandings changed because of reading others' comments.
- Jigsaw poster: draw pictures about a story and present them in sequence to a large group as the text is read aloud.
- Mini-conversation: exchange at least four remarks about a text with a partner.
- Read a text to others, observe responses and report to large group; read with a partner, respond and compare responses; read a novel as response to a culture or period of history being studied; read about a culture or historical period as response to a novel.
- Reciprocal teaching (Palinscar and Brown, 2000): discuss a text by using four strategies:

1. Asking classmates for answers to questions.
2. Summarizing by finding a topic sentence or creating one.
3. Clarifying by using context clues.
4. Predicting upcoming content by noting clues (i.e., structure of a text).

- Revisiting the text: turn to a specific page to discuss or answer questions.
- Title display: construct a bulletin board or other display about books.
- Top ten: poll other students about favorite books and tabulate results.

*(S)Written*

- Annotate a list of web sites that relate to a text; write a letter or e-mail to the author, do further research and write a biography.
- Book diary: write down responses as you read; reread and note your changes of opinions.
- Change genre, setting, point of view, ending, or microculture of a character.
- Compare texts in various media (i.e., TV drama with short story); compare texts that have the same theme.
- Create graphic organizer, board game or quiz-show questions.
- Create an acronym from letters in a book's title or characters' names.
- Write a parody, a letter to an advice column/editorial page, an interview, a dialogue with a character or a letter to a character from another character's point of view.
- Write a book review like a movie review; write a prequel or sequel.
- Reading to write: use a story's key ideas, characters, verbs and/or objects for writing a new story; compare the new story with the original story.

## Researching/Recording Strategies

Conducting research and recording their findings is one way learners are introduced to the world of scholarship. By investigating how someone else has used information and how teachers themselves use information, students discover how they too can use information. They question, listen, look things up and observe by using the five senses (and sense-extenders like microscopes). They research and record by using multiple print and nonprint resources, relating what is known to what is not known. They arrange information logically as a narrative or in chronological, alphabetical or numerical order, either quantitatively or qualitatively. The ideal result is that they not only literally interpret facts and concepts but also understand main ideas and important points, apply the research to their own lives, make meaningful connections and find new avenues to explore.

Sharon Healy (1992) adds that teachers facilitate note-taking for learners by doing the following before research begins (p. 11):

- Create a note-taking tool: distribute an outline, graphic organizer or another visual/kinesthetic aid (i.e., folding paper into quadrants for writing down a detail in each quadrant while watching a film in the dark).
- List key points on the chalkboard or overhead projector; teaching appropriate abbreviations.
- Permit a student with good note-taking skills to use carbonless paper to make an extra copy of notes for another learner who has difficulty taking notes; allow learners to tape instruction for review later.
- When note-taking from a speaker or audiovisual presentation, instruct learners to list facts and opinions, questions to ask, other possible sources; when note-taking from reading, read without writing paper present, then write down facts/opinions without reading material present.

### Types of Researching/Recording Strategies

(S) *General research* (Maxim, 1991): learner applies critical thinking skills and ability for self-regulation to research in the following ways (p. 34–42):

- Determine reliability of a source, accuracy of a statement and strength of an argument; distinguish between relevant/irrelevant information, verifiable facts/value claims, warranted/unwarranted claims; identify stated/unstated assumptions and ambiguous claims or arguments; recognize logical inconsistencies in a line of reasoning or evidence of bias; consider the mood of the times that may have influenced the content.

- Keep a research notebook in which is entered title, questions, resources and recorded notes of specific facts/opinions; or keep a log book in which is recorded observations, measurements, samplings and predictions.

- For a written research report, select facts/opinions worth sharing from notebook and write them as an acrostic poem, book, time line, letter, diary, script, poem, first-person sketch or newspaper account; for a visual research report, select facts/opinions and use them as captions for a shadow box, picture book, poster, mobile, bulletin board, game or photo collage.

- Before turning in a research assignment, go back over the directions and criteria to confirm that your product matches exactly what is expected, then ask such questions as, "Is this assignment finished? What have I learned? What possibilities for further work does this piece suggest? How is the work individual?"

*(S) Historical* (Minnesota State Board of Education, 1996): learner considers questions such as the following (p. 13):

- What are influences of geography and natural occurrences?
- What are dominant philosophies, ideas or beliefs?
- What are key events, interactions or conflicts?
- Who are important people and their contributions? What are major writings and/or publications?
- What are artistic works? What is the architecture? What are the technologies?
- What are social movements?
- What is daily life like and social customs?

*(S) Problem-solving:* learner defines a problem, represents the problem, collects data, forms an hypothesis, tests the hypothesis, forms a conclusion, applies the conclusion and evaluates the conclusion; also decision-making: defines a problem, collects data, identifies obstacles to reaching a goal, identifies alternatives, ranks alternatives, chooses the best alternative and evaluates decision. The Creative Problem-Solving (CPS) Process, based on research of Parnes and Osborn, is described by Joyce Juntune (1983) as the following pattern:

- Mess finding: describe a goal to achieve or a change to make.
- Fact finding: ask "who, what, when, where, why and how?"
- Problem finding: encourage alternative solutions by asking "In What Ways Might We…" ("IWWMW").
- Idea finding: brainstorm alternatives.
- Solution finding: establish criteria standards for the ideal.
- Acceptance finding: implement a plan of action.
- Action taking: make the plan of action work.

Students are encouraged to apply the following kinds of creative problem-solving strategies to their research:

- Make a model; draw a picture; make a chart; reenact an idea.
- Simplify it; find a pattern; work backwards; work from general to specific and back again.
- Apply rules or processes from another discipline.
- Split the work in half to see what it looks like.
- Restate the main idea in a different way; use analogies.

(S) *Scientific* (Minnesota State Board of Education, 1996): learner engages in an inquiry, discovery or project-based exploration that involves probing, collecting and analyzing published sources, experiments, personal observations and/or data collections while physically engaged in hands-on activities with materials, then forming conclusions, expressing what they have discovered and asking new questions (p. 7). The following are suggested steps:

- Identify and formulate a question by conducting a literature review, defining a problem, formulating a hypothesis or guessing, using available facts and designing an experiment.
- Gather data, using appropriate technological tools and methodologies, recording data and performing an experiment.
- Organize data by applying appropriate technology and selecting and applying statistical processes.
- Analyze data and make generalizations by replicating the experiment; identifying and considering alternative interpretations of results; formulating new questions based on investigation; comparing findings to theory, experience and current practice; using evidence to support ideas; developing conclusions from results; verifying, rejecting or changing initial guesses on basis of additional information; and formulating recommendations.

- Communicate results and conclusions by reporting findings in approved format; summarizing results and conclusions; and reporting self-reflections and generalizations.

## Writing/Print Reporting Strategies

All writing and reporting strategies in print form involve learners in stages of prewriting, drafting, revising, editing, finalizing and evaluating. Students may be asked to write about topic headings, topic sentences, provocative sentences, questions, fictional plots or characterizations. To hone skills in spelling, punctuation, grammar, sentence structure and fact-finding, creative teachers often present passages with errors for students to discover and correct.

However, students should also be given opportunities for informal freewriting without regard for mechanics. They should experiment with writing for different purposes (i.e., narration, description, conveying information and expressing a point of view or emotion). They may experiment with writing on unusual things (i.e., wrapping paper, place mats, paper plates) and perhaps write a report, using only objects or visuals for their resources, doing research in print materials afterward. Prewriting activities may include brainstorming, listing, webbing, clustering, mapping, outlining and responding to story starters or prompts.

## Types of Writing/Print Reporting Strategies

(S) *Additive:* learner engages in writing that expands on a text, such as the following:

- Add speech/thought/sound effect balloons or captions to historical photographs, science diagrams or math problems.
- Complete sentence stems (i.e., "I can't understand why…", "Inside this mystery box is a…", "The thing that worries me most is…").
- Complete sentences that have blanks to fill in or expand on bare-bones sentences.
- Create labels for things in a language other than your own
- Expand sentences in a text by adding descriptive words.
- Incorporate figurative language from sports, politics, the medical profession or popular culture in your writing.

- Make up jokes, riddles, puzzles or board games about characters or events in a text.
- Pretend to be a character in a book and write a continuation of events or a new chapter, ending or sequel.
- Revise a K-W-L-W chart to set personal goals in writing, such as "What I Do Well," "What I Want To Do Well," What I Learned To Do Well" and "What I Want to Learn To Do Well."
- Write text or labels for objects in photographs, wordless books or sequences of pictures.
- Write version of a text set in another place, culture or time period, from another intellectual or emotional perspective, using another voice or physical point of view, or as if it were an eyewitness newspaper account.

*(S) Collaborative:* learner engages in the following kinds of writing with peers:

- Card sort: a small group sorts and labels a series of cards with topic-related words or pictures into categories and uses information for writing activities.
- Class anthology: contribute to a volume of prose or poetry, dictionary, textbook, daily diary, alphabet book.
- Class letter: all students in a class offer ideas for an invitation, inquiry, complaint or note of praise to a public figure involved in a topic being studied.
- Community text: cowrite with family or community members about themes (i.e., family, dreams).
- Composite poem: all students in a class add a line to a poem describing a photo or picture.
- Mock conversation: write dialogue for characters in the same story or in different stories as if they had just sat down to dinner together.
- Newspaper publishing: write and illustrate factual accounts, editorials, columns and feature stories related to a topic for a class newspaper, literary journal or magazine; production staff might include copy editors, graphics staff, distribution/promotion staff as well as writers.
- One-sentence summary: share/compare a written sentence about a topic with another learner.
- Paired/dyadic: partners share responsibility for writing together and receive same evaluation; peer tutoring or mentoring.

- Partner-share: partners write, read aloud and discuss ideas with each other.
- Peer editing: read and comment on drafts of another learner's paper, with editing guidelines from a teacher that focus on particular aspects of writing which have been talked about in class; editing groups: one learner responds to first draft, different learner to the second and still another to third.
- Peer response: a small group compliments positive aspects of each other's work and suggests improvements.
- Reflective writing: write thoughts, ideas or feelings and share with a partner.
- Research group: members of a small group each research a different aspect of a topic, then share one written report with the whole class so that all learners are exposed to every aspect.
- Study group: a small group confers and supports each other in reading and exploring concepts; each learner responds individually in journals, presents insights to large group, reflects on and evaluates their own writing.
- Textbook writing: a small group reviews all material studied in a course, selects and organizes what should be included in a written text for the course and provides rationale for selections.
- Time capsule: a small group gathers items that are representative of a text, writes about each item and puts them into a sealed container for another group to open before they read the same text.
- Writing response group: a small group of writers provides feedback on strengths and limitations of one another's work during the revision stage, checking first for satisfactory ideas, then for correctness.

*(S) Genre-related:* learner engages in the following kinds of writing styles:

- Biography/autobiography: write about your life as if you were a character from history or fiction; create a diary you imagine a famous person or fictional character might have written; create an annotated family tree for yourself, a real or fictitious character.
- Book report (Berry, 1984): know what kind of book report is expected and decide beforehand what kind to do (i.e.,

traditional: story information, theme and opinion; alternative: artwork, drama or creative writing that stands alone or
supplements traditional report); note good passages and page
numbers as you read, outline or web the ideas; write a topic
sentence stating the main idea, support with passages, conclude with overview (p. 13–15).

- Critique/opinion essay/speech: decide on an opinion, list
  examples from a text that support that opinion, write a lead
  sentence that states the opinion followed by examples, conclude with your opinion stated another way; keep a collaborative journal in which comments, opinions or conclusions
  are written to share with other students for their support,
  constructive disagreement or suggestions.
- Essay: write a definition, comparison/contrast, facts and figures, persuasive argument, proof of a point, anecdote or summary; see Critique.
- Genre-to-genre: rewrite a prose selection in a new form, such
  as a speech, play, epic poem, dialogue, essay, song, mock interview, reader's theater script, picture book, TV or radio
  script.
- Journal: write down thoughts, doodle or draw to stimulate
  writing, thinking or personal expression.
- Miscellaneous: rewrite a well-known commercial to present
  an opposite meaning; transform an article into an advertise-
  ment; create a whimsical world-records book; write a slogan, riddle, rhyme, chant, jingle, rap or music video about a
  topic; write a how-to manual, field guide or annotated catalog about real or imaginary things; create a movie poster,
  book jacket, comic or storyboard about a story.
- Newspaper article: write facts about a person, place, thing,
  event or idea (i.e., who, what, when, where, why and how);
  editorial: write an opinion; feature: write from a human-
  interest angle; column: write from a specific perspective.
- Poem: write a story poem, ballad, cinquain, bio-poem or
  haiku about a topic.
- Report: pick a topic, list what you know and what you need
  to find out, use research strategies to gather new information, outline or web what you find, write lead sentence as an
  overview, support with information you knew or found out,

conclude with an overview stated in another way. "Eight Steps to Writing a Report" (Berry, 1984) offers the following advice: choose a topic; make an informal outline; research topic, take notes and make bibliography cards; make a formal outline and put notes in order; write the rough draft (i.e., introduction, body, conclusion); review the rough draft (i.e., content, style, spelling, punctuation and grammar); write the final draft and proofread each page; add final touches (i.e., title page, table of contents, bibliography) and put all pages in order (p. 20–37).

- Script: adapt a story or write an original story with a number and type of characters that fit the students who are available to perform; limit scenes with main characters or give them simpler, shorter lines; include a narrator to read prose sections, set the scene and occasionally describe action; use plain English and lines that are short or to the point except when flowery speeches are more fun; use echoes in dialogue as useful repetition for audience as well as actors; script some dialogue in a pattern (i.e., Kim, Robbie, Frank/Kim, Robbie, Frank) to cut down on missed cues.
- Story: rewrite traditional folklore to have a contemporary setting; write original folklore; turn a math problem or science project into a detective story; transform scientific or historic fact into fiction; retell a famous story as closely as possible to the original; write historical fiction; write an animal story in which fictional characterization and accurate natural information are both included.
- Summary: rethink the content in your own words; write main ideas as a smaller version of the entire original text.
- Web site: add your response to a personal, classroom or school web site.

*(S) Responsive:* learner responds to a topic or story in the following ways:

- Art project: create a two-dimensional or three-dimensional project illustrating a written response.
- Character sketch: describe a character; rewrite in your own words.
- Consider two characters from different books and write a story in which they meet.

- Empty head: draw a circle and fill it with thoughts a character in a story might have.
- Graphic organizer: create an outline, web, diagram, map, time line or flowchart about what you are reading.
- Historical letter: pretend to be an historical figure or character in a book and write to another famous person or character.
- Personal letter: write to peers, family members, teachers and friends about what you are reading and studying.
- Journal: write about a specific topic in a daily diary at the beginning of each class; keep a detailed response log, dialogue journal, scrapbook, field notes or word bank throughout an entire learning experience.
- Letter to the editor: write to the local or school newspaper, TV station, TV personality, author or other public figure about your concern, opinion or experiences concerning a current event or topic in the news.
- Open response: write an answer to a prompt about a topic that additionally asks you to explain your thinking about the topic (i.e., "Explain three ways that…", "Tell why you chose to…").
- Personal essay: write about the parts in a text that you remember the most vividly, parts that encouraged you to think in new ways and/or parts that affected you emotionally; turn your essay into a speech.
- Political activism: write a letter to a local, state or national official or politician requesting information, stating an opinion or calling for action concerning an issue in the news.
- Questions: write discussion, test or study questions for a text.
- Quick write: respond spontaneously to a question or a prompt by describing anything that occurs to you about a topic or by agreeing/disagreeing with what was said.
- True/false: write two sentences in response to what an ad, TV commercial or political candidate wants you to believe and what you know or think to be true.

# Bibliography

Ackerman, David (1992). Interdisciplinary learning. Interview by Scott Willis. *ASCD Curriculum Update*, November, 2, 6.

Adler, Mortimer J. (1982). *The Paideia proposal: An educational manifesto*. New York, NY: Macmillan.

———. (1983). *Paideia problems and possibilities*. New York, NY: Macmillan.

Algozzine, B. and J. Ysseldyke (1997). *Strategies and tactics for effective instruction*. Longmont, CO: Sopris West.

Ambrose, Jay (1996). Stupid. Minneapolis, MN: *Star Tribune*, August 5, A13.

*American Educator* (1992). What should elementary students be doing? Fall, 19–20.

American Federation of Teachers (1987). Education for democracy: A statement of principles. *American Educator*, Summer, 16.

———. (2000). Reforms that work show their worth in urban districts. *American Teacher*, December 2000/January 2001, 85/4, 3.

Anderson, R. C., E. H. Hiebert, J. A. Scott and I. Wilkinson, eds. (1985). *Becoming a nation of readers: The report of the commission on reading*. Washington, DC: National Institute of Education.

Bagha, Mohammed (1993). Mindworks: Kids say they want challenges, attention. Minneapolis, MN: *Star Tribune*, February 2, E2.

Banks, James A. (1991). Multicultural literacy and curriculum reform. *Educational Horizons*, Spring, 4, 138.

———. (1994). Transforming the mainstream curriculum. *Educational Leadership*, May, 51/8, 4–8.

———. (1997). *Educating citizens in a multicultural society*. New York, NY: Teachers College Press.

———. (1999). *An introduction to multicultural education*. 2nd ed. Boston, MA: Allyn and Bacon.

Barbe, Walter B. and Raymond S. Swassing (1979). *Teaching through modality strengths, concepts and practices*. Columbus, OH: Zaner-Bloser.

Baron, Joan Boykoff (1990). Performance assessment: Blurring the edges among assessment, curriculum and instruction. Paper. AAAS Forum for School Science.

Beane, James A. (1991). The middle school: The natural home of integrated curriculum. *Educational Leadership*, October, 49/2, 9, 12.

———. (1995a). Curriculum integration and the disciplines of knowledge. *Phi Delta Kappan*, 616.

———. (1995b). *Toward a coherent curriculum*. Alexandria, VA: ASCD.

Berliner, D. C. and B. V. Rosenshine (1987). *Talks to teachers*. New York, NY: Random House, 175.

Berry, Marilyn (1984). *Help is on the way for written reports*. Chicago, IL: Children's Press, 13–15, 20–37.

Betts, Frank (1992). How systems thinking applies to education. *Educational Leadership*, November, 50/3, 41.

Beyer, Barry K. (1984). Improving thinking skills: Practical approaches. *Phi Delta Kappan*, April, 559.

Bianculli, David (1992). *Teleliteracy: Taking television seriously.* New York, NY: Continuum.

Bloom, Benjamin S., and others (1974). *Taxonomy of educational objectives: Affective and cognitive domains.* New York, NY: David McKay.

Blythe, Tina and associates (1998). *The teaching for understanding guide.* San Francisco, CA: Jossey Bass.

Boucher, Michael (1994). Dimensions of learning cube. Handout August 29. Minneapolis, MN: Minneapolis Public Schools.

Brady, Marion (2000). The standards juggernaut. *Phi Delta Kappan*, May. Online. Available www.pdkintl.org/kappan.

Branigan, Cara (2000). Technology can improve education outcomes. *eSchool News*, November, 19.

Bransford, J. D., A. L. Brown and R. R. Cocking, eds. (1999). *How people learn: Brain, mind, experience, and school.* Washington, DC: National Academy Press.

Brendtro, Larry K., Martin Brokenleg and Steve Van Bockern (1990). *Reclaiming youth at risk: Our hope for the future.* Bloomington, IN: National Educational Service.

Brennan, Amber (1999). Teacher uses grad standards to help students see the big picture. In *Progress on graduation standards*. St. Paul, MN: Minnesota Department of Education.

Brilhart, John K. and Gloria J. Galanes (1997). *Effective group discussion.* 9th ed. New York, NY: McGraw Hill, 5.

Brooks, Jacqueline Grennon and Martin G. Brooks (1993). *The case for constructivist classrooms*. Alexandria, VA: ASCD.

Brown University (1983). Coalition of essential schools. Online. Available www.brown/edu; www.essentialschools.org.

Brown, A. L. and J. C. Campione (1986). Psychological theory and the study of learning disabilities. *American Psychologist*, 41, 1059.

Bruchac, Joseph (2000). How to build a multicultural library. *NEA Today*, November, 19/3, 29.

Bruner, Jerome (1960). *The process of education.* New York, NY: Vintage Books.

———. (1986). *Actual minds, possible worlds.* Cambridge, MA: Harvard University Press.

Caine, Geoffrey, Renate Nummela Caine and Sam Crowell (1994). *Mindshifts: A brain-based process for restructuring schools and renewing education.* 2nd ed. Tucson, AZ: Zephyr Press.

Caine, Renate Nummela and Geoffrey Caine (1990). Understanding a brain based approach to learning and teaching. *Educational Leadership*, October, 48/2.

———. (1994). *Making connections: Teaching and the human brain.* Alexandria, VA: ASCD.

Campbell, Joseph (1972). *Hero with a thousand faces.* Princeton, NJ: Princeton University Press.

Campbell, Linda, Bruce Campbell and Dee Dickinson (1998). *Teaching and learning through multiple intelligences.* 2nd ed. New York, NY: Allyn and Bacon.

Camper, Fred (1986). Film is not video/video is not film. *Release Print,* April.

Cannon, Lynn Weber (1990). Fostering positive race, class and gender dynamics in the classroom. *Women's Studies Quarterly 1 & 2,* 127.

Carbo, Marie (1995). *Reading style inventory: Intermediate.* RSI-I: Author.

Carbo, Marie, Rita Dunn and Kenneth Dunn (1986a). *Teaching students to read through their individual learning styles.* Englewood Cliffs, NJ: Prentice Hall.

———. (1986b). *Reading styles inventory.* Roslyn Heights, NY: Learning Research Associates.

Catterall, J. (1995). *Different ways of knowing 1991–1994.* Los Angeles, CA: Galef Institute.

Central Park East Secondary School (1995). Sub-essential questions. Handout, n.d.

Chall, J. S. (1996). *Stages of reading development.* 2nd ed. Fort Worth, TX: Harcourt Brace.

Chall, J. S., V. Jacobs and L. Baldwin (1990). *The reading crisis: Why poor children fall behind.* Cambridge, MA: Harvard University Press.

Chion-Kenney, Linda (1987). A report from the field: Coalition of essential schools. *American Educator,* Winter, 20.

Chodorow, Stanley (1994). Transformations in the humanities. In Perspectives on the humanities and school-based curriculum development. ACLS Occasional Paper 24. New York, NY: American Council of Learned Societies, 34.

Chu, Jocelyn (n.d.) *Synthesizing.* Handout. Moorestown, NJ: Hanson Silver.

Church, Susan M. (1991). Student empowerment: The view from the classroom. *Reading Today,* April/May, 24.

Cizek, Gregory J. (1999). Give us this day our daily dread: Manufacturing crises in education. *Phi Delta Kappan,* June. Online. Available www.pdk.org.

Clark, Barbara (1986). *Optimizing learning: The integrative education model in the classroom.* Columbus, OH: Merrill.

———. (1996). Integrative education. In *Creating the future: Perspectives on educational change.* Dee Dickinson, ed. Seattle, WA: New Horizons for Learning. Online. Available www.newhorizons.org.

———. (1997). *Growing up gifted: Developing the potential of children at home and at school.* 5th ed. Englewood Cliffs, NJ: Prentice Hall, 14.

Clinchy, Evans (1996). Reforming American education from the top to the bottom: Escaping academic captivity. *Phi Delta Kappan,* December.

Cohen, David K., Milbrey W. McLaughlin and Joan E. Talbert (1993). *Teaching for understanding: Challenges for policy and practice.* San Francisco, CA: Jossey Bass.

Cohen, Elizabeth G. (1986). *Designing groupwork: Strategies for the heterogeneous classroom.* New York, NY: Teachers College Press.

Coles, Robert (1990). *The spiritual life of children.* Boston, MA: Houghton Mifflin.

Comer, J. (1996). *Rallying the whole village: The Comer process for reforming education.* New York, NY: Teachers College Press.

Considine, David M. (1986). Visual literacy and children's books: An integrated approach. *School Library Journal,* 33/1, 38–42.

————. (1995). An introduction to media literacy: The what, why and how to's. *Telemedium: The Journal of Media Literacy*, 41/1, 5, 3. Online. Available www.ci.appstate.edu/programs/edmedia/medialit/article.html.

————. (1998). A healthy balance: Media literacy for preparation, protection and pleasure. *Telemedium: The Journal of Media Literacy*, 44/2, 16–19, 24–25.

————. (1999a). All in the family: Exploring media literacy through television families. *Telemedium: The Journal of Media Literacy*, 45/1, 12–13.

————. (1999b). The teen screen: Image, influence and the indies. *Telemedium: The Journal of Media Literacy*, 46/1, 6–9.

————. (2000a). Mastering the media: The Appalachian experience. *Telemedium: The Journal of Media Literacy*, 46/1, 22–23.

————. (2000b). Media literacy as evolution and revolution: In the culture, climate, and context of American education. In *Reconceptualizing literacy in the media age*. Ann Watts Pailliotet and Peter B. Mosenthal, eds. Stamford, CT: JAI Press, 299–327.

Considine, David M. and Gail E. Haley (1999). *Visual messages: Integrating imagery into instruction*. 2nd ed. Englewood, CO: Libraries Unlimited, xvi.

Considine, David M., Gail E. Haley and Lyn Ellen Lacy (1994). *Imagine that: Developing critical thinking and critical viewing through children's literature*. Englewood, CO: Libraries Unlimited, xviii, 23, 145, 147.

Cooper, Joanne (1991). Telling our own stories: The reading and writing of journals or diaries. In *Stories lives tell*. C. Witherell and N. Noddings, eds. New York, NY: Teachers College Press.

Cortes, Carlos E. (1990). A curricular basic for our multiethnic future. *Doubts and Certainties*, March/April, 3–5.

————. (1999). Searching for patterns: A conversation with Carlos Cortes. *Teaching Tolerance*, Fall, 16, 14.

————. (2000). *The children are watching: How the media teach about diversity*. New York, NY: Teachers College Press.

Costa, Arthur L., ed. (1991). *Developing minds: A resource book for teaching thinking*. Revised ed. Vol. 1. Alexandria, VA: ASCD.

Costa, Arthur L. and Robert Garmston (1993). *Cognitive coaching: A foundation for Renaissance schools*. Norwood, MA: Christopher Gordon, 104.

Costa, Arthur L., and Bena Kallick (1998). *Teaching and assessing habits of mind*. Search Model Unlimited, 2.

Costa, Arthur L. and Rosemarie Liebmann (1995). Process is as important as content. *Educational Leadership*, March, 52/6, 23–24.

Costa, Arthur L., James Bellanca and Robin Fogarty, eds. (1992). *If minds matter: A forward to the future*. Vols. 1 and 2. Palatine, IL: IRI/Skylight.

Crockett, Tom (1994). Visual information handling skills and portfolios. In *Portfolio 2000*. Dallas, TX: Polaroid Education Program.

Cronin, John (1996). Are you for real? *Learning*, August, 25/1, 73–74.

Cushman, Kathleen (1994). Technology in the essential school: Making change in the information age. *Horace*, January, 10/3, 3.

Del Mar, Malik (1995). Eye on the candidates: Minneapolis school board. Minneapolis, MN: *Star Tribune*, September 9, 6A.

Dewey, John (1916). *Democracy in education*. New York, NY: Macmillan.

Drummond, Steven (2000). Horace's compromise: A book review. *Teacher Magazine*, April, 55.

Dunn, Rita and Kenneth Dunn (1977). Seeing, hearing, moving, touching learning packages. *Teacher*, May/June, 48.

———. (1999). *Complete guide to the learning strategies inservice system*. Boston, MA: Allyn and Bacon.

Dunn, Rita, Kenneth Dunn and G. E. Price (1989). *The learning styles inventory*. Lawrence, KS: Price Systems, 4.

Dyrli, Odvard Egil and Daniel E. Kinnaman (1995). Teaching effectively with technology. *Technology and Learning*, March, 15/6, 53–57.

Ebersole, Ben (1992). Interdisciplinary learning. Interview by Scott Willis. *ASCD Curriculum Update*, November, 5, 7.

*Education Minnesota* (2001). National report delivers mixed bag for Minnesota. Online. Available www.educationminnesota.org.

Eisner, Eliot (1980). Future priorities for curriculum reform. *Educational Leadership*, March, 37/6, 455.

Elmore, Richard F. (1992). Why restructuring alone won't improve teaching. *Educational Leadership*, April, 49/7, 45.

Engel, Brenda (1994). Portfolio assessment and the new paradigm: New instruments and new places. *The Educational Forum*, Fall, 59, 22–27.

Farner, Conrad D. (1996). Mending the broken circle. *Learning*, August, 25/1, 27.

Fiderer, Adele (1988). Talking about books: Readers need readers. In *Focus on collaborative groups*. Jeff Golub, ed. Urbana, IL: NCTE.

Fielding, Elizabeth Nolan (1994). Reaching and teaching the ADD student. *Reading Today*, August/September, 27.

Fisher, Bobbi and Pat Cordeiro (1994). Generating curriculum: Building a shared curriculum. *Primary Voices K-6*, August, 2/3, 3.

Fitzgerald, Nancy (1996). Lifelong learning. *Parent Power Newsletter*, Summer, 2–3.

Fogarty, Robin (1991a). *The mindful school: How to integrate the curricula*. Palatine, IL: IRI/Skylight, 85–86, 95.

———. (1991b). Ten ways to integrate curricula. *Educational Leadership*, October, 49/2, 63.

Fogarty, Robin, ed. (1993). *Integrating the curricula: A collection*. Alexandria, VA: ASCD.

Fosnot, Catherine (1996). *Constructivism: Theory, perspectives and practice*. New York, NY: Teachers College Press.

Foxfire Fund, Inc. (1992). The foxfire approach: Perspective and core practices. *Hands On*, Spring/Summer, 35/36, 9–10.

Fredericks, Anthony D. (1991). Prompting new possibilities. *Learning91*, 51.

Friedman, Jerome (1999). The humanities and the sciences: Discussion. ACLS Occasional Paper 47. New York, NY: American Council of Learned Societies.

Frye, Billy E. (1999). The humanities and the sciences: Introduction. ACLS Occasional Paper 47. New York, NY: American Council of Learned Societies.

Fuhrman, Susan (1993). Education: Focus shifts from statehouse to school. Minneapolis, MN: *Star Tribune*, April 26, A8, A9.

Fullan, Michael (2000). The three stories of educational reform. *Phi Delta Kappan*, April.

Gaddy, Levonne (2001). Nearly 7 million Americans say they're multiracial. Minneapolis, MN: *Star Tribune*, March 13, A14.

Gagnon, Paul (1994). Standards: And bringing them to the classroom. *American Educator*, Fall, 15, 28.

Gandal, Matt (1994). Making standards good. *American Educator*, Fall, 15.

———. (1995). Not all standards are created equal. *Educational Leadership*, March, 52/6, 21.

———. (1996a). AFT criteria for high-quality standards. *American Educator*, Spring, 33.

———. (1996b). Standards: How's your state doing? *American Educator*, Fall, 20.

Garbarino, James (1997). Educating children in a socially toxic environment. *Educational Leadership*, April, 54/7, 12–14.

Gardner, Howard (1992). The two rhetorics of school reform: Complex theories vs. the quick fix. *Chronicle of Higher Education*, May 6, B2.

———. (1993). *Frames of mind: The theory of multiple intelligences*. 10th anniversary edition. New York, NY: Basic Books.

———. (1997). The first seven...and the eighth. Interview by Kathy Checkley. *Educational Leadership*, September, 55/1, 11.

———. (1998). Melding progressive and traditional perspectives. In *Teaching for understanding: Linking research with practice*. Martha Stone Wiske, ed. San Francisco, CA: Jossey Bass, 14.

———. (1999a). *The disciplined mind: What all students should understand*. New York, NY: Simon and Schuster.

———. (1999b). *Intelligence reframed: Multiple intelligences for the 21st century*. New York, NY: Basic Books.

Gardner, Howard and Veronica Boix-Mansilla (1994). Teaching for understanding: Within and across the disciplines. *Educational Leadership*, February, 52/5, 16–18.

Garelick, Sonya (1997). Mindworks: Hungry minds. Minneapolis, MN: *Star Tribune*, December 1, E5.

Garmston, Robert J. and Bruce M. Wellman (1992). *How to make presentations that teach and transform*. Alexandria, VA: ASCD, 16, 32–34, 74.

Gerber, Alex (1991). Synergy, holistic education and R. Buckminster Fuller: Education for a world in transformation. Pamphlet. Online. Available www.rwgray projects.com/rbfnotes.

Gerzon, Mark (1997). Teaching democracy by doing it! *Educational Leadership*, February, 54/5, 6, 9.

Gilligan, Carol, ed. (1989). *Making connections: The relational worlds of adolescent girls at Emma Willard School*. Troy, NY: Dodge Foundation.

Gitomer, Drew H. (1994). Learning by doing what? *American Educator*, 18/3, 35.

Glasser, William (1969). *Schools without failure*. New York, NY: Harper and Row, 122.

———. (1987). The key to improving schools: An interview with William Glasser. Interview by Pauline B. Gough. *Phi Delta Kappan*, May, 656, 661.

Glazer, Nathan (1998). *We are all multiculturalists now.* Cambridge, MA: Harvard University Press.

Goldstein, A. P. and E. McGinnis (1997). *Skillstreaming the adolescent: New strategies and perspectives for teaching prosocial skills.* Revised ed. Champaign, IL: Research Press.

Goleman, Daniel (1995). *Emotional intelligence: Why it can matter more than IQ for character, health and lifelong achievement.* Garden City, NY: Doubleday.

Gollnick, Donna M. and Philip C. Chinn (1998). *Multicultural education in a pluralistic society.* 5th ed. New York, NY: Macmillan, 14, 275.

Golub, Jeff, ed. (1988). *Focus on collaborative learning.* Washington, DC: NCTE.

Good. T. L. (1987). Teacher expectations. In *Talks to teachers.* D. C. Berliner and B. V. Rosenshine, eds. New York, NY: Random House, 175.

Gordon, Greg (2001). Overhauling education. Minneapolis, MN: *Star Tribune,* June 15, A1.

Gordon, Robin L. (1997). How novice teachers can succeed with adolescents. *Educational Leadership,* April, 54/7, 56–58.

Gormley, Denny (1995). Aiming to learn in a changing world. *Excellence for Education in Minnesota,* Winter, 3/2, 1.

Goswami, Dixie and Peter Stillman, eds. (1987). *Reclaiming the classroom: Teacher research as an agency for change.* Upper Montclair, NJ: Boynton Cook.

Greenfield, Patricia M. (1985). Multimedia education: Why print isn't always best. *American Educator,* Fall, 9/3, 18.

Gregorc, Anthony F. (1982a). *Transaction ability inventory.* Maynard, MA: Gabriel Systems.

———. (1982b). *An adult's guide to style.* Maynard, MA: Gabriel Systems.

Guild, Pat Burke (1997). Where do the learning theories overlap? *Educational Leadership,* September, 55/1, 30.

Guilford, J. P. (1967). *The nature of human intelligence.* New York, NY: McGraw Hill.

Guilford, J. P. and R. Hoeptner (1971). *The analysis of intelligence.* New York, NY: McGraw Hill.

Haley, Gail E. (1994). Planning an author/artist visit: Guidelines by Gail E. Haley. In *Imagine that: Developing critical thinking and critical viewing through children's literature.* Considine, David M., Gail E. Haley and Lyn Ellen Lacy, coauthors. Englewood, CO: Libraries Unlimited, 136.

Hamer, Irving (1994a). Multiculturalism and cross-culturalism in the curriculum. *The Multicultural Link,* 2/1, 2.

———. (1994b). There are no exemptions for multicultural content. *The Multicultural Link,* 1/4, 2.

Hammerman, Donald R. and William M. Hammerman (1983). *Teaching in the outdoors.* Minneapolis, MN: Burgess.

Hancock, Vicki E., Brian Moore and Bernard Schwartz (1993). Technology and the visual and performing arts. *Educational Leadership,* February, 50/5, 8, 68.

Harris, Douglas E. and Judy F. Carr (1996). *How to use standards in the classroom.* Alexandria, VA: ASCD.

Hartle-Schutte, David (1993). Literacy development in Navajo homes. *Language Arts*, 70, 652.

*Harvard Education Letter* (1988). Learning from children: Teachers do research. Cambridge, MA: Harvard University Press, July/August, 4/4, 3.

Harvard Graduate School of Education (1993). Project zero. Online. Available pzweb.harvard.edu.

———. (2002). Teaching for understanding: Putting understanding up front. Online. Available learnweb.harvard.edu/alps/tfu.

Healy, Jane (1992). *Endangered minds: Why our children don't think and what we can do about it.* New York, NY: Simon and Schuster.

Healy, Sharon (1992). Improving those lectures. *American Federation of Teachers Newspaper*, December/January, 11.

Herbert, Frank (1965). *Dune.* New York, NY: Putnam.

Herman, Joan L., Pamela R. Aschbacher and Lynn Winters (1992). *A practical guide to alternative assessment.* Alexandra, VA: ASCD.

Herreman, David (1988). None of us is as smart as all of us. In *Focus on collaborative learning.* Jeff Golub, ed. Washington, DC: NCTE, 5.

Hesse III, Joseph J. (1996). Stretched analogies and school reform. *Educational Leadership*, February, 54/5, 62.

Hillerman, Tony (1982). *The dark wind.* New York, NY: Harper and Row.

Hirsch Jr., E. D. (1993). The core knowledge curriculum: What's behind its success. *Educational Leadership*, May, 50/8, 23–25.

Hopfenberg, W. S., H. M. Levin and associates (1993). *The accelerated schools resource guide.* San Francisco, CA: Jossey Bass.

Hotakainen, Rob (1997). Reward excellence in schools, forum says. Minneapolis, MN: *Star Tribune*, January 21, B1.

Howe, Kenneth R. (1995). Wrong problem, wrong solution. *Educational Leadership*, March, 52/6, 22.

Hughes, Linda Hazard (1991). An invitation to bake bread. *American Educator*, Fall, 33.

Hunt, David E. (1977). *Assessing conceptual level by the paragraph completion method.* Toronto, ON: Ontario Institute for Studies in Education.

Iggers, Jeremy (1993). Participants raise other tough issues on education. Minneapolis, MN: *Star Tribune*, April 19, E2.

*Insights in Ink* (2001). Minnesota Youth Series. Minneapolis, MN: *Star Tribune*, May 16.

Ivins, Molly (1996). Blaming teachers for the problems in our schools is simply wrong and unfair. Minneapolis, MN: *Star Tribune*, September 4, A17.

Jackson, Megan (1993). Mindworks: Kids say they want challenges, attention. Minneapolis, MN: *Star Tribune*, February 2, E3.

Jackson, Tony (1995). Mindworks: What's the right size for a class? Minneapolis, MN: *Star Tribune*, January 3, E1.

Jacobs, Heidi Hayes (1991a). The integrated curriculum. *Instructor*, September, 23.

———. (1991b). On interdisciplinary curriculum: A conversation with Heidi Hayes Jacobs. *Educational Leadership*, October, 49/2, 24.

———. (1992). Interdisciplinary learning. Interview by Scott Willis. *ASCD Curriculum Update*, November, 2, 6.

————. (1997). *Mapping the big picture: Integrating curriculum and assessment K-12.* Alexandria, VA: ASCD.

Jacobs, Heidi Hayes, ed. (1989). *Interdisciplinary curriculum: Design and implementation.* Alexandria, VA: ASCD, 7–8.

Jacobs, Heidi Hayes and James H. Borland (1986). The interdisciplinary concept model: Theory and practice. *Gifted Child Quarterly*, Fall, 30/4, 161–162.

James, P. D. (1986). *A taste for death.* New York, NY: Warner, 162.

Jehlen, Alain (2001). A nation at risk? *NEA Today*, 19/4, January, 29.

Jennings, John F. (1995). School reform based on what is taught and learned. *Phi Delta Kappan*, June, 767.

Jensen, Eric (1998). *Teaching with the brain in mind.* Alexandria, VA: ASCD.

Johnson, David W. and Roger T. Johnson (1987). *Learning together and alone: Cooperative, competitive and individualistic learning.* Englewood Cliffs, NJ: Prentice Hall.

Johnson, David W., Roger T. Johnson and E. J. Holubee (1991). *Cooperation in the classroom.* Edina, MN: Interaction Books.

Johnson, Jean and John Immerwahr (1995). First things first: What Americans expect from the public schools. *American Educator*, Winter 1994–1995, 18/4, 11–13.

Jones, Susan C. (1995). *Memory aids for math.* Fayetteville, AR: Educational Memory Aids, 2.

Joyce, Bruce, Marsha Weil with Beverly Showers (1996). *Models of teaching.* 5th ed. Needham Heights, MA: Allyn and Bacon, 96, 183–191, 301.

Joyce, Bruce, Beverly Showers and Carol Rolheiser-Bennett (1987). Staff development and student learning: A synthesis of research on models of teaching. *Educational Leadership*, October, 44/2, 13.

Jung, Carl G. (1964). *Man and his symbols.* Garden City, NY: Doubleday.

————. (1927). *Theory of psychological type.* Princeton, NJ: Princeton University Press.

Juntune, Joyce E. (1983). *Creative problem solving for the classroom teacher.* Circle Pines, MN: 120 Creative Corner, 1.

Kagan, J. (1965). *Matching familiar figures test.* Cambridge, MA: Harvard University Press.

Kameenui, E. J. and D. W. Carmine, eds. (1998). *Effective teaching strategies that accommodate diverse learners.* Upper Saddle River, NJ: Prentice Hall.

Kameenui, E. J. and D. C. Simmons (1990). *Designing instructional strategies: The prevention of academic learning problems.* Columbus, OH: Merrill.

Kamii, Mieko (1996). Standards and assessment: What we've learned thus far. *The Web*, September, 14/7, 7, 2.

Kamil, Michael L. and others (2000). *Handbook of reading research.* 3rd ed. West Haven, CT: NEA.

Karp, Stan (1997). Educating for a civil society: The core issue is inequality. *Educational Leadership*, February, 54/5, 42.

Katz, Stanley N. (1993). The humanities in the schools, 1986–1997. ACLS Occasional Paper 20. New York, NY: American Council of Learned Societies, 2–4, 7, 8, 10.

————. (1998a). Computing and the humanities: Summary of a roundtable meeting. ACLS Occasional Paper 41. New York, NY: American Council of Learned Societies.

————. (1998b). What are the humanities? In Computing and the humanities. ACLS Occasional Paper 41. New York, NY: American Council of Learned Societies.

Keirsey, David and Marilyn Bates (1984). *Please understand me: Character and temperament types*. Del Mar, CA: Prometheus Nemesis.

Kennedy, M. M. (1997). The connection between research and practice. *Educational Researcher*, 27/7, 4–12.

Kieren, T. E. (1997). Theories for the classroom: Connections between research and practice. *For the Learning of Mathematics*, 17/2, 31–33.

Kierstead, Janet (1993). Direct instruction and experiential approaches: Are they really mutually exclusive? *Educational Leadership*, May, 50/8, 46.

Kincheloe, Joe L. (1999). The struggle to define and reinvent whiteness: A pedagogical analysis. *College Literature* 26, Fall, 57, 162.

Kincheloe, Joe L. and Shirley R. Steinberg (1993). A tentative description of postformal thinking: The critical confrontation with cognitive theory. *Harvard Educational Review*, Fall, 63/3, 296.

————. (1999). *Rethinking intelligence: Confronting psychological assumptions about teaching and learning*. London: Routledge.

Kinder, Melvyn (1992). *Going nowhere fast*. New York, NY: Fawcett.

Koestler, Arthur (1972). *Roots of coincidence*. New York, NY: Vintage.

Kohl, Herbert (1986). *On teaching*. New York, NY: Shocken.

Kolb, David A. (1971). *Individual learning styles and the learning process*. Cambridge, MA: M.I.T. Press.

————. (1984). *Experiential learning: Experience as the source of learning and development*. Englewood Cliffs, NJ: Prentice Hall.

————. (1985). *Learning style inventory*. Boston, MA: McBer.

Krogh, Suzanne (1992). Interdisciplinary learning. Interview by Scott Willis. *ASCD Curriculum Update*, November, 2–3.

Kurth-Schai, Ruthanne (1988). The roles of youth in society: A reconceptualization. *The Educational Forum*, Winter, 52/2, 114–116, 124–128.

Lacy, Lyn Ellen (1986a). *Art and design in children's picture books: An analysis of Caldecott award-winning illustrations*. Chicago, IL: American Library Association.

————. (1986b). *Visual education: An interdisciplinary approach for students K-12 using visuals of all kinds*. Minneapolis, MN: Minneapolis Public Schools.

————. (1994). About TV: What do you know about, think about, do about television? Handout. Minneapolis, MN: Minneapolis Public Schools.

————. (2000). Integrating standards in K-5 media literacy. In *Reconceptualizing literacy in the media age*. Ann Watts Pailliotet and Peter B. Mosenthal, eds. Stamford, CT: JAI Press, 243.

Lampert, M. and C. M. Clark (1990). Expert knowledge and expert thinking in teaching: A response to Floden and Klinzing. *Educational Researcher*, 19/4, 21–23.

Lasswell, H. D. (1948). The structure and function of communications in society. In *Communication of ideas*. L. Bryson, ed. New York, NY: Harper and Row, 37.

Lawrence, Gordon (1982). *People types and tiger stripes: A practical guide to learning styles*. Gainesville, FL: Center for Applications of Psychological Types.

————. (1997). *Looking at type and learning*. Gainesville, FL: Center for Applications of Psychological Types.

Lazear, David (1991). *Seven ways of knowing: Teaching for multiple intelligences*. 2nd ed. Palatine, IL: IRI/Skylight, 93–94.

————. (1994). *Multiple intelligence approaches to assessment: Solving the assessment conundrum*. Tucson, AR: Zephyr, 11.

Lear, Rick (1992). Interdisciplinary learning. Interview by Scott Willis. *ASCD Curriculum Update*, November, 3.

*Learning90* (1990a). Great teaching's many faces. September, 19/2, 2.

————. (1990b). Spotlight on innovation. September, 19/2, 29.

Lehr, Art and Joe Bauers (1993). What we think of the standards project. *The Council Chronicle*, November, 3/2, 18.

Leshin, Cynthia B., Joelleyn Pollock and Charles M. Reigeluth (1992). *Instructional design strategies and tactics*. Englewood Cliffs, NJ: Educational Technology Publications, 146–151.

Levitsky, Ronald (1990). The not-so-good old days. *Teacher*, June/July, 73.

Lewis, Anne C. (1995). An overview of the standards movement. *Phi Delta Kappan*, June, 746, 750.

Lipman, Matthew (1984). The cultivation of reasoning through philosophy. *Educational Leadership*, September, 42/1, 51.

Lipman, Matthew, Ann Margaret Sharp and Frederick S. Oscanyan (1980). *Philosophy in the classroom*. Philadelphia, PA: Temple University Press.

Lippitt, Linda (1996). The mission of About Learning, Inc.'s Research Division. Online. Available www.aboutlearning.com.

Lockwood Summers, Sue (2000). *Media alert! 200 activities to create media-savvy kids*. Littleton, CO: Media Alert!

Lonetree, Anthony (2001). Elementary schools scramble to reinstate Profile standards. Minneapolis, MN: *Star Tribune*, January 10, B1.

Lowery, Lawrence (1998). How new science curriculums reflect brain research. *Educational Leadership*, November, 56/3.

MacDonald, Joseph (1992). *Teaching: Making sense of an uncertain craft*. New York, NY: Teacher's College Press.

MacMullen, M. M. (1996). *Taking stock of a school reform effort: A research collection and analysis*. Providence, RI: Annenberg Institute for School Reform.

Mairson, Alan (1995). Saving Britain's shore. *National Geographic*, October, 188/4, 56.

Marsh, Ngaio (1941). *Death and the dancing footman*. New York, NY: Jove.

Marzano, Robert J. (1992). *A different kind of classroom: Teaching with dimensions of learning*. Alexandria, VA: ASCD, 7, 71.

————. (1998). Dimensions of learning. Online. Available www.mcrel.org.

Marzano, R. J. and Debra Pickering (1997). *Dimensions of learning: Teacher's manual*. 2nd ed. Alexandria, VA: ASCD.

Marzano, Robert J., Debra Pickering and Jay McTighe (1993). *Assessing student outcomes: Performance assessment using the Dimensions of Learning model*. Alexandria, VA: ASCD, 10, 13–14, 18–24, 126–131.

Marzano, Robert J., Debra Pickering and Jane E. Pollock (2001). *Classroom instruction that works: Research-based strategies for increasing student achievement*. Alexandria, VA: ASCD.

Maxim, Donna (1991). Beginning researchers. *American Educator*, Spring, 34–42.

McCarthy, Bernice (1987). *The 4MAT system: Teaching to learning styles with right/left mode techniques*. Barrington, IL: Excel, 122.

————. (1991). *The 4MAT system: Awareness workshop materials*. Barrington, IL: Excel.

————. (1996a). *About learning*. Barrington, IL: Excel.

————. (1996b). About learning. Online. Available www.aboutlearning.com.

————. (1997). A tale of four learners: 4MAT's learning styles. *Educational Leadership*, March, 54/6, 50.

McCarthy, Bernice and Susan Morris (1995a). *4MAT in action: Sample units K-6*. Barrington, IL: Excel.

————. (1995b). *4MAT in action: Sample units 7–12*. Barrington, IL: Excel.

McCarty, Willard (1998). Computing and the humanities: Summary of a roundtable meeting. ACLS Occasional Paper 41. New York, NY: American Council of Learned Societies, 10, 12.

McCown, Karen Stone and others (1998). *Self science: The subject is me*. 2nd ed. San Mateo, CA: Six Seconds.

McGinnis, E. and A. P. Goldstein (1997). *Skillstreaming the elementary school child: New strategies and perspectives for teaching prosocial skills*. Rev. ed. Champaign, IL: Research Press.

Meeker, Mary (1969). *Structure of the intellect: Its interpretation and its uses*. Columbus, OH: Merrill.

Miller, Patrick W. (1988). *Nonverbal communication*. West Haven, CT: NEA, 10.

Minnesota Department of Children, Families and Learning (1997a). Minnesota's K-12 graduation standards. Handout. St. Paul, MN: State Printing Office.

————. (1997b). *Plan for technology education*. St. Paul, MN: State Printing Office.

Minnesota Department of Education (1986). Thinking through technology program. Handout. St. Paul, MN: Curriculum and Technology Section.

————. (1989). *Classroom instructional design: Options for teacher/student interaction*. White Bear Lake, MN: Curriculum Services Center.

*Minnesota Educator* (2000). Fallout continues from scoring snafu. August 25, 3/2, 13.

Minnesota State Board of Education (1996). *Graduation standards*. St. Paul, MN: Capitol Square, 5, 7, 13.

Moll, L., C. Velez-Ibanez and J. Greenberg (1990). *Community knowledge and classroom practice: Combining resources for literacy instruction*. Arlington, VA: Development Associates.

Morse, Jodie (2000). Sticking to the script. *Time*, March 6, 60–61.

Murphy, Amanda (1997). Mindworks: Hungry minds. Minneapolis, MN: *Star Tribune*, December 1, E5.

Myers, Isabel Briggs (1980). *Gifts differing*. Palo Alto, CA: Consulting Psychologists Press.

Myers, Isabel Briggs and K. C. Briggs (1977). *Myers-Briggs type indicator*. Palo Alto, CA: Consulting Psychologists Press.

Myers, Miles (1986). When research does not help teachers. *American Educator*, Summer, 18–23.

National Commission on Teaching and America's Future (1997). What matters most: Teaching for America's future. Paper. Woodbridge, VA.

National Council of Teachers of English (1996). *On viewing and visually representing as forms of literacy*. Urbana, IL: NCTE.

Nebgen, Mary K. and Kate McPherson (1990). Enriching learning through service. *Educational Leadership*, November, 48/3, 91.

Nelson, Annabelle (1994). *The learning wheel: Ideas and activities for multicultural and holistic lesson planning*. Tucson, AZ: Zephyr, 41–44.

Nelson, M. Rae (2001). High speed learning. *Cable in the Classroom*, January, 11/1, 10.

Nidds, John and James McGerald (1995). Corporate America looks at public education. *Principal*, March, 22–23.

Norris, Stephen P. (1985). Synthesis of research on critical thinking. *Educational Leadership*, May, 42/8, 40.

O'Connor, Stephen (1993). What standards can't solve: Death in the everyday schoolroom. *The Nation*, May 24, 704.

Ohmann, Richard (1994). Humanities and the public schools: Perspectives from inside the ACLS project. In Perspectives on the humanities and school-based curriculum development. ACLS Occasional Paper 24. New York, NY: American Council of Learned Societies, 6.

Oliver, Donald (1990). Grounded knowing: A postmodern perspective on teaching and learning. *Educational Leadership*, September, 48/1, 65.

O'Neil, John (1995). On lasting school reform: A conversation with Ted Sizer. *Educational Leadership*, February, 52/5, 4 6.

Owen, Linda (2001). Why we got an "F" for accountability. *Minnesota Educator*, January 26, 3/10, 1.

Pachon, Harry (2001). Census says numbers of Hispanics, blacks equal. Minneapolis, MN: *Star Tribune*, March 7, A4.

Paige, Rod (2001). Tests paint U. S. students as underachievers. Minneapolis, MN: *Star Tribune*, April 5, A4.

Palinscar, Annemarie and Ann Brown (2000). Reciprocal teaching. Online. Available www.mdk12.org/practices/goodinstruction.

Palinscar, A. S., D. S. Ogle, B. F. Jones, E. G. Carr and K. Ransom (1985). *Facilitator's manual for teaching reading as thinking*. Washington, DC: ASCD.

Parker, Walter C. (1997). The art of deliberation. *Educational Leadership*, February, 54/5, 18.

Parnes, Sidney and Alex Osborn (1983). *Creative problem-solving process*. San Diego, CA: Creative Problem Solving Institute.

Partridge, L. (1998). There's academic rigor in state's Profile of Learning. Minneapolis, MN: *Star Tribune*, March 28, A19.

Paul, Richard W. (1985). Bloom's taxonomy and critical thinking instruction. *Educational Leadership*, May, 42/8, 36–39.

———.(1990). *Critical thinking*. Sonoma, CA: Sonoma State University, 147.

Paulson, Pie (1998). Mindworks: Indelible influences. Minneapolis, MN: Star Tribune, April 6, E10.

Perkins, David (1986a). *Knowledge as design*. Mahwah, NJ: Lawrence Erlbaum.

————. (1986b). On creativity and thinking skills. Interview by Ronald S. Brandt. *Educational Leadership*, May, 43/8, 14.

————. (1992). Interdisciplinary learning. Interview by Scott Willis. *ASCD Curriculum Update*, November, 2, 5, 6.

————. (1993). Teaching for understanding. *American Educator*, Fall, 17/3, 3, 32.

————. (1995). *Outsmarting IQ: The emerging science of learnable intelligence*. New York, NY: Free Press.

Perrone, Vito (1988). *Alternative assessment*. Alexandria, VA: ASCD.

————. (1991). *A letter to teachers: Reflections on schooling and the art of teaching*. San Francisco, CA: Jossey Bass.

————. (1994). How to engage students in learning. *Educational Leadership*, February, 52/5, 13.

————. (1998). Why do we need a pedagogy of understanding? In *Teaching for understanding: Linking research with practice*. Martha Stone Wiske, ed. San Francisco, CA: Jossey Bass.

Perrone, Vito, ed. (1999). *Expanding student assessment*. Alexandria, VA: ASCD.

Peterson, David (2001). Diversity here is modest, but finely balanced. Minneapolis, MN: *Star Tribune*, April 3, B1.

Peterson, Sandra (2001). Where are our leaders? Look in the mirror. *Minnesota Educator*, May 25, 3/18, 2.

Pewewardy, Cornel D. (1994). Culturally responsible pedagogy in action: An American Indian magnet school. In *Teaching diverse populations: Formulating a knowledge base*. Etta R. Hollins, Joyce E. King and Warren C. Haymon, eds. Buffalo, NY: State University of New York Press.

————. (1998). Our children can't wait: Recapturing the essence of indigenous schools in the United States. *Cultural Survival Quarterly*, Spring, 22/1, 31.

————. (1999). The holistic medicine wheel: An indigenous model of teaching and learning. *Winds of Change*, Autumn, 14/4, 28, 31.

————. (2000a). Holistic circle. Online. Available busboy.sped.ukans.edu/~rreed/NAedPhilosophy.html.

————. (2000b). Native American educational philosophy. Online. Available busboy.sped.ukans.edu/~rreed/NAedPhilosophy.html.

Pewewardy, Cornel D. and Donald J. Willower (1993). Perceptions of American Indian high school students in public schools. *Equity and Excellence in Education*, April, 26/1, 55.

Pfeiffer, Andy (1997). Mindworks: The value of virtue. Minneapolis, MN: *Star Tribune*, January 9, E12.

Pinnell, G. S. (1995). Reading recovery: A review of research. *Educational Report #23, Special Topics Issue*. Columbus, OH: Martha L. King Language and Literacy Center.

Pogrow, S. (1995). Making reform work for the educationally disadvantaged. *Educational Leadership*, February, 52/5, 20–24.

Pratt, Jon (1996). Minnesota: It's colder than you think. Minneapolis, MN: *Star Tribune*, July 6, B10.

Prawat, Richard S. (1992). From individual differences to learning communities—our changing focus. *Educational Leadership*, April, 51/7, 11–12.

Purrington, Sandra Sanchez (1994). Panel discussion on school-based curriculum development. In Perspectives on the humanities and school-based curriculum development. ACLS Occasional Paper 24. New York, NY: American Council of Learned Societies, 17–18.

Randall, Patsy A. (1993). Twin Cities educators should recognize all children as gifted. Minneapolis, MN: *Star Tribune*, November 21, A33.

Ravitch, Diane (1995). *National standards in American education*. Washington, DC: Brookings Institution, 163.

Raywid, Mary Anne (1994). Alternative schools: The state of the art. *Educational Leadership*, September, 52/1, 26–29.

Reichert, Matt (1997). Mindworks: The value of virtue. Minneapolis, MN: *Star Tribune*, January 9, E12.

Reiff, Judith C. (1992). *Learning styles: What research says to the teacher series*. West Haven, CT: NEA.

Rifkin, Jeremy (1997). Preparing students for "the end of work." *Educational Leadership*, February, 54/5, 30–31.

Rifkin, Jeremy and Ted Howard (1989). *Entropy: Into the greenhouse world*. New York, NY: Viking, 28, 252.

Roberts, Wayne (1994). Life, math tournament doesn't follow textbook. Minneapolis, MN: *Star Tribune*, April 12, B7.

*Unit of study template: Concepts for curriculum* (1995). Handout November 13. Rochester, NY: Rochester City School District.

Rose, Lowell C. and Alec M. Gallup (1999). 31st annual PDK/Gallup poll of the public's attitudes toward the public schools. *Phi Delta Kappan*, April.

Rose, Lowell C. and Dana Rapp (1997). The future of the public schools: A public discussion. *Phi Delta Kappan*, June.

Rosenshine, B. V. (1986). Synthesis of research on explicit teaching. *Educational Leadership*, April, 43/7, 63.

Rosenshine, B. V. and R. Stevens (1986). Teaching functions. In *Handbook on research and teaching*. M. C. Wittrock, ed. 3rd ed. New York, NY: Macmillan.

Ross, A. C. (1989). *Mitakuye oyasin*. Denver, CO: Bear, 47–50, 190.

Ross, Ann and Karen Olsen (1993). *The way we were...the way we can be: A vision for the middle school through integrated thematic instruction*. 2nd ed. Kent, WA: Books for Educators.

Roth, Kathleen J. (1994). Second thoughts about interdisciplinary studies. *American Educator*, Spring, 44–48.

Sandholtz, Judith Haymore, Cathy Ringstaff and David C. Dwyer (1997). *Teaching with technology: Creating student-centered classrooms*. New York, NY: Teachers College Press.

Sawochka, Max (1998). Mindworks: Intriguing individuals. Minneapolis, MN: *Star Tribune*, June 1, E10.

Sawyer, Alan (1975). Mystery of the ancient Nazca lines. *National Geographic*, May, 147/5, 724.

Schmidt, Gary (2000). The last taboo: The spiritual life in children's literature. *The Five Owls*, November/December, 15/2, 26.

Schwahn, Charles and William Spady (1998). Why change doesn't happen and how to make sure it does. *Educational Leadership*, April, 55/7, 45–47.

*The Science Teacher* (1990). Code of practice on animals in school. Washington, DC: National Science Teachers Association.

Semali, Ladislaus, and Ann Watts Pailliotet, eds. (1999). *Intermediality: The teachers' handbook of critical media literacy*. Boulder, CO: Harper Collins.

Senge, Peter M. (1990). *The fifth discipline: The art and practice of the learning organization*. Garden City, NY: Doubleday.

Shah, Allie (2001). Minneapolis dropout study helps spark overhaul effort. Minneapolis, MN: *Star Tribune*, May 29, B1.

Shah, Allie and Duchesne Paul Drew (2001). Superintendent forges a legacy of gains in Minneapolis schools. Minneapolis, MN: *Star Tribune*, June 24, B1.

Shannon, Patrick (1991). How long has it been since you taught? *Reading Today*, October/November, 32.

Shaubach, Judy (2001). Supporters rally in the rain for students. *Minnesota Educator*, May 11, 3/17, 1.

Shepard, Lorrie A. (1991). Psychometricians' beliefs about learning. *Educational Researcher*, 20/7, 2–16.

———. (1995). Using assessment to improve learning. *Educational Leadership*, February, 52/5, 42–43.

———. (2000). The role of classroom assessment in teaching and learning. Occasional report. Santa Cruz, CA: University of California, Center for Applied Linguistics/Center for Research on Education, Diversity and Excellence.

———. (2001). How to fight a death star. *NEA Today*, January, 85/4, 19.

Shulman, Lee S. (1986). Those who understand: A conception of teacher knowledge. *American Educator*, Spring, 13–15, 44.

Silver, H. F. and J. R. Hanson (1995). *Learning styles and strategies*. Woodbridge, NJ: Thoughtful Education Press.

Silver, Harvey, Richard Strong and Matthew Perini (1997). Integrating learning styles and multiple intelligences. *Educational Leadership*, September, 55/1, 23.

———. (2000). *So each may learn: Integrating learning styles and multiple intelligences*. Trenton, NJ: Silver Strong.

Silverblatt, Art (2001). *Media literacy: Keys to interpreting media messages*. Westport, CT: Praeger.

Silvers, Penny (1994). Everyday signs of learning. *Primary Voices K-6*, April, 2/2, 26.

Simmons, Rebecca, Vito Perrone, David Perkins, Howard Gardner and Tina Blythe (1993). Teaching for understanding: Enhancing student learning and performance. Handout March 25–26. ASCD Pre-Conference Institute, Washington, D. C. Cambridge, MA: Harvard Graduate School of Education, 2–7, 16–17.

Sizer, Theodore R. (1984). *Horace's compromise: The dilemma of the American high school*. Boston, MA: Houghton Mifflin.

———. (1992). *Horace's school: Redesigning the American high school*. Boston, MA: Houghton Mifflin, 13, 21, 76, 81, 104.

———. (1995a). Making the grade. *Washington Post Education Review*, April 2, 12.

———. (1995b). On lasting school reform: A conversation with Ted Sizer. *Educational Leadership*, February, 52/5, 7.

———. (1996). *Horace's hope: What works for the American high school*. Boston, MA: Houghton Mifflin.

Sizer, Theodore R. and Bethany Rogers (1993). Designing standards: Achieving the delicate balance. *Educational Leadership*, February, 50/5.

Slavin, R. E. (1983). *Cooperative learning*. New York, NY: Longman.

———. (1986). *Using student team learning*. 3rd ed. Baltimore, MD: Johns Hopkins University.

———. (1990a). *Cooperative learning: Theory, research and practice*. Englewood Cliffs, NJ: Prentice Hall.

———. (1990b). Mastery learning reconsidered. *Review of Educational Research*, 60, 300–302.

Slavin, R. E., N. A. Madden, L. J. Dolan and B. A. Wasik (1996). Success for all: A summary of research. *Journal of Education for Students Placed At-Risk*, 1/1, 41–76.

Slavin, R. E., N. A. Madden and M. Leavey (1984). Effects of team assisted individualization. *Journal of Educational Psychology*, 76, 813.

Smetanka, Mary Jane (1992). Teaching overload? Society's ills put schools under pressure. Minneapolis, MN: *Star Tribune*, April 12, A8.

———. (1993). Hands-on testing. Minneapolis, MN: *Star Tribune*, April 29, B1.

———. (2001a). Schools still a top priority. Minneapolis, MN: *Star Tribune*, June 25, A1.

———. (2001b). A student of learning: Howard Gardner. Minneapolis, MN: *Star Tribune*, January 10, E2.

Smiley, Tavis (2001). Bridging the divide. *USA Weekend*, February, 2–4, 10.

Smith, Billie Jo (1990). Applying principles of learning: Activity packet. Handout. Newport, OR: Lincoln County School District.

Smith, Lisa (1993). Mindworks: Kids say they want challenges, attention. Minneapolis, MN: *Star Tribune*, February 12, E2.

Smith, M. (1996). The national writing project after 22 years. *Phi Delta Kappan*, 77/10, 688–692.

Smith, Marshall S. and Ramon Cortines (1993). Clinton proposals will challenge students and the school systems. *Philadelphia Inquirer*, June 24, 767.

Snow, Misti (2001). Mindworks editor Misti Snow bids farewell. Minneapolis, MN: *Star Tribune*, June 4, E1.

Sousa, David A. (1995). *How the brain learns: A classroom teacher's guide*. Reston, VA: National Association of Secondary School Principals.

Sowder, Judy (2000). Relating research and practice. Pre-session address. Chicago, IL: NCTM.

Sparks-Langer, Georgea Mohlman and Amy Berstein Colton (1991). Synthesis of research on teachers' reflective thinking. *Educational Leadership*, March, 48/6, 40–41.

Sternberg, Robert J. (1988). *Triarchic mind: A new theory of intelligence*. New York, NY: Viking.

232 Creative Planning Resource

————. (1990). Practical intelligence for success in school. *Educational Leadership*, October, 48/2, 35, 38, 135.

————. (1994). Allowing for thinking styles. *Educational Leadership*, November, 52/3, 36–37.

————. (1995). Investing in creativity: Many happy returns. *Educational Leadership*, December 95/January 96, 53/4, 81–84.

————. (1997). *Successful intelligence: How practical and creative intelligence determine success in life*. New York, NY: Simon and Schuster.

Storm, Hyemeyohsts (1972). *Seven arrows*. New York, NY: Harper and Row, 5.

Stovsky, Renee (1992). Expert says kids have 'different brains' shaped by TV, fast pace. Minneapolis, MN: *Star Tribune*, February 9, F8.

*Sub-essential questions* (1995). Handout November 13. New York, NY: Central Park East Secondary School.

Suddeth, Gary (2001). Stop tinkering with a worn-out educational system. Minneapolis, MN: *Star Tribune*, April 1, A14.

Sylwester, Robert (1995). *A celebration of neurons: An educator's guide to the human brain*. Alexandria, VA: ASCD.

Tanner, Daniel (1992). Interdisciplinary learning. Interview by Scott Willis. *ASCD Curriculum Update*, November, 5.

Teacher and Instructional Services (2000). Following teacher vote, board approves phased-in Profile of Learning implementation. Minneapolis, MN: Minneapolis Public Schools.

Tharp, Roland G. and Ronald Gallimore (1989). Rousing schools to life. *American Educator*, Summer, 23.

Thomas, Chadwin (1996). U.S. students still far from the top in math and science. Minneapolis, MN: *Star Tribune*, November 21, A6.

Thorne, Rich (1996). The fourth R is research. *Electronic Learning*, October, 58.

Torrance, E. P. (1966). *Torrance tests of creative thinking*. Princeton, NJ: Personnel.

Tyner, Kathleen (1998). *Literacy in a digital world: Teaching and learning in the age of information*. Mahwah, NJ: Lawrence Erlbaum.

————. (2000). Foreword: Expanding literacy in a shrinking world. In *Reconceptualizing literacy in the media age*. Ann Watts Pailliotet and Peter B. Mosenthal, eds. Stamford, CT: JAI Press.

Tyner, Kathleen and Donna Lloyd-Kolkin (1991). *Media and you: An elementary media literacy curriculum*. Englewood Cliffs, NJ: Educational Technology Publications.

Unger, Chris (1997). Teaching for understanding: Questions to ask yourself and your students. Online. Available www.newhorizons.org.

Utke, Nicholas (1997). Mindworks: Lessons learned. Minneapolis, MN: *Star Tribune*, June 5, E12.

Vana, Craig (2001). Director's notes. Minneapolis Public Schools: TIS Express, 1.

von Oech, Roger (1992). Creative whack pack. Stamford, CT: U.S. Games Systems.

Vygotsky, L. S. (1962). *Thought and language*. Cambridge, MA: M.I.T. Press.

————. (1978). *Mind in society: The development of higher psychological processes*. M. V. Cole, J. Steiner, S. Scribner and E. Souberman, eds. Cambridge, MA: Harvard University Press, 57.

Wahl, Mark (1999). *Math for humans: Teaching math through 8 intelligences.* Langley, WA: LivnLern Press.

Wang, Margaret C. (1992). *Adaptive education strategies: Building on diversity.* Baltimore, MD: Paul H. Brookes.

———. (1997). *Community for learning implementation manual.* Philadelphia, PA: Temple University Center for Research in Human Development and Education.

Wang, Margaret, Geneva Haertel and Herbert Walberg (1994). What helps students learn? *Educational Leadership,* December 1993/January1994, 51/4, 74–79.

———. (1997). *Characteristics of twelve widely implemented educational reforms.* Philadelphia, PA: Laboratory for Student Success.

———. (1998). Models of reform: A comparative guide. *Educational Leadership,* April, 55/7, 66–67.

Wasley, Pat (1992). Interdisciplinary learning. Interview by Scott Willis. *ASCD Curriculum Update,* November, 7.

Watts Pailliotet, Ann (2000). Introduction. In *Reconceptualizing literacy in the media age.* Ann Watts Pailliotet and Peter B. Mosenthal, eds. Stamford, CT: JAI Press.

Watts Pailliotet, Ann and Thomas A. Callister, Jr. (1999). Preparing postformal practitioners: Pitfalls and promises. In *Rethinking intelligence: Confronting psychological assumptions about teaching and learning.* Joe Kincheloe and Shirley Steinberg, eds. London: Routledge.

Watts Pailliotet, Ann and Peter B. Mosenthal, eds. (2000). *Reconceptualizing literacy in the media age.* Stamford, CT: JAI Press.

Weaver, W. T. and G. M. Prince (1990). Synectics: Its potential for education. *Phi Delta Kappan,* January, 380.

Weiss, Patricia F. (1992). Paideia principles. Handout. Minneapolis, MN: Augsburg College Paideia Institute.

West, Charles K., James A. Farmer and Phillip M. Wolff (1991). *Instructional design: Implications from cognitive science.* Englewood Cliffs, NJ: Prentice Hall.

Whitworth, Richard (1988). Collaborative learning and other disasters. In *Focus on collaborative learning.* Jeff Golub, ed. Washington, DC: NCTE, 19.

Wiggins, Grant P. (1987). Creating a thought-provoking curriculum. *American Educator,* Winter, 11/4, 11–15.

———. (1989). The futility of trying to teach everything of importance. *Educational Leadership,* November, 47/3, 44–48.

———. (1991). CLASS. Handout November 13.

———. (1992). Interdisciplinary learning. Interview by Scott Willis. *ASCD Curriculum Update,* November, 4, 5.

———. (1993a). *Assessing student performance: Exploring the purpose and limits of testing.* San Francisco, CA: Jossey Bass, 3.

———. (1993b). Assessment to improve performance, not just monitor it: Assessment reform in the social sciences. *Social Science Record,* Fall.

Willcox, Don (1986). *Hmong folklife.* Hmong Association of North Carolina, 33.

Williams, Wendy M., Tina Blythe, Noel White, Jin Li, Robert J. Sternberg and Howard Gardner (1997). *Practical intelligence for school.* New York, NY: Harper Collins.

Willis, Scott (1992). Interdisciplinary learning: Movement to link the disciplines gains momentum. *ASCD Curriculum Update,* November, 2, 4–5.

Wiske, Martha Stone, ed. (1998). *Teaching for understanding: Linking research with practice*. San Francisco, CA: Jossey Bass.
Witkin, Herman A. and D. R. Goodenough (1981). *Cognitive styles: Essence and origins*. New York, NY: International Universities Press.
Wood, George H. (1990). Teaching for democracy. *Educational Leadership*, November, 48/2, 33–37.
Wynne, Edward A. and Kevin Ryan (1993). Curriculum as a moral educator. *American Educator*, Spring, 24.
Zemelman, Steven, Harvey Daniels and Arthur A. Hyde (1998). *Best practice: New standards for teaching and learning in America's schools*. Portsmouth, NH: Heinemann.

# Index

# Studies in the Postmodern Theory of Education

*General Editors*
*Joe L. Kincheloe & Shirley R. Steinberg*

Counterpoints publishes the most compelling and imaginative books being written in education today. Grounded on the theoretical advances in criticalism, feminism, and postmodernism in the last two decades of the twentieth century, Counterpoints engages the meaning of these innovations in various forms of educational expression. Committed to the proposition that theoretical literature should be accessible to a variety of audiences, the series insists that its authors avoid esoteric and jargonistic languages that transform educational scholarship into an elite discourse for the initiated. Scholarly work matters only to the degree it affects consciousness and practice at multiple sites. Counterpoints' editorial policy is based on these principles and the ability of scholars to break new ground, to open new conversations, to go where educators have never gone before.

For additional information about this series or for the submission of manuscripts, please contact:

> Joe L. Kincheloe & Shirley R. Steinberg
> c/o Peter Lang Publishing, Inc.
> 275 Seventh Avenue, 28th floor
> New York, New York 10001

To order other books in this series, please contact our Customer Service Department:

> (800) 770-LANG (within the U.S.)
> (212) 647-7706 (outside the U.S.)
> (212) 647-7707 FAX

Or browse online by series:

> www.peterlangusa.com